Education in Canada: Recent Trends and Future Challenges

ungov

Education in Canada: Recent Trends and Future Challenges

Neil Guppy

Department of Anthropology and Sociology

University of British Columbia

and

Scott Davies

Department of Sociology

McMaster University

Published by authority of the Minister responsible for Statistics Canada

© Minister of Industry, 1998

Canadian Cataloguing in Publication Data

Guppy, L. Neil, 1949-
    Education in Canada: recent trends and
future challenges

Issued also in French under title: L'éducation au Canada :
tendances récentes et défis à relever.
ISBN 0-660-17668-8
CS96-321-MPE no. 3

1. Education – Canada. 2. Education – Canada – Statistics.
3. Teachers – Canada. 4. Postsecondary education – Canada.
I. Davies, Scott. II. Statistics Canada.

LA412 G86 1998   370'.0971
C98-988018-4

DEDICATION

Edward Thomas Pryor, 1931–1992

This series of census analytical volumes is dedicated to the memory of Dr. Edward T. Pryor, a respected and internationally acclaimed sociologist, demographer and author. Dr. Pryor served as Director General of the Census and Demographic Statistics Branch of Statistics Canada and was affectionately known as "Mr. Census." His scholarship, vision, leadership and unfailing dedication to his profession served as inspiration and guidance in the conception and development of this series.

Contents

LIST OF FIGURES

LIST OF TABLES

FOREWORD

Education in Canada: Recent Trends and Future Challenges is the third in a series of monographs produced by Statistics Canada as part of the 1991 Census Analytic Program. The 1991 Census monographs continue a tradition in census analysis that began with the 1931 Census and was repeated in 1961 and 1971. Although several studies were conducted following the 1981 Census, there has not been a formal monograph program associated with the census since 1971. Many of the 1971 series are still used today in university programs and by the general public.

It has always been the purpose of census monographs to provide analysis of topics related to Canadian social and economic life. To this end, the current series deals with some major issues of Canadian life in the 1990s that will continue to have ramifications into the 21st century. The themes covered by this series concern education, aging of the population, the changing Canadian labour market, families, immigrants, income distribution, women, and Aboriginal peoples. Using sophisticated analytic techniques, the monographs deal with the selected themes in a comprehensive way and complement the *Focus on Canada* series, which presents more general analyses.

I would like to express my appreciation to all the authors who contributed to this excellent series. I would also like to thank the staff of the Census Analytic Program of Statistics Canada, who so efficiently oversaw the program, as well as the Advisory Committee for their valuable expertise.

I hope the series will help Canadians understand the challenges our country faces as we approach the 21st century, and contribute to informed discussion of how to deal with them.

DR. IVAN FELLEGI
Chief Statistician, Statistics Canada

FOREWORD

As the 20th century draws to a close, schooling is increasingly significant for individuals and for Canadian society. Human resource development, productivity enhancement and skill training are becoming the cornerstones of public and private sector policies dealing with Canada's competitive position in international commerce. Governments currently spend in excess of $50 billion on education. Furthermore, a significant proportion of the Canadian labour force is engaged in education-related activities. *Education in Canada: Recent Trends and Future Challenges* is a comprehensive analysis of education in Canada, both from the perspective of the clients of the system and the providers.

Education in Canada: Recent Trends and Future Challenges examines current and historical patterns of education in Canada. This analysis shows how the linkage between educational attainments and labour market outcomes has changed in the past 50 years. This volume also documents and analyses the differences among groups of Canadians with respect to their educational experiences. The analysis concludes with an examination of the current state of education in Canada from an international perspective, highlighting the challenges for the future.

As part of the 1991 Census Monograph Series, *Education in Canada* joins the other volumes in providing substantive, in-depth analyses of selected themes, and demonstrating the power and value of census data on their own and when analytically coupled with other data sources. Topics in the series include aging, income distribution, immigration, the family, women, the labour force and Aboriginal peoples. The monographs are designed to be integrated into a variety of academic programs and to serve as background in formulating and developing public policy.

Planning and overseeing the 1991 Census monograph program was the responsibility of the Census Analysis Division of Statistics Canada. The program manager and those responsible within the division were assisted by the Advisory Committee, whose members reflect the broad interests and professional backgrounds of Canada's socio-economic research community. The committee provided advice on all aspects of the monograph program, including topic suggestions, methodology for competitions, assessment of proposals, and the process for peer review. In the Acknowledgments page of this volume is a list of Advisory Committee members as well as Statistics Canada personnel who gave generously of their time and effort to the monograph series.

The invitation to submit research proposals was extended by the Chief Statistician to all members of the Canadian research community, both new scholars and those with proven track records. Proposals were assessed on the basis of their relevance to socio-economic issues facing Canada, the scope of the analytical approach, the suitability of the analytical techniques and methodologies, and the importance of census data to the study. The authors selected represent the full spectrum of Canada's social science research community. They come from universities across Canada as well as from Statistics Canada.

By encouraging investigations of the trends and changes in Canadian society, the 1991 Census monograph program continues a valuable tradition in census analysis. As we approach the millennium, many social issues will persist and possibly intensify. Canada, and all Canadians, will benefit from insight provided by the 1991 Census Monograph Series. Persons interested in economic and social issues related to the educational systems will find *Education in Canada* an informative analysis of the impact they have had on Canada's labour market in a global economic environment.

DR. MONICA BOYD

Chair, Census Monographs Advisory Committee

ACKNOWLEDGEMENTS

Statistics Canada wish to acknowledge the following for their excellent efforts on behalf of the Census Monograph Series:

FOR THE ADVISORY COMMITTEE ON CENSUS MONOGRAPHS

Monica Boyd (Chair)
Florida State University
Visiting Research Fellow,
Statistics Canada

Paddy Fuller
Canada Mortgage and Housing Corporation

Réjean Lachapelle
Statistics Canada

Jacques Légaré
Université de Montréal

Ramona MacDowell
Human Resources Development Canada

Ian Macredie
Statistics Canada

Susan McDaniel
University of Alberta

Allan Maslove
Carleton University

John Myles
Florida State University
Visiting Research Fellow,
Statistics Canada

Elizabeth Ruddick
Citizenship and Immigration Canada

Tom Symons
Trent University

Derrick Thomas
Citizenship and Immigration Canada

James Wetzel
United States Bureau of the Census

Telmet Design Associates
Cover Design

FOR STATISTICS CANADA

Census Analysis Division
Gustave Goldmann (Manager)
Tom Caplan
Nicole Kelly
Sonia Latour
Patty Paul
Andy Siggner
Lyse St-Jacques
Claudette Trudeau

Official Languages and Translation Division
Sylvette Cadieux

Library and Information Centre
Brian Drysdale
Glen Gagnon
Mary McCoy
Michele Sura

Communications Division— Editorial Services
Gaye Ward (Head, English Unit)
Martha Armstrong
Janis Camelon
Tom Vradenburg
Nathalie Turcotte (Head, French Unit)
Julie Bélanger
Valérie Catrice

Dissemination Division—Production Integration
Danielle Baum (Manager)
Production and Interior Design

Acknowledgements
by the Authors

We are grateful to many bright and supportive people who helped us complete this monograph. We are deeply indebted to Ravi Pendakur (Carleton University and Secretary of State) for suggesting this project and helping us with both the acquisition and analysis of the census data on which this work is based. His help has been of the superior, extra-strength variety. Mireille Laroche worked with us as a data analyst for two successive summers. Her skill, savvy, and professionalism at data management and analysis were indispensable. Others helped with the work at different stages, including Helen Bent, Barbara Gauthier, Mike Gifford, and especially Chantelle Marlor. Several other people were helpful in more indirect ways, especially Brian Elliott, Fiona Kay, Ralph Matthews, Martin Meissner, and Nico Stehr, each of whom, with well-timed advice, steered us in useful directions.

At Statistics Canada we had help and advice from Gustave Goldmann, Tom Caplan, Patty Paul, and Nicole Kelly. Gustave and Tom provided us with ideas and encouragement while Patty and Nicole supplied vast quantities of data files to help us pursue the ideas. We also benefited from the opinions of six anonymous (to us) referees. Their reviews contained some excellent suggestions, all of which we have incorporated in the final version as best we could.

This work would not have been completed without the continual support and understanding of our families. We are immensely grateful both to our wives, Jean Gillies and Helen Luzius, and our daughters, Emma Guppy and Tatyana Davies.

Neil Guppy
and
Scott Davies

THE SCHOOLED SOCIETY

Whatever epithets best describe the emerging world of the 21st century—information society, knowledge age, credential society, post-industrial era—the contours of that world are now coming into focus and education is in the central foreground. Knowledge work will be pivotal work. More than ever before, both personal and societal prosperity will depend upon effectively applying knowledge to generate innovative solutions to all manner of problem. In every country this realization has dawned. Schooling is increasingly seen as a key investment, a competitive advantage both for the nation and for the individual.

Two interrelated principles lie behind this recognition of education's growing importance. First, a flourishing competitiveness in international commerce has focused attention on human resource development, productivity enhancement, and skill training. As the idea that knowledge is essential to production gains acceptance, unanimity is emerging over the need to strengthen training and education. Second, in a world of growing complexity, awareness of the necessity for citizenship training, in its broadest sense, has matured. Many agree that education plays a pivotal role in making people aware of, and sensitive to, today's difficult ethical, political, and moral choices. Schools must integrate these complementary mental and moral goals.

Schools have never been more central to Canadians' lives. Government spending on education and training now exceeds $50 billion annually and a sizeable proportion of the Canadian labour force works in education-related jobs. Not only do schools help shape the lives of individual students, they also play a vital role in determining what counts as knowledge thus shaping the very structure of modern society. Education helps constitute and legitimate new jobs—such as economist, computer scientist, forensic accountant—and reinforces the importance of new concepts, such as human rights, environmentalism and multiculturalism. Beyond these functions, schooling is often called on to help unify a fragmenting nation and provide channels that will lead to equal opportunity in Canadian society.

Although formal, public schooling is a relatively recent social invention, dating from the middle of the 1800s in Canada, it has become fundamental both to our national community and to the makeup of our personal identities. Today, schooling is so important that young people are legally required to attend school until the age of 16. While people may criticize specific issues in the delivery of education, few ever question the wisdom of mandatory schooling (but see Gallagher 1995, 45).

The impact of schooling goes far beyond this minimum legal requirement—it penetrates into the fabric of our lives. As youth, we spend countless hours attending class or pursuing school activities. Even when our schooling ends, our lives are shaped profoundly by what we learned at school, by the level of scholastic performance we attained, and by the type of institutionalized education we undertook.

Beyond these obvious impacts, however, "school," in the guise of student–instructor relationships, prescribed curricula, and formal certification, has been exported to other institutional domains to deal with a myriad of social phenomena. These include prisoner rehabilitation, John school, anti-sexist/racist education and other "sensitivity training" schemes, various types of job re-training—from McDonald's Hamburger University to executive Outward Bound programs[1]—and even self-help movements epitomized by Weight Watchers and stop smoking groups. All represent new, more "educational" solutions to old problems and extend far beyond reading, writing, and arithmetic. Indeed, almost any policy initiative aimed at fixing societal problems, from environmental damage to poverty, involves education at some point.

Our premise is that Canada, like other developed nations, has become a *schooled society*. While education as an institution has been expanding for some time, and while the use of schooling to solve a variety of social ills is not new, the continual intensification of these processes over recent decades has had a very real impact.

We are, inescapably, members of a "schooled society."

As a result, schooling is touted as ever important in Canadian society. Many Canadian politicians and policy-makers are calling for schools to be re-shaped to meet difficult modern challenges, such as the need to enhance economic productivity while simultaneously reinforcing ethical reasoning and assuaging the insecurities of parents worried about their children's futures. Reform is not proving easy, and debate rages over how best to confront these challenges. No miraculous solutions have appeared on the horizon, and so we anticipate the lively debate over possible educational futures will continue for some time. Such debate is healthy and ought to be encouraged.

I.1   ABOUT THIS MONOGRAPH

In this monograph, we step back from these debates, important as they are, to provide details about the recent history of schooling in Canada. Our mandate from Statistics Canada was to show how and why the educational profile of Canadians has changed, relying on the Census of Canada as much as possible. The census provides a valuable barometer for measuring accomplishments in education and training, permits an assessment of our collective success in delivering education to *all* Canadians, and enables comparisons with earlier periods of Canadian history. Combined with other data, also collected by Statistics Canada or by international governmental agencies, such as the Organisation for Economic Co-operation and Development (OECD), this information helps us paint a rich picture of the changes and challenges facing Canadian education.

We document the size, distribution, and composition of schooling in Canada, showing changes in various education patterns in recent decades. We provide context for the current reform discussions by showing how educational attainments, the size of the teaching profession, and the link between educational attainments and labour market outcomes have changed during this century and, in particular, the last 50 years. As well, we document differences among groups of Canadians, examining the differing educational experiences of women and men over time, the provincial variations in high school drop-outs, and the fields of study students from different backgrounds pursued in college and university.

All this offers a perspective on future challenges by highlighting current weaknesses that require attention. Those challenges include building on the system's strengths, while simultaneously addressing areas of concern for Canadian education.

We begin our look at education in Canada with a simple question. If education is increasingly important, is our nation ensuring that *all* Canadians are able to participate in the schooling process? By examining changes in Canadians' education levels, particularly the levels of those in the labour force, we can see if our delivery of education has kept pace with the expanding knowledge base necessary for full participation in modern societies. As we began this project, there was some suggestion that the pace of *growth* in educational attainment had slowed (Mori and Burke 1989). This implied that just as we move into a schooled society, Canadians are slowing down their pursuit of further schooling, at least relative to the 1970s and 1980s.

Much recent attention in educational debates has focused on the content of the school curriculum. In Chapter 1, our attention is directed to an equally fundamental, but frequently neglected aspect of that larger debate—how many Canadians are exposed to the school curriculum at various levels of education? For us the content of the curriculum, and its utility, is a separate issue from who participates in, or is exposed to, that curriculum. Even the best curricular reform will be inefficient if the students most able to benefit from new approaches to learning are restricted from participating.

Who are the educators responsible for the various forms of schooling in Canada? Chapter 2 explores this question in various ways, principally by looking at historical changes in the size and composition of the teaching profession. We examine various topics, including remuneration, student–teacher ratios, labour market change, and demographic profiles. We devote an entire chapter to updating our knowledge about Canada's largest profession (Lockhart 1991; King and Peart 1992).

Many observers say we must ensure that the skills and abilities of all Canadians have an opportunity to flourish if we are to remain competitive in international commerce. Access to education helps Canadians develop their full range of talents. Likewise, a basic level of education must be distributed evenly for all citizens to participate in modern society's complex ethical, political, and moral debates. Meaningful democracy demands nothing less. Chapters 3 and 4 focus on education distribution.

It is useful to examine schooling profiles across both social and geographic boundaries. For some time we have known that Canadians living in rural areas leave school at younger ages than their urban counterparts. The average level of schooling also differs provincially. In Chapter 3 we explore reasons for, and changes in, these rural–urban and inter-provincial distributions. As well, we ask whether differences between people of distinct social categories, such as language groups and ethnic communities (both variously defined), translate into differences in schooling attainments.

The Royal Commission on Equality in Employment (Commission of Inquiry on Equality in Employment 1984) identified four groups of Canadians—native people, visible minorities, disabled persons, and women—who share disproportionately in the *dis*advantages of Canadian society. They were, according to commissioner Rosalie Abella, "on the lower rungs of the ladder to society's benefits" (p. 3). Education is frequently seen as one way to move up the ladder of success, and so in Chapter 4 we explore the changing educational fortunes of groups designated as disadvantaged and thus deserving of assistance. We pay particular attention to whether their collective educational achievements are keeping pace with, catching up to, falling behind, or surpassing the attainments of other Canadians. Since Statistics Canada collects data using those equity categories, we investigate the rationale underlying the Employment Equity Act by asking, "do the expected patterns of advantage and disadvantage arise in education?"

In recent decades postsecondary education has become more important for an ever-growing number of Canadians. Currently, more than 50% of all secondary school graduates go on to college or university. In Chapter 5, therefore, we examine recent trends among Canadians entering higher education.

Both the size and differentiation of postsecondary institutions have changed dramatically in the last five decades. There are more, and bigger, universities now than in 1950. The community colleges and technical/vocational institutes have grown to represent a critical part of the higher education system in many, but not all, provinces (see Dennison 1995). As postsecondary institutions have proliferated, so too have the programs they offer. Our examination of the postsecondary sphere therefore incorporates a look at student choices about fields of study, full- or part-time status, and the pursuit of postgraduate degrees. Increasingly, the educational differences between Canadians are evident in the types and levels of postsecondary education they attain (Anisef, Ashbury, and Turrittin 1992; for an American comparison see Davies and Guppy 1997a).

We also examine what people do with their educational qualifications once they leave school. While we have no direct information from the census on the actual skills and abilities that Canadians acquire in school, we do have a wealth of data on the credentials they obtain. In Chapter 6 we examine how the relationship between credentials and various labour market outcomes has changed. We also briefly examine some of the non-economic consequences of educational attainment, particularly political participation.

Comparing Canadian education delivery with achievements in other countries, as we do in Chapter 7, can offer useful insights. Education has been a central priority in many nations for some time. With processes of globalization continuing unabated, it is important to see if our schooling attainments are meeting the levels achieved by our key economic competitors. Certainly simple exposure to a school curriculum is not a sufficient comparative measure (outcome measures such as standardized test scores are relevant here), but attendance at school is a marker of comparative standing. Especially when viewed in relation to other countries, these findings add to our awareness of the challenges we will face in the next century.

Before turning to these chapters, some context is necessary. Students' lives, in and out of the classroom, are influenced by the wider societal sphere of the economy, the labour market, and the political milieu. Changes in this wider ambit are an important backdrop for any study of education. Though we are unable to pursue these issues in sustained detail, in the next section we focus on key changes in the last few decades that have influenced schooling and school outcomes. We then turn to an examination of changes in the childhood experience.

I.2 CONTEXTUALIZING EDUCATIONAL CHANGE: TECHNICAL UPGRADING, LABOUR MARKET COMPETITION, AND THE POLITICIZATION OF EDUCATION

I.2.1 Globalization and the service economy

What social forces have led to the advent of our schooled society? Why is education increasingly seen as important? To address these issues, consider the Canadian economy's transformation over the past century. It has evolved from an agriculturally based, resource economy to a manufacturing-driven, industry-dominated economy, through to a service economy. Roughly 70% of all jobs in 1991 were in the service sector (Krahn and Lowe 1993, 44). This shift has resulted in the continual upgrading of required literacy and numeracy skills (see Hunter 1988).

More recently, this upgrading, according to many observers, has taken a quantum leap. Technological advances and increasingly competitive international trade are creating a new economic order. These forces will further upgrade most jobs, making knowledge work[2] more pivotal while promoting deindustrialization. Service and high technology jobs will continue to replace routine and low-skill occupations. According to many commentators, the locus of economic activity is shifting from material production to information processing. Knowledge is emerging as the key resource of the next century (see e.g., Beck 1995; Bell 1973; Stehr 1994).

Policy-makers are near unanimous in arguing that, since knowledge is key to production, training and education need strengthening. In an updated version of the human capital theory (which informed policy in the 1960s and 1970s), many argue that both personal and societal prosperity will depend, even more so than now, on effectively applying knowledge to generate innovative solutions to all types of problems (see Lockhart 1979). As a reflection of this growing trend, an estimated 20% of gross national product (GNP) in Western industrial countries currently goes to producing and distributing knowledge via education, on-the-job training, and research and development (Drucker 1993, 186).

I.2.2 More labour market competition

Not all of the pressure to increase educational attainment comes from rising technical requirements in the economy. Other, more supply-side, factors also pressure Canadians to acquire more and more credentials. As farm ownership and most other forms of propertied self-employment dwindled over this century, fewer and fewer Canadians had options other than working in the labour force. Additionally, women aged 15 and over have greatly increased their participation in paid employment, from only 16% at the turn of this century to over 58% in 1991 (Krahn and Lowe 1993, 62). As we show in Chapter 5, Canadian postsecondary education expanded mainly because of greater female participation. These twin forces have made the labour market increasingly crowded. The movement towards a service economy also means job seekers need higher credentials because the service sector demands more education than other sectors. Additionally, changes in Canada's immigration policy have also heightened competition. Today's immigrants are on average far more educated than in previous decades and most compete in the service sector at a variety of levels.

These trends, along with greater technical requirements, inflate the amount of schooling expected in most jobs. This is indeed the conclusion of some analysts who downplay the direct relevance of much schooling for the workplace. Credentialists (e.g., Collins 1979) look instead to market forces, arguing that a large supply of job seekers allows employers (who have limited time and knowledge to make smart hiring decisions) to use education credentials as a socially accepted and convenient device to limit pools of job candidates within a glutted market of applicants. Many firms, for instance, now expect cashiers or salespersons to have high school diplomas or university degrees, though there is little evidence of rising skill requirements in those jobs. Growing credential requirements, in turn, cause younger people in particular to seek a competitive edge by collecting ever-more credentials, thereby reinforcing credential inflation and giving employers an even larger pool of well-educated applicants. This paper chase, the "diploma disease" as Dore (1976) calls it, is an educational equivalent to the arms race of the Cold War era.

A related understanding of rising educational attainments comes from the work of Ulrich Beck (1992) and Anthony Giddens (1990). In their eyes, the increasing complexity of the world creates greater levels of uncertainty, causing people to plan more for the future, especially in an effort to minimize risk. People go to financial planners, they set up RRSPs, they install security systems in their homes and cars, and they engage in preventative–maintenance exercise programs, all with the intent of reducing risk. For a parent, a principal way to enhance their child's future security is to encourage educational development. Parents arrange a formidable array of "shadow" education practices (e.g., private tutors, art classes, computer camps) and education planning ventures, including registered education savings plans. Education is an essential commodity in a high-risk society. By engaging in these education-related, risk-reducing strategies, the uncertainty spawned by the modern world's complexity and competitiveness further entrenches the pervasiveness of schooling in our lives.

I.2.3   More politicization

The twin pressures of ever-changing economic conditions and keener labour market competition are ushering in a new, more intense politics of education. In Canada, as elsewhere, policy debates are infused with the imagery of globalization and economic competitiveness. Freer trade, more international migration, and greater deregulation—each a factor under-girding the uncertainties of a higher-risk society—lie behind the forces of globalization. Most political parties in Canada presume we must compete for increasingly mobile investment dollars by stressing our labour force's skills and the innovative capacity of our scientific and technical workers. The result is that all aspects of schooling, from assessment and evaluation, to curricular content and school governance, are claimed to be in need of reform. Many see our schools as "behind the times" and "out of touch." As low-skill jobs vanish due to automation or job exporting, they argue, most future jobs will require a minimal skill level that must be guaranteed by education systems (see for instance, Ontario Premier's Council 1988; Liberal Party of Canada 1993; Human Reources Development Committee 1991; Steering Group on Prosperity 1992). Others, particularly teacher unions and their advocates, have strongly disputed this vision, portraying it as an unfounded, barely concealed attempt to further "vocationalize" the content of schooling, instil commercial values in students, and shift blame for economic stagnation onto schools and away from industry (e.g., Barlow and Robertson 1994).

But it is not just business, politicians, and teacher unions that are politicizing education. Today there is an historically unprecedented range of activists and interest groups vying to influence public education. For instance, Ontario's recent Royal Commission on Learning witnessed an amazing array of interest groups and individuals submitting proposals. "Parent power" in education, is now a force to be recognized in Canada (Davies and Guppy 1997b). Today's cohort of parents, the most educated and informed in history, are less deferential toward the educational establishment and are more likely to feel entitled to challenge experts. With a greater ability to get involved in school issues, and with higher expectations regarding schooling, coalitions of taxpayers, ethnic and religious minorities, and other groups are demanding publicly funded schools tailored to their curricular, ethnic, or linguistic wants.

Changing economic conditions throughout the second half of the 20th century have made Canadian society more unequal in terms of wealth, income and employment distribution. Labour income, especially for low and middle-income earners, has remained fairly stable for some time, but the gap between Canada's richest and poorest has widened (Morissette, Myles, and Picot 1994). This means schooling is increasingly seen as a way to level the playing field, and as a result, educational equity has become a central issue. In part, the latter trend highlights the rise of "identity politics," which refers to politics based largely on visible characteristics such as race, ethnicity and gender as opposed to region, class or socio-economic status. These politics shape public policy concerns. Indeed, they have influenced the types of questions and categories we investigate in this monograph. For instance, the Abella report, in prescribing remedies for social inequality, focused only on groups categorized by physical characteristics—gender, race, ancestry, and disability—and ignored class, socio-economic status, or region as forces that shape disparities. As a result, increasingly, the politics of educational equity centre on Abella's categories, even though disparities by class, for instance, are comparably more entrenched than those focused on by Abella (see Guppy and Arai 1993; Siedule 1992; Wanner 1996).

In sum, economic changes, greater labour market competition, and greater politicization are crucial influences on Canadian education. However, a contextualization of education would be incomplete if it did not include an examination of the lives of children. The shift to a service economy, growing inequalities, and greater numbers of women in the work force all affect the lives of children in and out of the classroom. Though schools serve everyone, their largest and most immediate constituency is children. Virtually all Canadian children between the ages of 5 and 15 are full-time students. To understand changes in education delivery over time, and the impact of all of the trends discussed above, we need to document the evolving nature of childhood in Canada (see also Ross, Scott, and Kelly 1996).

I.3   The changing context of childhood

Over the past few decades, the world of children has altered in fundamental ways. Table I.1 illustrates some major shifts in Canada. Demographically, children today represent a smaller proportion of the population. In 1961, children under age 15 comprised more than a third (33.9%) of the Canadian population. By 1994, their representation had fallen to just over one-fifth (20.3%). This has occurred partly because older people live longer, but also because the birth rate fell from an average of 3.8 children per woman in 1960 to 1.7 children per woman in 1993. For today's children this will mean moving into their working lives as part of a relatively small cohort, while having to support both the non-working elderly and their own children.

Not only do children compose a smaller population segment, but also the family arrangements in which they live have been changing dramatically in recent years. Now they have fewer siblings than in earlier decades (from 0.9 siblings, on average, in 1961 to 0.2 in 1991), and they are also more likely to live in families headed by a female lone-parent (the latter represented 9.0% of all families with children in 1961 and 16.4% in 1991). For children living in two-parent families, the probability that the mother is working has soared from 29.1% in 1971 to 66.5% in 1992, thereby reducing the amount of time children spend with their parents. Divorce rates have also risen sharply since the Second World War, quintupling between 1968 and 1992, and thereby increasing stress upon children. Not all divorced couples had children, of course, and although the proportion of divorces involving marriages with dependent children did not change dramatically between 1971 and 1992, children are still involved in over one-half of all divorces.

Over recent decades Canadians' geographic mobility has increased and this too has added to the stresses and strains children face. In the five-year time-span between 1956 and 1961, 41.2% of all children aged 5 to 14 changed their place of residence. This mobility rate increased to 51.5% in the interval between 1986 and 1991.

One area of improvement is the mortality rate. Infant death rates have plummeted and suicide rates for 10- to 19-year-olds, while high, have not grown significantly since 1981 (in the 1970s the rates increased for females and males among 10- to 14-year-olds and 15- to 19-year-olds). Injury death rates have also dropped by more than half for children aged 1 to 4 between 1970 and 1990.

Pregnancy rates for females between 15 and 19 have also fallen—from 5.3% of females in 1975 reporting at least one pregnancy, down to 4.0% by 1992. Certainly not all such pregnancies were unwanted, but many were, and so the declining rate means young parents experience less pregnancy-related tension.

Economic changes have also had a major impact on the lives of children. Over the past decade children living in low income families have increased for both two-parent and lone-parent families. (While Statistics Canada publishes data on low income cut-offs, these are not designed or intended to be used as measures of poverty. Also note that the definition of poverty is contested, see Sarlo 1996 and Ross, Shillington, and Lochhead 1994.) In 1981, 763,400 children under the age of 18 lived at or below the low income cut-off, while 10 years later the number had risen to 1,211,900 (see also Picot and Myles 1996). The social safety net is an increasingly important source of income for low-income families; social transfer payments made up 63% of all income for such families in 1991, compared with only 36% in 1973. Whatever the exact reasons for this shift (and the reasons are debated—is it falling employment income or rising welfare payments?), a sizeable number of children are vulnerable to claw-backs by the welfare state.

While there is no consistent evidence that the material lives of children have worsened in an absolute sense, it does appear that fewer of today's children can realistically share in the North American dream of continually rising affluence from one generation to the next. Many children do not experience the rising affluence their parents enjoyed growing up in the 1950s, 1960s, and early 1970s. As previous generations progressed from childhood to adulthood, the family holidays got longer, the presents more expensive, the lifestyle more plush and this had a big impact on how people approached the future. Economic insecurity (e.g., unemployment) in the family was much less a problem then than it is today.

Even for children not living in low-income families, economic changes have meant the rising prosperity of previous decades is not something they experience (Morissette, Myles, and Picot 1994). For example, after adjusting for inflation, the average income for two-parent families with children remained almost constant between 1980 and 1993, while average family income declined for lone-parent families headed by women. Falling birth rates have, of course, softened the impact of this income stabilization, since families are now smaller than in previous decades.

Finally, the percentage of young people charged with violent crimes has more than doubled in the last eight years, and overall rates of crime have increased, although less dramatically. As well, the fear of crime has risen, and children have become much more conscious of potential dangers, as a host of family and school safety initiatives signal, from "don't talk to strangers" slogans to school identification badges.

In combination, all the indicators listed in Table I.1 suggest that, on balance, childhood has become a more stressful period of life in recent decades. Not all of the indicators point in the same direction. Mortality rates have improved substantially, for example, but there is no disputing the fact that most other indicators suggest Canadian children's quality of life has deteriorated over the period (for a U.S. comparison on which we base our examples, see Haveman and Wolfe 1994).

The halcyon days of increasing material prosperity are "on hold." The next generation of Canadians, more than any other, will attend school for a greater number of years, accumulating more degrees, diplomas, and certificates, but it is not likely to earn greater real incomes. This affects education in many ways. Though it does not follow that coming from a family living below the low income cut-off or headed by a single mother renders a child less educable, it does suggest that cultural themes with which Canadian education has been historically associated— themes of upward social mobility, the pursuit of ever-rising material affluence—may now be strained, and may not motivate as many students and parents as in the past.

These contextualizing factors, and their impact on children, set the stage for the remainder of this book. In the next chapter we review key elements of educational change in historical perspective. Following that, we turn to more contemporary aspects of education, pointing especially to recent changes and future challenges.

---

1. Outward Bound programs involve groups of executives or young offenders, for example, pursuing wilderness challenges designed to enhance personal qualities such as teamwork, leadership and self-confidence.

2. In knowledge work we include jobs focused on one or more of the following: acquiring, analysing, interpreting, refining and producing ideas and information.

APPENDIX I

TABLE I.1

CHANGES IN CHILDREN'S LIVES IN CANADA

A. DEMOGRAPHICS

1. PERCENTAGE OF POPULATION UNDER AGE 15

	(%)
1961	33.9
1971	29.5
1981	22.5
1991	20.8
1994	20.3

Source: Statistics Canada, *Population: Age, Sex and Marital Status, 1982;* Statistics Canada, *Annual Demographic Statistics, 1994,* 1995.

2. TOTAL FERTILITY RATE

1960	3.8
1980	1.8
1985	1.7
1990	1.8
1993	1.7

Source: Canadian Institute of Child Health 1994.

3. PERCENTAGE OF YOUTHS UNDER 15 WHOSE MOTHER TONGUE IS NEITHER FRENCH NOR ENGLISH

	(%)
1961	7.9
1971	8.3
1981	7.5
1991	10.3

Source: Statistics Canada, *Home Language and Mother Tongue,* 1992.

B. FAMILY

4. AVERAGE NUMBER OF CHILDREN PER FAMILY

1961	1.9
1971	1.8
1981	1.4
1991	1.2

Source: Statistics Canada, *Women in Canada: A Statistical Report,* 1995.

5. DIVORCES PER 100,000 POPULATION

1968	54.8
1971	137.6
1981	278.0
1992	277.9
1993	270.3

Source: Statistics Canada, *Women in Canada: A Statistical Report*, 1995; Statistics Canada, *Divorces, 1992,* 1995.

6. PERCENTAGE OF ALL FAMILIES HEADED BY LONE-PARENTS

	Female-headed (%)	Male-headed (%)
1961	9.0	2.5
1971	10.4	2.8
1981	13.7	2.9
1991	16.4	3.5

Source: Statistics Canada, *Women in Canada: A Statistical Report,* 1995.

7. AVERAGE NUMBER OF CHILDREN PER FEMALE LONE-PARENTS

1976	2.0
1981	1.7
1986	1.6
1991	1.6

Source: Statistics Canada, *Annual Demographic Statistics, 1994,* 1995.

8. PERCENTAGE OF MARRIED FEMALES IN THE LABOUR FORCE WITH CHILDREN UNDER AGE 6

	(%)
1971	29.1
1991	59.7
1992	66.5

Source: Statistics Canada, *Labour Force Activity of Women by Presence of Children*, 1993.

9. PERCENTAGE OF DIVORCES INVOLVING DEPENDENT CHILDREN

	(%)
1971	55.4
1981	51.1
1986	45.4
1992	55.6

Source: Statistics Canada, *Women in Canada: A Statistical Report*, 1995; Statistics Canada, *Divorces, 1992*, 1995.

C. GEOGRAPHICAL MOBILITY

10. PERCENTAGE OF CHILDREN AGED 5 TO 14 WHO CHANGED RESIDENCE OVER A FIVE-YEAR TIME SPAN

	(%)
1956–1961	41.2
1966–1971	46.1
1976–1981	48.5
1986–1991	51.5

Source: Statistics Canada, *Mobility and Migration*, 1993; Statistics Canada, *Population: Mobility Status*, 1983.

D. MORTALITY

11. CHILDREN'S DEATH RATES (PER 1,000)

	Under 1 year	10–14 years
1961	27.2	0.4
1971	17.5	0.4
1981	9.6	0.3
1991	6.4	0.2
1992	6.1	0.2
1993	6.2	0.2

Source: Statistics Canada, *Annual Demographic Statistics, 1994, 1995.*

12. Suicide rates (per 100,000)

	10–14 years		15–19 years	
	Female	Male	Female	Male
1971	0.35	1.09	3.00	12.32
1981	0.95	2.52	3.70	20.55
1991	0.97	1.94	3.83	22.02
1992	0.85	2.62	5.42	20.08

Source: Health Canada, *Suicide in Canada*, 1994.

13. Children's injury death rates (per 100,000)

	1–4 years	10–14 years
1970	34	25
1974	36	24
1978	29	22
1982	20	17
1986	18	12
1990	15	13
1992	12	10

Source: Canadian Institute of Child Health 1994; Statistics Canada, *Mortality*, 1995.

E. Pregnancy

14. Estimated pregnancy rates for women aged 15 to 19 (per 1,000)

1975	53.4
1981	45.7
1987	40.6
1990	44.0
1992	40.4

Source: Wadhera and Silins 1994; Statistics Canada, *Births, 1992*, 1995.

15. Fertility rates for women aged 15 to 19 (births per 1,000)

1974	34.8
1981	25.9
1987	22.8
1992	25.7

Source: Statistics Canada, *Births, 1992*, 1995.

F. ECONOMICS

16. PERCENTAGE OF LOW INCOME FAMILIES AMONG TWO-PARENT FAMILIES WITH CHILDREN

	(%)
1980	9.6
1988	9.2
1991	11.0
1993	12.5

Source: Statistics Canada, *Women in Canada: A Statistical Report,* 1995.

17. PERCENTAGE OF LOW INCOME FAMILIES AMONG LONE-PARENT FAMILIES WITH FEMALES AS THE HEAD OF THE HOUSEHOLD

	(%)
1980	56.7
1988	55.1
1991	61.1
1993	59.6

Source: Statistics Canada, *Women in Canada: A Statistical Report,* 1995.

18. AVERAGE FAMILY INCOME FOR TWO-PARENT FAMILIES WITH CHILDREN (1991 CONSTANT DOLLARS)

1980	58,747
1988	61,725
1991	60,992
1993	59,658

Source: Statistics Canada, *Women in Canada: A Statistical Report,* 1995.

19. AVERAGE FAMILY INCOME FOR LONE-PARENT FAMILIES WITH FEMALES AS THE HEAD OF THE HOUSEHOLD (1991 CONSTANT DOLLARS)

1980	24,592
1988	23,707
1991	22,930
1993	23,301

Source: Statistics Canada, *Women in Canada: A Statistical Report,* 1995.

20. NUMBER OF CHILDREN UNDER 18 YEARS OF AGE LIVING BELOW THE LOW INCOME CUT-OFF

1981	763,400
1987	1,057,800
1991	1,211,900

Source: Canadian Institute of Child Health 1994.

21. SOCIAL TRANSFER INCOME AS PERCENTAGE OF ALL INCOME FOR POOR FAMILIES WITH CHILDREN 0 TO 6

	(%)
1973	36.0
1981	45.0
1988	56.0
1991	63.0

Source: Picot and Myles 1995.

G. YOUNG OFFENDERS

22. PERCENTAGE OF YOUTHS (AGED 12 TO 17) CHARGED FOR VIOLENT CRIME

1986	0.4
1990	0.7
1994	0.9

Source: Hendrick, 1995.

23. PERCENTAGE OF YOUTHS CHARGED FOR PROPERTY CRIME

1986	3.5
1990	3.7
1994	2.9

Source: Hendrick, 1995.

24. PERCENTAGE OF YOUTHS CHARGED UNDER THE CRIMINAL CODE

1986	4.8
1990	5.6
1994	5.1

Source: Hendrick, 1995.

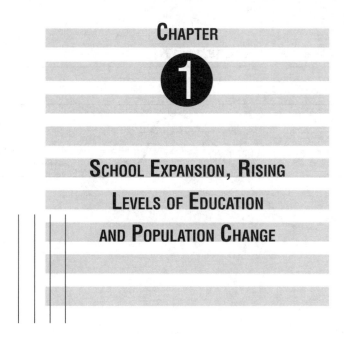

CHAPTER 1

SCHOOL EXPANSION, RISING LEVELS OF EDUCATION AND POPULATION CHANGE

The central place education now occupies in the lives of Canadians has gradually developed over the past century. This chapter describes the developmental phases of our schooled society. We begin by outlining the growth of the teaching work force, using this as a key measure of the education system's evolution in Canada. We also use early census data on school attendance to pinpoint when various transitions in Canada's education system occurred. By examining selected milestones in the development of the education system, we can better understand key historical transitions in educational change. We focus on several milestones in this chapter—the points at which it became the norm for children to attend elementary and secondary school on a regular basis and the point at which it became the norm for the vast majority of teenagers to complete high school.

Beyond these defining transitional moments, schools are also profoundly affected by demographic shifts. This is especially so in the elementary grades and in the early years of high school where attendance is mandated by the minimum school-leaving age. Undoubtedly, the baby boom had a significant impact on Canada (see Figure 1.1). Starting in 1947, the number of births grew year upon year, reaching a peak in 1959 when there were 479,275 newborns. Births then fell steeply and even though the population nearly doubled from 17.5 million in 1959 to 29.2 million in 1994 the annual number of births in Canada has never exceeded the 1959 total. This rapid increase and subsequent decrease in births led a pattern of "boom, bust, and echo," as described by Foot (1996), with the boomers of the 1950s creating their own "echo boom" when they reached prime childbearing ages in the 1980s and 1990s. The fluctuating size of the school-age population, perhaps exemplified most dramatically through "portable classrooms," has been instrumental in shaping the education system of recent decades. Demographic shifts are likely to influence future changes in schooling and so population projections play an important role for school planners.

FIGURE 1.1

POPULATION UP TO 1 YEAR OF AGE, CANADA, 1921 TO 1994

thousands

Source: Statistics Canada, Catalogue nos. 91-537; 91-213.

In the introductory chapter, we discussed the emerging information age and the suggestion that education levels in Canada must rise if we are to keep pace with recent social and economic changes. We explore this idea more fully here by examining various measures of the average amount of schooling that Canadians have received, paying particular attention to whether the growth in the level of schooling has accelerated in recent decades. Besides probing average levels of schooling, we also explore the two extremes—early school leavers and postsecondary graduates.

1.1 OVERVIEW

According to the 1991 Census, more than 550,000 Canadians worked in education-related jobs. Representing approximately 4% of the entire Canadian labour force, this is a strong indicator of our massive labour investment in schooling. In addition, there were over 6 million full-time students in the elementary and secondary school system during the 1991–92 school year. Among Canadians aged 15 and over, 3,781,165 or 17.7% attended school either full or part time in 1991. Finally, Statistics Canada estimates that more than 5.8 million Canadian adults, although not attending school full time, were enrolled in some form of adult education or structured training (Statistics Canada, *Education in Canada* 1996, 88). The number of all the education workers, grade school and high school learners, and adult students combined reflects the importance of schooling in Canadians' lives. Currently, approximately 10 million Canadians—about one-third of the population—are directly involved in some part of our education system.

Formal schooling was not always so central for Canadians. It began later in Canada than in many European societies but, by the mid-1800s, schooling had a noticeable presence. One historical indicator of the collective importance we place on schooling is the number of elementary and secondary school teachers hired. In 1870, there were just over 13,000 full-time teachers in Canada. By 1970 this number had swollen to just over 260,000, an increase of 1,900%. In 1995, close to 300,000 full-time elementary and secondary school teachers were employed across Canada (Guppy and Davies 1996).

1.2 GROWTH IN THE TEACHING WORK FORCE

By the late 19th century, schools were well established in most regions of Canada (see Phillips 1957; Wilson, Stamp and Audet 1970; Curtis 1988). From the mid-1800s until the 1920s, literacy and elementary education were widely promoted and the teaching labour force expanded accordingly. However, because of the Depression and the Second World War, school expansion slowed and the early momentum of the "school promoters" was not maintained (see Prentice 1977). Between 1930 and 1950, fewer than 20,000 new teaching jobs were added to the school system, representing a growth rate of only 28% (see Table 1.1). That rate was well below the 69% growth experienced between 1870 and 1890 or the 74% growth experienced between 1910 and 1930. In sharp contrast, after the Second World War, over 170,000 new teaching jobs were introduced between 1950 and 1970, and the growth rate soared to 193%.

TABLE 1.1

FULL-TIME TEACHERS IN PUBLIC ELEMENTARY AND SECONDARY SCHOOLS, AND CANADIAN LABOUR FORCE, SELECTED YEARS, 1870 TO 1994

Year	Number of teachers	% change	Total Canadian labour force	Teachers as % of labour force
1870	13,323	…	..	..
1890	22,550	69	..	..
1910	40,476	79	..	..
1930	70,245	74	4,060,000	1.7
1950	89,682	28	5,198,000	1.7
1970	262,457	193	8,395,000	3.1
1990	296,271	13	13,681,000	2.2
1994	306,227	3	14,928,000	2.1

.. figures not available

… figures not applicable

Source: Number of teachers for 1870 to 1970 taken from Leacy 1983, Series W-152; for 1990 and 1994 the numbers are from Statistics Canada, *Education in Canada*, various years. Total Canadian labour force estimates for 1930 to 1950 are from Urquhart and Buckley 1965, Series C-50; for 1970 to 1992 the estimates are from Statistics Canada, "Annual Labour Force Estimates 1946–1994," *Canadian Social Trends*, 1995 (Spring), 34. Earlier comparable estimates of the Canadian labour force are unavailable.

The teaching profession's fluctuating growth cycle has been sluggish in recent decades, with the rate of change falling to 13% between 1970 and 1990, its lowest level since Confederation. This slowing of growth in the full-time teaching work force is partly because the baby boom generation has passed through the school system, thus reducing the demand for teachers. School boards have also begun using more part-time and temporary teachers to cope with mounting financial constraints, and this too has slowed the growth of full-time teaching jobs. For example, part-time teachers in the elementary and secondary system have grown from 1 in 40 teachers in the early 1970s to 1 in 10 in the 1990s (see Table 2.2).

Any growth in the teaching work force is partly a function of population change. As the Canadian population grows so does the demand for teachers. Canadians are also spending more time in school, especially at the upper levels. These two factors have been the primary forces behind the expansion of the teaching profession.

1.3   SCHOOL ATTENDANCE: EARLY CENSUS REPORTS

At the time of Confederation, 723,000 students were enrolled in public elementary and secondary schools (Leacy 1983, W-67). However, many children, especially in rural areas, did not attend full time because they still helped with family obligations. For this reason, education historians focus more attention on attendance rates than enrolment figures (Gidney and Millar 1985; Harrigan 1990). In 1867 the average daily attendance at school was estimated at approximately 41%, meaning that on any given day only about 4 in 10 registered pupils would typically be attending. Most provinces introduced minimum school-leaving ages in the 1870s, requiring students between ages 7 and 12 to be in school for some portion of the year. Enforcement was lax, though, and children were routinely used as family workers.[1] With most Canadian families dependent on agricultural, hunting, trapping, and fishing occupations, children were valuable assistants at peak times in these seasonal industries. This practice inhibited the growth of full attendance at school.

The 1921 Census reported that "[f]or Canada (exclusive of Yukon and Northwest Territories), out of every 1,000 children, 7 to 14 years of age, 886 attended school for some period in 1921, as against 798 in 1911" (Dominion Bureau of Statistics 1925, xxi). By 1931, the authors of the census could claim that "practically every person in the population goes to school at some period of life . . ." (Dominion Bureau of Statistics 1936, 268). For example, more than 95% of boys and girls between ages 9 and 12 attended school in 1931. Even in rural areas attendance rates were high, with more than 90% of children aged 9 to 12 attending school. And, as the census authors note, the reason for the marginally lower attendance rate is not because families in rural areas "are unwilling to send their children to school but that they are unable to send them" (p. 270). Schools were often not available in rural areas, especially in remote rural areas (see Harrigan 1988).

While these figures show that schooling, by the 1930s, was a shared experience for most Canadian youngsters, the normal age for starting school was later than it is now. For example, in 1931 the census showed that over 90% of 7- to 14-year-olds attended school, but just over 50% of 6-year-olds and less than 20% of 5-year-olds attended. The census authors wrote that it was "remarkable" that "any person attends [school] at 5 years . . . since this age is manifestly considered abnormal for school attendance" (Dominion Bureau of Statistics 1936, 269). Most provinces with compulsory schooling required attendance at age 7 or 8 and it was some years until compulsory starting ages for schooling dropped to 5 and 6. It is important to emphasize, however, that government intervention was not required to force parents to send their children to school. Legislation enshrined what was already common practice. As Harrigan (1990, 805) notes, "compulsory school legislation" simply enforced "what had become a common experience for almost all Canadian boys and girls."

It is also important to stress that although provincial legislation in the early 20th century mandated school attendance for children between the ages of 7 and 14 (depending on the province), it was not abnormal for students to attend sporadically. For example, even though 80% of children between the ages of 7 and 14 attended school for some period in 1911, 13% of these children attended for six months or less. However, this too changed over the next two decades such that by 1931 most students were attending school regularly for at least eight months of the year. In this sense the 1930s are an important milestone in the history of Canadian schooling, since by the start of that decade elementary schooling had become a common experience for all young people—it was the first transition point in the shift to mass schooling.

Attendance rates over a longer time period are shown in Figure 1.2, which charts average daily attendance at public elementary and secondary schools between 1870 and 1960. Daily school attendance increased by an average of just under 5% every decade from 1870 to 1910, but the rate of increase more than doubled in the period 1915 to 1930 as attendance rates grew from 64% to 86% in 15 years. However, complementary to the period of slow growth in the teaching profession noted in the previous section, the rising attendance rates seen earlier in the century stagnated during the Depression and Second World War, so that by 1950 the daily attendance rate was still around 86%. The rate of change accelerated again after 1950, and by the 1960s full attendance in public elementary and high school was almost the norm.[2]

FIGURE 1.2

AVERAGE DAILY SCHOOL ATTENDANCE IN PUBLIC ELEMENTARY AND SECONDARY SCHOOLS, CANADA, 1870 TO 1960

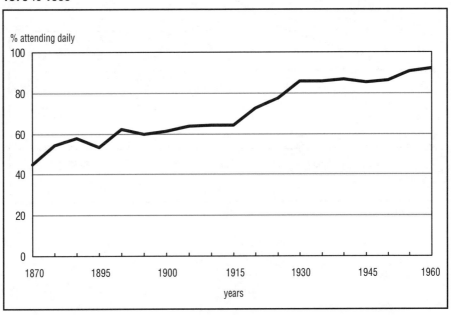

Source: Leacy (1983), Series W-68.

By 1960, it was routinely expected that most children would attend elementary and secondary school regularly, the second milestone on the road towards mass schooling in Canada. The Canadian population was largely urban at this point and less than 15% of the labour force was employed in primary occupations, such as fishing and logging. By 1960 all Canadian provinces had elementary and secondary school attendance rates greater than 90% (the low was Prince Edward Island at 90.2% and the high was Alberta at 95.2%).[3] This meant that mass schooling, the idea that all young children between specific ages would be formally educated in a publicly sanctioned school, was accomplished only within the last four decades in Canada.

Figure 1.3 captures in even finer detail this second transition to mass schooling by showing the daily attendance rates between 1951 and 1974 for children aged 14 to 17. This chart has the advantage of narrowing the age range to students in the secondary school system. As the figure clearly shows, it was not until the late 1960s that most young people regularly attended secondary school full time. It is important to stress here, as we note below, that regular attendance does not mean that all young people graduated from secondary school.

FIGURE 1.3

AVERAGE DAILY SCHOOL ATTENDANCE, 14- TO 17-YEAR-OLDS, CANADA, 1951 TO 1974

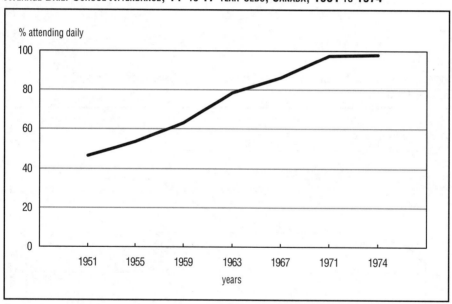

Source: Leacy (1983), Series W-14.

1.4 SCHOOLING THE BABY BOOMERS

Before the 1950s it was mainly the rate of enrolment—the proportion of school-aged children actually attending school—that affected class sizes. However, as the first and second transitions to universal or mass schooling took hold, changes in population size, as opposed to enrolment rates, had the greatest impact on elementary and secondary education. For a variety of reasons, birth rates in Canada soared in the late 1940s and 1950s, the era of Canada's baby boom. Canadian immigration numbers also increased in the 1950s, causing the size of the school-aged population to rise dramatically.

The Second World War had disrupted families and so a postwar boom in marriages and children was expected. The baby boom, however, only really took hold in the 1950s. Canadian troops returned home slowly in the latter part of the 1940s and it took some time for life to return to normal. Many veterans took advantage of government sponsorship to complete their schooling and therefore many delayed marriage. Furthermore, immediately following the war many Canadians still harboured fears of a return to the economic ravages of the Great Depression of the 1930s, and so many delayed starting families. Provincial and federal governments began campaigns to enhance family values; a tactic designed at least in part to encourage women to leave factory work (so returning veterans could find jobs) and begin families. Fuelled by world demand for Canadian exports, the economy was extremely buoyant in the 1950s and memories of the Depression faded. In combination, these changes gradually encouraged increasing numbers of Canadians to raise families that were relatively large by today's standards.

This led to 459,275 births in 1959, the peak of the baby boom. Figure 1.1 charts the changing fertility patterns in Canada by highlighting the number of children between 0 and 1 for each calendar year. As the chart shows, the baby boom occurred between the late 1940s and the early 1960s. A sharp decline in birth rates followed the boom's peak. The so-called baby bust stretched from the mid-1960s to the late 1980s. In 1973 only 343,373 children were born, more than 100,000 fewer babies than in 1959. Despite a small echo baby boom in the early 1990s, the 1959 birth total still has not been surpassed.

Although the rate of increase was not constant, starting in the late 1940s through to the late 1960s, school administrators experienced 20 years of uninterrupted growth in enrolment. As Kettle describes it:

> Architects learned to design for expansion, with bolt-on wall panels and movable partitions. Portable classrooms were distributed by the hundreds and thousands to fill gaps while the builders rushed in to slap on yet another new wing. (1976, 35)

To alleviate crowded classrooms, some schools were forced to teach one group of students in a morning shift (for example from 8 a.m. to 1 p.m.) and another in the afternoon (for example from 1 p.m. to 6 p.m.). As we noted above, teacher hiring accelerated through the period at a furious rate. This continued until the late 1960s, when growth slowed substantially. As Figure 1.1 shows, the growth had been relatively steep and steady, but the decline was precipitous and short. The actual effect on enrolment is shown in Figure 1.4. Both elementary and secondary school enrolments grew through the 1960s until 1969, when the number of elementary students began to decline. The decline continued through the 1970s, and only since the late 1980s has there been modest growth in the number of students in Grades 1 to 8.

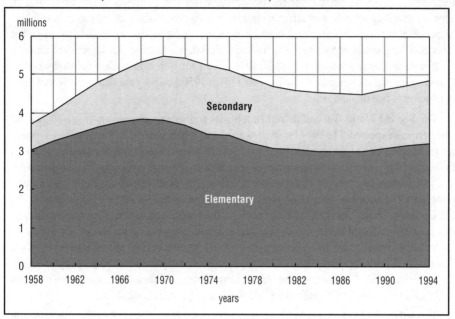

Source: Statistics Canada, Catalogue no. 81-229.

At the elementary level, the size of the school-age population (5 to 13 years) is an almost perfect predictor of school enrolments, largely because children must attend until age 16 unless home schooling or other permission is granted. At the secondary level, the minimum school-leaving age is important for the more junior grades, but most Grade 10 or 11 students are not legally required to remain in school. This means that both population size and voluntary participation rates are key factors affecting enrolment numbers in secondary schools.

Secondary school enrolments peaked in the early 1970s. This was partly because the size of the age cohort of 14- to 17-year-old students peaked in the mid-1970s, and partly because participation rates for 16- and 17-year-olds soared to over 95%, compared with 75% in the early 1960s. This greater participation rate helps explain the steeper slope in the ascending line for secondary enrolments than elementary enrolments in Figure 1.4. By the mid-1970s the number of secondary school students had begun to decline, as the 14- to 17-year-old cohort began to shrink.

As with elementary enrolments, secondary-level enrolments began to climb again in the last decade. This is a consequence of the same two phenomena, although more recently it is the participation rate rather than the cohort size that has been the major factor. The 17-year-old population peaked at 494,000 in 1978, declined to 376,900 in 1991, and has since rebounded to 390,400 in 1994. The enrolment figures started climbing earlier, in 1987, and the rise has again been steeper than cohort size alone would predict. The reason is that, once again, in the late 1980s and early 1990s, participation rates grew. More and more teenagers responded to the concern that a high school graduation certificate was a minimal labour market credential (see below for more detail on secondary school graduation).

Beaujot and McQuillan have referred to the ebb and flow of students in the elementary and secondary system as "roller coaster enrolment" (1982, 122). This roller coaster has not been evident at the other two levels of schooling—pre-elementary and postsecondary. At the pre-elementary level, the number of students registering in public schools has increased annually since the Second World War. In 1958, 132,000 students, or just 5% of Canada's full-time student population, attended public pre-elementary schools (see Figure 1.5). By 1994 more than 490,000 students, or 10% of enrolments, were in pre-elementary schools. By contrast, in 1958 about 75% of all Canadian full-time students were in Grades 1 to 8. This figure declined to roughly 50% in 1994. The major reason the baby boom and bust have not created an enrolment roller coaster at the pre-elementary level is that more school boards are offering kindergarten classes. Now, virtually all regions of all provinces and territories provide at least one year of pre-elementary schooling.

FIGURE 1.5

FULL-TIME ENROLMENT, PERCENTAGES, BY LEVEL OF EDUCATION, 1958 TO 1994

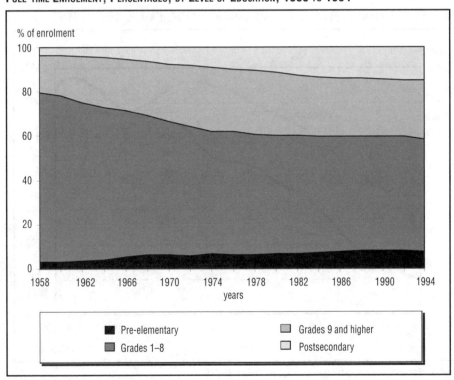

Source: Statistics Canada, Education in Canada, 1988 and 1995, Catalogue no. 81-229; Leacy, *Historical Statistics of Canada*, 1983, series W1–9.

At the postsecondary level, enrolments have continued to rise in the face of the baby bust. Looking at the trends up to the 1980s, Beaujot and McQuillan (1982, 124) remarked that if "trends continue, the 1980s will see a marked decline in postsecondary enrolment, especially after 1982 when the population aged 18 to 24 will have peaked." As Figure 1.5 shows, prior to the 1980s postsecondary enrolments had grown steadily. Approximately 75% of the increase in the 1960s and 1970s was due to the growing age cohort of 18- to 24-year-olds, while the other 25% was due to greater participation rates. After the early 1980s, although the size of the 18-to-24 cohort shrank, a greater and greater percentage of that age group completed high school and enrolled in postsecondary schooling. Figure 1.6 shows this trend even more directly. The size of the 18- to 24-year-old cohort is displayed on the right vertical axis, while the size of the postsecondary school enrolment is registered along the left vertical axis. The enrolment line continues to grow, unabated by the decline in the 18- to 24-year-old population. The reason for the continued growth is that as more and more teenagers complete high school, many of them continue on to postsecondary institutions. In 1985–86, 25.2% of 18- to 24-year-olds were enrolled full time at a postsecondary college or university, a figure that rose to 33.1% by 1993–94 (Statistics Canada, *Education in Canada* 1995, 89).

FIGURE 1.6

FULL-TIME POSTSECONDARY ENROLMENT AND POPULATION 18 TO 24, CANADA, 1958 TO 1996

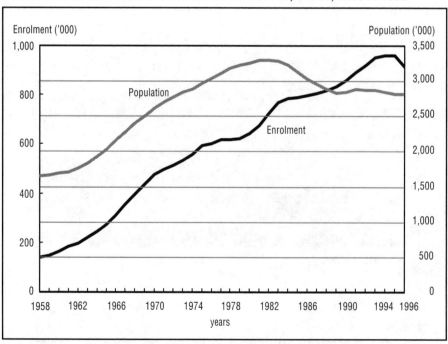

Source: Statistics Canada, Catalogue nos. 81-568; 81-220; 81-229.

One alternative explanation needs to be considered. Postsecondary enrolments could continue to expand, even if the 18- to 24-year-old cohort's participation rates remained stable and its size declined. This could occur if colleges and universities recruited a growing proportion of students from outside the traditional 18- to 24-year-old age group. This has happened to a modest degree, mostly by the growth of graduate student populations, many of whom are older than 24. However, this increase plays only a minor part in the overall growth of postsecondary enrolments. As well, although more individuals are returning to college or undergraduate university programs after age 24, this too has only a minor effect on enrolments. In 1985–86, less than 4% of the 25-to-29 age group were enrolled full time in the postsecondary system, a figure that grew to just over 4% in 1993–94 (Statistics Canada, *Education in Canada*, various years).

By separating the types of institutions, we can see whether the trend is common to the entire postsecondary sector. Figure 1.7 shows the relation between cohort size and participation levels, but this time with college and university distinguished. Here we focus on annual percentage changes. For the 18- to 24-year-old cohort, the line tracks year-upon-year changes in the size of the cohort, expressing this change as a percentage increase or decrease relative to the immediately preceding year. In the first half of the 1970s this age cohort grew by 2% to 3% annually, with growth slowing to between 1% and 2% later in the decade. By the early 1980s, however, the 18-to-24 cohort had begun to shrink and year upon year this decrease has continued into the 1990s. The other two lines show what has happened to college and university enrolments through the same period. First, it is important to note that there is no correspondence between the population cohort line and the enrolment lines—they vary independently of each other. Second, college and university enrolments have increased almost every year since the 1970s (although the rate of increase varied). There are two minor exceptions to this. University enrolments declined in the late 1970s and college enrolments decreased for several years in the late 1980s. Third, at both the college and university level, there is substantial volatility in enrolment increases and decreases. Early in the 1980s, during an economic recession, enrolments rose in colleges by as much as 8% a year and in universities by as much as 6% a year as many "discouraged workers" left the depressed labour market in favour of postsecondary education. Just four years later the increase for college was zero and for universities it was just above 1%. In the face of such volatility, making predictions about future changes in postsecondary enrolment patterns is difficult.

FIGURE 1.7

ANNUAL RATE OF GROWTH IN COLLEGE AND UNIVERSITY FULL-TIME ENROLMENT VERSUS GROWTH
IN 18-TO-24 COHORT, CANADA, 1971 TO 1993

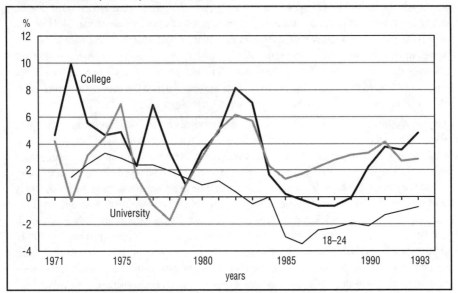

Source: Statistics Canada, Catalogue nos. 81-568, 81-229 and 81-220; Leacy, *Historical Statistics of Canada, 1983.*

1.5 TRANSITION PROBABILITIES

A different perspective on changes in the education system comes from examining in greater detail the progress people make in moving from one education level to the next. Over the decades, the likelihood of young Canadians completing a particular level of schooling has typically increased. In the early 1900s the percentage of youngsters completing grade school was relatively low, but over time this completion rate rose so that now virtually everyone advances through the grade structure at least to Grade 7 or 8. As the rate of successful completion of elementary school rose, more and more children went to secondary school. After the Second World War, as the proportion of young people completing secondary school grew, the pool of potential participants for postsecondary education expanded. The basic point here, as expounded by Pineo and Goyder (1988), is that retention rates in education are cumulative, in the sense that one level of education typically requires the successful completion of an earlier one. The education system, from kindergarten to doctoral studies can be thought of as "laddered"; to make transitions up the rungs, students must successfully negotiate a series of earlier steps.

This idea of "transition probabilities" is captured in Table 1.2, which shows completion rates for different levels of education, by birth cohorts and sex. The entry in the top left cell (0.87) means that for everyone born prior to 1917 and counted in the 1991 Census, 87% had attended school through at least Grades 5 to 8. The values for women (0.88) and men (0.86) show women are slightly more likely than men to reach this level of schooling. Going down the column, the entry for "some high school" (0.63) means that *of those who entered Grades 5 to 8, 63%*

continued to high school. The probabilities down each column are transition probabilities based on the subset of individuals who survived each earlier transition (that is, the probability is analogous to a survival rate). The beauty of these transition rates is their ability to show the cumulative impact of retention changes in the school system.

Transition probabilities can help identify and explain trends. For example, two different explanations can account for why more and more Canadians are graduating from high school. First, it could be that the likelihood of graduating from high school, once a student has entered high school, has risen. Second, it could simply be that more people are continuing to high school, but the same proportion is graduating. Notice that for men the transition probabilities for high school graduation increased for each birth cohort until the 1947-to-1951 group. Subsequently the probabilities have remained relatively stable. This means that the likelihood of a man graduating from high school has not changed for several decades. In absolute terms, more men have been graduating simply because the propensity of men to continue to some high school has increased, although only slightly, over the last few decades. For women, the rates tell a different story. Among women who do continue to high school, the graduation rate has continued to expand and, in the last birth cohort, 84% of women who entered high school were graduating. In comparison with the United States (see Mare 1981), where about 90% of those who entered high school subsequently graduated, the corresponding figure for Canada is 81% (84% for women, 79% for men).

The transition probabilities also show a clear increase in the likelihood that high school graduates will continue on to some form of postsecondary schooling. For the oldest cohort, 62% of high school graduates made the transition to the postsecondary system (63% of men and 62% of women). In the final cohort, the transition rate is 75%, with more women (77%) than men (72%) continuing to postsecondary institutions. A growing proportion of people are seeking out postsecondary opportunities but the growth is relatively modest, rising by only 13% over five or more decades. Basing their findings on 1981 Census information, Pineo and Goyder (1988, 43) reported "little trend in the propensity to seek out or complete training at any level beyond high school." The 1991 Census data suggest the take-up rate for postsecondary education has risen, although the pattern is not always consistent.

This lack of consistency is seen most dramatically when comparing the rates by which women and men complete university once they have begun. Among men in the oldest cohort the rate was 62%. By the 1962-to-1966 cohort, it was virtually unchanged at 61% (the last cohort has to be discounted here because by 1991 many people born in 1967 to 1971 would not have completed their schooling). For women, however, the pattern is much different, with only 38% of women in the earliest birth cohort completing university (given their entry into university) but 61% of women in the 1962-to-1966 cohort graduating. At least for men, then, universities in Canada have not managed to increase the prospects of their new entrants continuing through to graduation. Furthermore, only about 6 in 10 students who are admitted to university eventually graduate.

TABLE 1.2

PROBABILITY OF PROCEEDING TO THE NEXT LEVEL OF SCHOOLING, BY BIRTH COHORT AND SEX, 1991 CENSUS

Level of schooling	Prior to 1917	1917– 1926	1927– 1931	1932– 1936	1937– 1941	1942– 1946	1947– 1951	1952– 1956	1957– 1961	1962– 1966	1967– 1971
Grades 5–8											
Total	0.87	0.92	0.94	0.95	0.97	0.98	0.99	0.99	0.99	0.99	1.00
Male	0.86	0.92	0.94	0.95	0.97	0.98	0.99	0.99	0.99	0.99	0.99
Female	0.88	0.92	0.94	0.95	0.97	0.98	0.99	0.99	0.99	0.99	1.00
Some high school											
Total	0.63	0.69	0.72	0.77	0.83	0.88	0.93	0.96	0.97	0.97	0.98
Male	0.62	0.69	0.72	0.77	0.83	0.88	0.93	0.96	0.96	0.97	0.97
Female	0.63	0.69	0.73	0.77	0.83	0.88	0.93	0.96	0.97	0.98	0.98
Graduated from high school											
Total	0.57	0.60	0.64	0.67	0.72	0.78	0.81	0.80	0.79	0.81	0.81
Male	0.60	0.64	0.68	0.71	0.74	0.79	0.81	0.80	0.78	0.79	0.79
Female	0.56	0.57	0.61	0.64	0.69	0.76	0.80	0.81	0.80	0.83	0.84
Postsecondary											
Total	0.62	0.62	0.64	0.65	0.68	0.71	0.72	0.72	0.73	0.75	0.75
Male	0.63	0.65	0.64	0.66	0.69	0.72	0.75	0.74	0.74	0.74	0.72
Female	0.62	0.60	0.63	0.64	0.67	0.69	0.69	0.70	0.71	0.75	0.77
Some university											
Total	0.44	0.45	0.44	0.45	0.48	0.51	0.53	0.50	0.46	0.46	0.51
Male	0.52	0.51	0.49	0.49	0.52	0.55	0.54	0.51	0.46	0.46	0.51
Female	0.39	0.38	0.39	0.39	0.43	0.47	0.51	0.62	0.46	0.45	0.51
Complete university											
Total	0.49	0.53	0.56	0.57	0.60	0.62	0.62	0.61	0.60	0.61	0.30[1]
Male	0.62	0.62	0.64	0.65	0.67	0.68	0.66	0.63	0.62	0.61	0.27[1]
Female	0.38	0.40	0.45	0.47	0.50	0.54	0.58	0.58	0.58	0.61	0.32[1]
Postgraduate											
Total	0.21	0.23	0.26	0.28	0.30	0.29	0.24	0.20	0.17	0.11	0.03[1]
Male	0.24	0.24	0.29	0.31	0.35	0.33	0.27	0.23	0.19	0.12	0.03[1]
Female	0.17	0.19	0.20	0.22	0.23	0.23	0.19	0.18	0.14	0.09	0.02[1]

1. See text for an explanation of these low transition probabilities.

Source: Census of Canada, 1991, special tabulations.

1.6 FUTURE POPULATION SIZES

What will the size of the school system look like in the future? As the preceding analysis has shown, the size of the 5- to 12-year-old cohort is the major factor influencing elementary level enrolment. Cohort size also plays a significant role at the secondary school level, especially as the participation rate for 16-year-olds approaches 100%. However, only about 75% of 17-year-olds attend school full time (either at secondary or postsecondary institutions) and for this age group, participation-rate increases or decreases will influence both secondary and postsecondary enrolments. At the postsecondary levels, where the minimum school-leaving age does not apply, the participation rate as opposed to cohort population size has become a key factor behind growth.

It is exceedingly difficult to accurately project the size of the Canadian population, let alone age groups within it, especially for any long-range view. However, it is precisely the long-range view that is the most interesting, at least for present purposes.

Some of the best projections for Canada are developed by the Population Projections Section of Statistics Canada's Demography Division. In preparing its most recent national estimates, it considered changes in fertility, mortality, immigration, emigration, returning Canadians, and non-permanent residents (see George et al. 1994). Based primarily on changes in natural increase (births minus deaths) and net migration (immigration minus emigration), the demographers project Canadian population figures for selected age groups.

As they argue, fertility is still "the single most important demographic component influencing population growth" (George et al. 1994, 7). This is especially true for the school-aged population, since the vast majority of children now attending Canadian schools, especially at the elementary and secondary levels, were born in Canada. In 1994, for example, 27,633 Canadian immigrants were between the ages of 0 and 14, as compared with 5.9 million Canadians in the same cohort (see Statistics Canada, *Annual Demographic Statistics 1994*, 1995). Of course, immigration is fluid and so a single-year estimate fails to capture the number of children who immigrated to Canada and are in the school system. Nevertheless the above figures suggest the number of immigrants in the school system must be relatively low in comparison to the size of entire age cohort.

Statistics Canada's *Education Quarterly Review*, as part of its series "Education at a Glance," reports population figures over time for "youth immigrants." This group is defined as "the number of persons aged 0 to 19 who are, or have been, landed immigrants in Canada" (1995 Winter, 83). In 1971 the youth immigrant population was 35,708 (p. 77), which represents less than half of 1% of the entire 0-to-19 age cohort in Canada. For 1992 (the latest available data), the number of youth immigrants is estimated to have risen to 53,488 or 0.68% of the 0-to-19 age cohort. In comparison to Canadian births, immigration contributes a relatively small flow to the number of school-aged children in this country (see Chapter 3).

Predicting future school-aged populations hinges, then, on being able to predict both the number of women of childbearing age, and the number of children they are likely to bear. We already know, with some certainty, the number of Canadian women who will be of childbearing ages (15 to 49) early in the next century, since most of these women have already been born. Their numbers will be affected mainly by immigration over the next few decades. Far less certain are the likely fertility rates of these women. In 1974 the total fertility rate was 1.8 children.[4] The rate declined to 1.57 by 1987 and has subsequently rebounded slightly to 1.7 in the early 1990s. The Canadian rates are currently typical for advanced industrial economies and most observers expect this rate to remain reasonably stable over the next few decades.

George et al. (1994) predict that the total fertility rate will vary between 1.5 and 1.9 from now until 2016. They base this estimate on the likelihood that women will continue to increase their participation in the labour force, that knowledge and effective use of various contraceptive methods will continue, and that higher divorce rates, declining marriage rates, and the postponement of both marriage and childbearing will persist.

Immigration levels are the other significant contributor to school-aged populations, both directly in the guise of school-aged children, and indirectly through the recruitment of young, potential parents. In 1993–94 an estimated 225,000 immigrants entered Canada. George et al. (1994, 36) note that immigration levels may revert toward the levels of the 1980s (approximately 150,000). This may occur because of public concern with unemployment, especially if that is coupled with sluggish economic growth. Conversely, as they argue, immigration levels may continue at about 1% of the population, such that by 2016 the number of newcomers entering the country could be around 330,000 annually.

Low, medium and high projections for the Canadian population aged 5 to 14 are shown in Figure 1.8. Assuming that both fertility and immigration rates will decline from present levels until 2016, the 5- to 14-year-old cohort will decline from 2.1 million in 1996 to 1.8 million in 2016 and 1.7 million in 2041. Conversely, under the assumption that fertility will increase to 1.9 and annual immigration will be close to 1% of population, then the 5- to 14-year-old cohort will rise from 2.1 million in 1996 to 2.5 million by 2016 and 3.0 million by 2041.

FIGURE 1.8

POPULATION PROJECTIONS FOR 5- TO 14-YEAR-OLD COHORT, CANADA, 1996 TO 2041

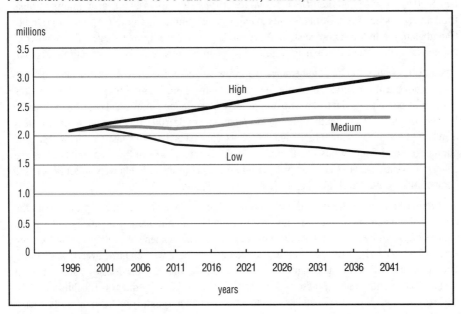

Source: Statistics Canada, Catalogue no. 91-520.

The population for the 15- to 24-year-old cohort is projected to rise through 2006 (see Figure 1.9). We can have more confidence in these projections than in those for the 5- to 14-year-old cohort because all of the people in the 15- to 24-year-old cohort have already been born. The low projection then predicts a 14% decline in the cohort between 2011 and 2021, followed by a period of equilibrium. The high projection foresees sustained growth in the 15-to-24 cohort. How these population numbers will correspond to actual enrolments is, as we have noted above, tough to predict for the postsecondary level. If the competition for jobs continues to be intense, and if educational credentials continue to be used by employers as signals of ability or as screening devices, then participation rates are likely to remain stable and perhaps even grow.

FIGURE 1.9

POPULATION PROJECTIONS FOR 15- TO 24-YEAR-OLD COHORT, CANADA, 1996 TO 2041

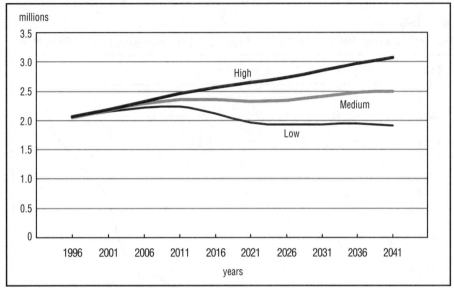

Source: Statistics Canada, Catalogue no. 91-520.

1.7   UNIVERSITY DEGREES

The growing importance of postsecondary credentials is reflected by the increasing number of Canadians who have stayed in school to complete a university degree. Good records on degree recipients only began in the mid-1800s, even though the first independent university charter in Canada was granted in 1802, to the University of King's College in Nova Scotia. Figure 1.10 plots the number of bachelor and first professional degrees awarded in Canada from 1851 to 1995.[5] Growth in the number of degrees awarded was slow but reasonably steady throughout the later part of the 1800s, increasing at a faster rate only after the First World War.

It is at the close of the Second World War, however, that the number of university degrees was most affected. On the one hand the war had reinforced the importance of scientific research in the minds of many (indeed there was a proposal to suspend the teaching of social science and humanities during the Second World War). On the other hand, the war's end also created a management problem for the federal government. How was the country going to reintegrate the returning veterans into Canadian society? Among a variety of initiatives connected with the

Veterans' Rehabilitation Act, the federal government agreed to pay the university tuition fees of qualifying veterans as well as a special sum of $150 to each university for every veteran enrolled (see Cameron 1991, 44). As a result, university enrolments soared in the immediate postwar years. For example, veteran enrolments at universities across the country peaked at approximately 35,000 in 1946–1947, swelling attendance by 44% in that year alone. This explains the noticeable rise in degrees awarded in the late 1940s and early 1950s. A subsequent dip occurred as the number of degrees granted settled back toward pre-war levels in the mid-1950s. However, since 1955, degree attainment has skyrocketed, with growth levels remaining high in subsequent decades.

FIGURE 1.10

BACHELOR'S AND FIRST PROFESSIONAL DEGREES AWARDED BY CANADIAN UNIVERSITIES, 1850 TO 1995

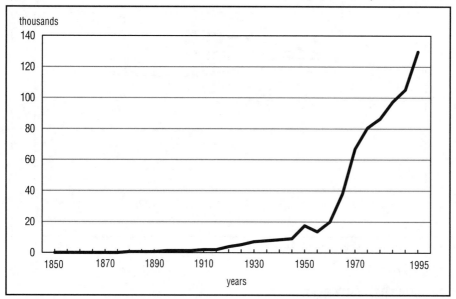

Source: Leacy, *Historical Statistics of Canada,* 1983; *Education in Canada,* various years.

1.8   RISING LEVELS OF EDUCATION: 1951 TO 1991

Comparing data from the 1951 and 1991 Censuses vividly illustrates the acceleration of degree attainment in the postwar period. In 1951 fewer than 200,000 Canadians, or fewer than 2 in every 100 people aged 15 and over, had a university degree. By 1991, only 40 years later, more than 2.4 million, or more than 10 in 100 people aged 15 and over, had a university degree. Put another way, while the population 15 years and over increased by just over 100% between 1951 and 1991, the number of university graduates grew by nearly 1,200%.

Rising levels of education were not just a consequence of people choosing to pursue university degrees. As the transition probabilities showed, the practice of staying in school longer also meant that far fewer Canadians left school before completing at least elementary school and more recently high school. Table 1.3, showing changes in educational levels since the Second World War, reveals the acute decline in the percentage of Canadians with less than Grade 9 education and the correspondingly sharp upward trend in the percentage of Canadians with university degrees. The biggest percentage changes occur in the earlier decades, with a distinct tailing off in the pace of educational advance in the most recent decade. In the 1950s, 1960s, and 1970s, the pace of educational upgrading increases no matter which dimension of schooling is examined (that is, the percentage of people with less than Grade 9 or the percentage of people with a university degree). Almost 53% more Canadians held a university degree in 1961 than in 1951 and between 1971 and 1981 the number of degree-holders increased by 67%. However, the rates of change slowed in the 1980s, when the growth rate for Canadians earning university degrees was only 43%.

TABLE 1.3

NUMBER AND PERCENTAGE OF POPULATION 15 AND OVER WITH LESS THAN GRADE 9 OR WITH A
UNIVERSITY DEGREE, BY YEAR

	Less than Grade 9			University degree		
Year	Number	%	% change	Number	%	% change
1951	5,069,134	51.9	...	188,783	1.9	...
1961	5,313,584	44.1	− 15.0	352,876	2.9	52.6
1971	4,858,295	32.3	− 26.8	718,775	4.8	65.5
1981	3,851,285	20.7	− 35.9	1,490,185	8.0	66.7
1991	3,051,900	14.3	− 30.9	2,419,750	11.4	42.5

... figures not applicable

Source: Statistics Canada, *Educational Attainment and School Attendance*, 1993, 11.

Does this mean that the rate at which Canadians are attaining university degrees is decreasing? At a time when the value of education is being stressed more and more, any decrease of this sort would be worrisome. Intuitively, it would be tempting to conclude from the figures in Table 1.3 that the rate of university-degree attainment is slowing, but this would be a mistake.

The apparent slowing of the relative increase or percentage change in degree attainment in the 1980s is partly a function of two demographic changes. First, the peak of the baby boom cohort attended university in the late 1970s and early 1980s. Even though the propensity of subsequent cohorts to go on to attain university degrees remained high, they made less of an impact on overall levels of education simply because of their smaller cohort size. Coupled with this, Canada's population continued to age throughout this period and relatively more Canadians over 65 were living longer. Since elderly Canadians tend to have lower levels of schooling than do the young, this too dampened the rate of increase in educational attainment of the population 15 and over. Therefore, even though the absolute number of people with university degrees grew by 929,565 in the 1980s as compared with 771,410 in the 1970s, the size of this group, relative to the rest of the Canadian population, was smaller. This gives the impression that the pace of educational attainment is decelerating.

There is an additional factor at work here, however. The Canadian postsecondary system experienced unprecedented expansion from the late 1960s through to the end of the 1970s. This was a time in which new universities were born while others rapidly expanded. Consequently, there was a healthy spurt in the number of degrees granted in this period. The 1980s, in contrast, were a time of consolidation and, in the vernacular of university presidents, a period of retrenchment. Funding was tighter and expansion slowed.

1.9 EDUCATION STOCKS AND FLOWS

Although subsequent chapters will explore various reasons for the changes in educational attainment discussed above, it is useful to consider, in a general way, the processes that underlie the changes illustrated so far. Changes in the levels of educational attainment, or in the *stock* of schooling possessed by the entire Canadian public, can be thought of as a consequence of four population *flows*. There are two inward flows affecting the stock of schooling. One inflow is from young people moving through the school system. A second inflow results from immigrants moving into the country. The two other flows, both outward, are emigration and mortality. Inflows of more and more young people increase the average stock of schooling since younger people tend to attain more schooling than their parents and grandparents. The mortality outflow also contributes to a rising average stock of schooling since older people have, on average, less schooling than the young. The contribution of net migration (immigration minus emigration) is not so easily summarized. Historically more people have arrived in Canada than have left the country in any one year, and so in this century net migration has been positive. And, as we will see in Chapter 3, the education of our immigrant population has always been equal to, and sometimes better than, that of the Canadian population. We know far less about emigration but it seems that emigrants tend to have above average levels of schooling, largely because these are the people who are recruited for, or are attracted to, jobs abroad (pursuit of employment is probably a main reason why Canadians leave the country, although some no doubt return).

In total, however, these four flows are relatively small in relation to the size of the entire population and so it takes some time for changes in the stock of schooling to be manifest. Even over a decade, inflows and outflows do not represent a sizable proportion of the population, meaning that the net changes in the stock of schooling are relatively minor over short- or even medium-term intervals. This is especially the case for the emigrant population which, while estimated to run between 50,000 and 100,000 people annually, is only a tiny fraction of the entire Canadian population.

Seen as a whole, the era after the Second World War was one of unparalleled growth in Canadian schooling. This extraordinary growth is exactly what we would expect in an era often depicted using the imagery of a knowledge explosion or an information age (Bell 1973). However, in the context of our educational history before the Second World War, this growth can be seen as somewhat surprising. As John Porter lamented in *The Vertical Mosaic*, "Canada entered the post World War II industrial boom with a poorly educated labour force" (1965, 155). Historically Canada had relied on immigration as the mechanism to inflate the necessary stock of educated labour essential for the industrial era. It was this inflow from abroad, as opposed to the expansion of schooling for Canadian youngsters, that had been used to stoke the talent pool of the Canadian labour force.

In its first annual report, the Economic Council of Canada (1964) placed education at the top of the list of factors essential to attaining faster and better productivity growth in Canada. Improving the stock of education was deemed essential to keeping pace with the dynamic American economy, and this report signaled one of the first moves to look at inflows of Canadian youth as the key component of growth for an even better-educated work force. That the Canadian education system reacted more slowly than some experts anticipated was evident as late as 1976 when the Organisation for Economic Co-operation and Development (OECD) was lamenting how poorly Canada had done in fostering the growth of schooling. Engaging in a bit of hyperbole, the Commission concluded that Canadian education was, at that time, "clearly approaching a danger zone" (OECD 1976, 102).

While it would be disconcerting to learn that levels of schooling in Canada had not accelerated after the Second World War, it is important to remember that in the 1950s the government's conviction to fund postsecondary schooling was not strong (Cameron 1991). As well, further education beyond high school was not a high priority for most families. What made it essential for Canadians to reverse their thinking about schooling was the intense globalization occurring in the latter half of this century. As revealed by the very presence of an OECD commission examining national education programs, international comparisons of educational progress were seen as imperative. Increasingly, national progress was being measured on a world scale, whether in terms of GDP, infant mortality rates, or university participation figures (see Davies and Guppy 1997b).

Another part of the story about levels of education, and a worry in the context of both international competitiveness and national poverty levels, was a concern about school drop-outs. Although average or typical attainment levels may have been rising, there was a fear that some were not keeping abreast of the trend toward more and more schooling.

1.10   LOW EDUCATIONAL ATTAINMENT AND SCHOOL DROP-OUTS

A focus on school drop-outs or early school leavers (Gilbert and Devereaux 1993; Tanner, Krahn, and Hartnagel 1995) reveals a key debate in Canadian education. The extraordinary growth in the number of Canadians with university degrees is matched by a stagnant number of Canadians without high school completion. For example, according to the 1991 Census, 55,610 people between the ages of 20 and 24—56.7% of them men—had an education below the Grade 9 level. At a time when many social commentators speak of the need for a high school graduation certificate as a *minimum* qualification for the labour force, having a schooling level below Grade 9 is problematic. Young people who leave the school system that early are seen by some, in the context of a global economy, as a serious potential drain on society. Without having the rudimentary skills many deem necessary for functioning successfully in 21st century jobs and society, these school leavers could face bleak futures individually and act as a collective anchor on society by failing to contribute positively to social debate and economic prosperity.

TABLE 1.4

NUMBER AND PERCENTAGE OF POPULATION WITH LESS THAN GRADE 9, BY AGE, 1951 TO 1991

Year	15–24 years		25 years and over	
	Number	%	Number	%
1951	892,582	41.6	4,176,552	54.9
1961	714,659	27.3	4,598,925	48.8
1971	491,865	12.4	4,366,430	39.4
1981	255,485	5.5	3,595,800	25.7
1991	145,740	3.8	2,906,160	16.6

Source: Statistics Canada, *Educational Attainment and School Attendance*, 1993, 11.

As Table 1.4 shows, 55% of Canadians aged 25 and over had less than Grade 9 in 1951. This pattern has changed dramatically in recent decades, however, and now only 1 in 6 Canadians aged 25 or over have attained less than Grade 9. Restricting the age range to individuals between 15 and 24, we see, from 1951 to 1991, a decline in the percentage of those with less than Grade 9. (At 15 most young people would be expected to have completed Grade 9.) In 1951, 42 out of every 100 men in this age cohort had not completed Grade 9, but this number dropped sharply, to 4 in every 100 men, by 1991. Men have always been more likely than women to leave school before completing the ninth grade, and this trend has continued up to the present. Given the resource-based nature of Canada's economy earlier in this century, many men had found that leaving school early did them little immediate harm since jobs in the primary sector and blue collar occupations were easy to find, especially in logging, mining, fishing, and farming. However, even by 1951 only about 20% of the Canadian work force was employed in the primary sector (and that percentage dropped to about 5% in 1991). Consequently, by 1991 slightly less than 15% of Canadians aged 15 and over had less than Grade 9, and most of those with low levels of schooling were among the more elderly. However, a substantial proportion of Canadians still lack high school graduation certificates.

TABLE 1.5

NUMBER AND PERCENTAGE OF POPULATION WITHOUT HIGH SCHOOL GRADUATION, BY AGE GROUP, 1991

Age group	Total population	Population without high school graduation[1]	%
20–24	1,960,595	415,085	21.2
25–34	4,840,340	1,113,410	23.0
35–44	4,353,575	1,083,260	24.9
45–54	2,960,445	1,101,170	37.2
55–64	2,385,235	1,275,280	53.5
65 and over	2,932,320	1,887,875	64.4

1. Excludes individuals with secondary school-level trades certificates and diplomas.

Source: Census of Canada, 1991, special tabulations.

The high school drop-out rate has declined dramatically in this country (see Table 1.5), but as of 1991, more than 1 in 5 Canadians between the ages of 20 and 24 still left high school before attaining a graduation certificate. If one of the indicators of mass schooling today is the near universal completion of the secondary tier of education, then Canada is close to accomplishing this transition. However, Table 1.5 shows that the reduction in school drop-outs, by age group, has slowed considerably in recent times. There is a sizable gap of more than 39% between the oldest cohort in the table (those 65 and over) and the cohort aged 35 to 44. However, in comparing the 35- to 44-year-old group with the two younger cohorts in the table, the percentage differences are not nearly so noticeable. Figure 1.11 shows this trend a different way. The percentage of individuals without secondary school graduation dropped substantially between 1971 and 1981. For example, more than 60% of 25-year-olds in 1971 had not received a secondary school graduation certificate, whereas only a decade later the percentage had dropped to below 30. The decline continued to 1991 (20.4%) but the size of the reduction over the decade was greatly reduced compared with the change between 1971 and 1981.

FIGURE 1.11

PERCENTAGE OF INDIVIDUALS WITHOUT A SECONDARY SCHOOL GRADUATION CERTIFICATE, BY AGE, CANADA, 1971, 1981 AND 1991

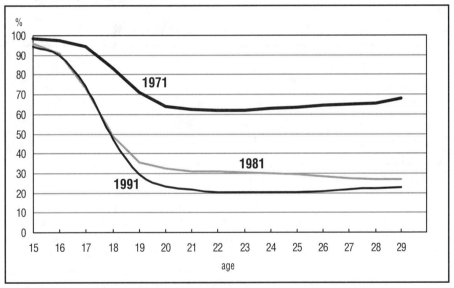

Source: Census of Canada, 1971, 1981 and 1991.

These data suggest that the universal completion of high school may be well in the distance, a finding that accords with the earlier analysis based on transition probabilities. Unfortunately, we cannot expect every Canadian to attain a secondary school graduation certificate. Learning impairments and other factors will prevent some from finishing high school. Nevertheless, as we noted earlier, our graduation rate remains substantially below the rate achieved in the United States.

Both provincial and federal governments have introduced policies aimed at improving high school completion rates. These have ranged from the federal Stay-in-School initiative to curriculum content revisions aimed at making school more relevant and attractive to younger students deemed to be "at risk" of dropping out. What makes these programs and the issue they seek to remedy so important is that those with low levels of schooling are being left behind in an era where educational credentials have been, and continue to be, important for both labour market success and civic participation (see Chapter 6).

1.11 MEDIAN LEVELS OF SCHOOLING IN CANADA

The number of years of schooling completed by Canadians provides a final indicator of increasing educational attainment. A good measure of this is provided by median years of schooling.[6] In 1971 the median number of years of schooling for the population 15 and over was 10.6, and in two decades this has risen to 12.5 (see Table 1.6). However, while school attainment continues to rise, it may be that the pace of this increase has slowed. Over the decade 1971 to 1981 the median number of years of schooling rose by 1.2, but from 1981 to 1991 the increase was only 0.7 years. This deceleration in the growth of the median years of schooling has been taken as a possible indication that "the pace of growth is slowing" (Mori and Burke 1989, 12).

TABLE **1.6**

MEDIAN YEARS OF SCHOOLING BY SEX, POPULATION **15** AND OVER, **1971** TO **1991**

Year	Males		Females	
	Median years	% change	Median years	% change
1971	10.5	...	10.6	...
1976	11.3	7.6	11.4	7.5
1981	11.9	5.3	11.8	3.5
1986	12.2	2.5	12.2	3.4
1991	12.5	2.5	12.5	2.5

... figures not applicable

Source: Census of Canada, various years.

As we saw earlier, there are several explanations for this apparent slowing in the pace of growth. First, the slowdown could simply be a result of population change. The cohort born at the demographic peak of the baby boom completed secondary school between the years 1978 and 1982. Cohorts since then have been smaller and therefore have had less impact on overall median years of schooling. Second, the slowing of the growth rate of median years of schooling may be simply a ceiling effect caused by the near universal completion of high school coupled with the breadth of, but not necessarily the lengthening of, higher education options.

Recent median levels of educational attainment for women and men are almost identical, but their patterns of schooling have typically differed (see Table 1.6). Men appeared at the ends of the schooling distribution more often than women did. That is, while the sexes had similar average years of schooling, men were more likely either to drop out of high school or to complete a university degree. This pattern has changed noticeably in the last two decades. In 1971 more men than women had less than Grade 9 education, but by 1991 the percentage of women and men with less than Grade 9 was identical (14.3%). At the other end of the distribution, 6.6% of men aged 15 and over had a university degree in 1971 compared with only 3% of women. However, between 1971 and 1991 women's degree attainment tripled so that 1 in 10 women aged 15 and over had a university degree by 1991. The number of men receiving degrees also increased over the same two decades and, although the rate only doubled, 12.8% of men 15 and over held a university degree in 1991 (see further detail in Chapter 4).

1.12 CONCLUSION

In this chapter, we provided a brief history of Canadian education, as seen through the demographic changes in the student and teacher populations. This history, especially the timing of key milestones in the transformation of Canadian schooling, shows the importance of population change in understanding the development of Canadian education. This chapter has explored the consequences of this century's sharp swings in population composition, spatial distribution and, especially, size. If birth rates continue on the steady path that they have followed over the past three decades, then natural increase is unlikely to provide the volatility in school enrolments that occurred in the past half-century. Furthermore, if the federal government maintains immigration levels at some fixed percentage of the national population, then this too may quell the erratic population changes of the 20th century. (Should responsibility for immigration revert to the provinces, as some hope, then this stability may not come to pass because the provinces may have different policies on immigration levels.)

Besides population numbers, participation rates, especially for individuals beyond the minimum school-leaving age, become the driving force of school enrolments. At the postsecondary level, where these rates are the most significant predictors of enrolment, the steady increase in participation has led to an expanding higher education sector. This bubble of expansion cannot continue at a steady pace forever, but it is impossible to predict exactly when the growth in participation will slow, although early enrolment estimates for 1995 and 1996 already suggest that enrolments are plateauing, if not dropping.

Canadians' rising levels of education and the consequences of this for the school system have had a profound impact on the teaching work force, the topic to which we turn next. Just who is teaching all of these students and how has the profession changed in recent decades?

ENDNOTES

1. Quebec is an important exception here. That province did not introduce regulations on compulsory school attendance until well into the next century, largely because the churches regulated schooling. Hunter (1986) reports that Quebec and Newfoundland established compulsory schooling in 1943.

2. Full daily attendance (100%) is never anticipated since some students will always be absent for various reasons (for example personal sickness, death or injury in the family or family travel). The routine publication of average daily attendance figures in Statistics Canada reports stopped in the 1970s, presumably because "full attendance" had been achieved by then.

3. In contrast, sharp regional differences in rates of school attendance existed earlier, underscoring the fact that the development of education was uneven. For example, in 1920 attendance rates in public elementary and secondary school varied from a low of 60.8% in Newfoundland to a high of 79.8% in British Columbia.

4. The total fertility rate is an estimate of the average number of children born to a woman.

5. In the early years, records of degrees conferred do not distinguish between bachelor and first professional degrees. For consistency this combination has been maintained up to 1995.

6. The median is the point in a distribution above which one half the population falls and below which the other half falls.

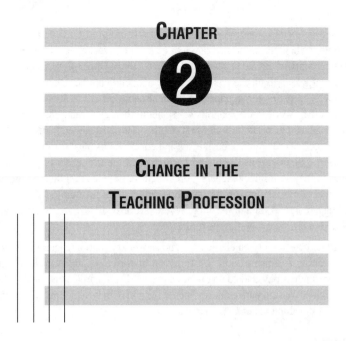

CHAPTER

2

CHANGE IN THE

TEACHING PROFESSION

In our introduction we developed the theme of the "schooled society" to illustrate the increasingly important role formal education plays in our economy and national community. This chapter focuses on the role teachers have played, and continue to play, in transforming Canada into an increasingly schooled society. An integral part of this change has been the professionalization and specialization of teaching. The development of this occupation—overseen chiefly by provincial governments and the churches—in tandem with the creation of a large, full-time student body, has been a central element in the institutionalization of schooling.

The vast size of the contemporary public education system reflects its importance to our economy and public life. The sector now employs hundreds of thousands of Canadians, including more than 300,000 full-time elementary and secondary school teachers. Teaching is one of the largest occupations in the country, and it continues to grow relative to others (Coish 1994; Guppy and Davies 1996). Elementary and secondary school teachers are more numerous than any other profession, ahead of accountants, auditors, and other financial officers, and far more numerous than lawyers and notaries. Only two other occupational fields— secretaries and stenographers, and bookkeepers and accounting clerks—have larger work forces.

Canada's teaching environment is constantly changing, especially since demand for teachers fluctuates with demographic shifts. But in recent years teachers have had to work under a new set of pressures and they face challenges that are more intense than in previous times. Budgetary cutbacks, a more demanding public, an expanding knowledge base, technological changes, and greater demographic diversity have all put the profession under stress. Many critics suggest teachers are overpaid and of questionable quality (for examples, see Lewington and Orpwood 1993). Expressions of public confidence in education, while remaining positive in general, have declined in recent years (Guppy and Davies 1997).

As we discussed in our introductory chapter, qualms about public education are hardly surprising given both the heightened politicization of education in recent years and the growing complexity and uncertainty of the modern world (Giddens 1990). Uncertainty, as Giddens uses the term, is caused largely by both the pace and scope of social change. One consequence is increased concern with preparing for an uncertain future. Businesses worry about future markets and the suitability of their work forces; parents worry about their children's schooling because school credentials enhance prospects for long-term stability. This heightened focus on education is, however, a two-edged sword. Parents, businesses and governments must trust teachers to give students the skills and dispositions they need to prosper in the modern world. In times of uncertainty, however, they scrutinize teachers more. Such scrutiny is embodied by the various task forces and royal commissions throughout the country that have called for reforms to education, including a reorganization of teaching. Where reforms will take teaching is unclear at this time, but these pressures are clouding its future.

In this chapter we focus mainly on elementary and secondary school teachers to sketch the development of teaching as a profession. We focus on historical changes in the number of teachers, fluctuations in their pay, and some of the labour market dynamics that move people in and out of the profession. We summarize our findings at the end of the chapter by identifying four distinct periods in the development of Canadian teaching.

2.1 DEFINITIONS

Exactly which occupations should be included in a definition of the teaching profession is not easy to decide. Many occupations might be defined as teaching (see Figure 2.1), but the two largest groups are Elementary School and Kindergarten Teachers (175,965 in 1991) and Secondary School Teachers (136,005 in 1991).[1] Elementary and Secondary School Administrators are the sixth largest group, and typically would be included in any discussion of the teaching profession. School and Guidance Counsellors and Public School Teaching Assistants could also be included, although often the latter are not (e.g., Lockhart 1991; King and Peart 1992).

Two other large groups are College and Other Vocational Instructors, and University Professors, although for both groups teaching is often complemented by research duties (research is more common at universities but not unknown in college and vocational institutes). These groups are complemented by two others—Postsecondary Administrators and Postsecondary Teaching and Research Assistants. The latter group is particularly difficult to include because it comprises students employed as research assistants as well as students employed in teaching roles. A similar form of ambiguity occurs for individuals employed as Instructors and Teachers of Disabled Persons because some of these people work in public or private schools, while others work in rehabilitation centres and might more easily be described as health professionals. Early Childhood Educators, employed largely in day-care or nursery school settings, are rarely considered part of the teaching profession. Finally, Other Instructors includes driving instructors and teachers at finishing and modeling schools. While these types of employment clearly involve teaching, they are rarely considered part of the teaching profession. We follow common practice and restrict our attention mainly, but not exclusively, to the largest groups. The key exception here is Early Childhood Educators, which we include wherever possible even though the data on this group are scarce.

FIGURE 2.1

FULL-TIME TEACHERS, BY TEACHING OCCUPATION, CANADA, 1991

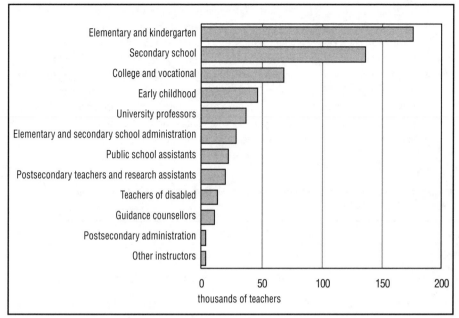

Source: Census of Canada, 1991, special tabulations.

2.2 A BRIEF HISTORY OF THE PROFESSION IN CANADA

Canada has not always had a relatively well paid and professionalized teaching force. Prior to the mid-1800s, Canadians learned most of the skills necessary for their occupational pursuits, community lives, and domestic duties outside schools. Most teaching was informal, unorganized, and unrecognized. Not until the latter part of the 1800s was schooling well established in most provinces, although not all regions, of the country (see Phillips 1957; Wilson et al. 1970; Curtis 1988). In these early days, teachers endured low social status and haphazard employment conditions. The history of Canadian education is sprinkled with stories of teachers lamenting the conditions under which they laboured to teach children basic reading, writing, and arithmetic (e.g., Wilson 1995). However, by the 1920s, literacy and elementary education were widely promoted by teachers, parents and governments, and the teaching labour force expanded accordingly. The number of new teachers ebbed and flowed in concert with the gradual universalizing of both elementary and secondary schooling. Canada was becoming, in every sense, a schooled society, and teacher preparation became a central concern of governments and education policy makers.

The years following the Second World War form the watershed in the history of Canadian teaching. We have noted already how the postwar expansion of the education system was brought on by the twin pressures of the baby boom bulge and the greater commitment to longer retention rates in secondary and postsecondary schooling. Below we examine how these pressures created a large postwar demand for teachers at all levels, from pre-school through to university.

Table 2.1 illustrates changes in the size of the elementary and secondary teaching work force from 1955 to 1993. The first row shows the absolute number of teachers for each year, while the second row shows the percentage change using 1955 as the base year, and the third row reports the percentage change since the previous interval. Between 1955 and 1965 the number of elementary and secondary teachers increased dramatically from 123,800 to 211,800, a growth of 71% in a mere 10 years. The elementary and secondary teaching work force reached a peak in the mid-1970s, when the number of teachers had more than doubled since 1955. Through the next decade the number of teachers declined year by year. This drop in demand occurred, in part, because the baby boom generation was moving out of the school system.

TABLE 2.1
INCREASE IN TEACHING FORCE IN COMPARISON WITH OTHER DEMOGRAPHIC AND INSTITUTIONAL VARIABLES, 1955 TO 1993

Base	1955	1960	1965	1970	1975	1980	1985	1990	1993
Elementary and secondary teachers ('000)	123.8	164.0	211.8	272.3	281.0	276.3	267.6	297.1	301.4
% change since base year	...	32	71	120	127	123	116	140	144
% change since previous interval	...	32	29	29	3	−2	−3	11	1
Elementary and secondary enrolment ('000)	3,291.4	4,204.4	5,201.3	5,836.1	5,594.7	5,106.3	4,927.8	5,141.0	5,363.2
% change since base year	...	28	58	77	70	55	50	56	63
% change since previous interval	...	28	24	12	−4	−9	−3	4	4
Total population ('000)[1]	16,081.0	18,238.0	20,015.0	21,568.0	22,993.0	24,574.0	25,309.3	27,296.9	28,753.0
% change since base year	...	13	25	34	43	53	57	70	79
% change since previous interval	...	13	10	8	7	7	3	8	5
Retention rate, 14- to to 17-year-olds	53.5	66.2	79.6	87.9	85.0	85.0	..	..	...
Student–teacher ratio	26.6	25.6	24.6	21.4	19.9	18.5	18.4	17.3	17.8

Note: Percentages have been rounded to nearest whole number.

1. For census years 1956, 1961, 1966, 1971, 1976, 1981, 1986, and 1991. For 1993, population comes from *Canadian Social Trends*, Summer 1994.

.. figures not available

... figures not applicable

Sources: Easton 1988; Lockhart 1991; Statistics Canada, *Education in Canada,* various years; Statistics Canada, *Advance Statistics of Education,* various years; Statistics Canada, *Age, Sex and Marital Status,* The Nation series, 1992; *Canadian Social Trends,* Summer 1994.

This stagnation continued until the mid-1980s, when an echo baby boom contributed to renewed growth in teaching jobs. Of the three largest occupational groups in the labour force, elementary and secondary school teaching grew fastest, by 7.1% between 1986 and 1991. If supply teachers, teaching consultants, private school teachers, and other occupations related to elementary and secondary school teaching are added, the size of the 1991 teaching work force increases to 419,810 and the five-year growth rate jumps to 14.1%.[2] It is doubtful, however, that we will ever revisit the booming expansion of the 1950s, 1960s, and 1970s.

FIGURE 2.2

NUMBER OF FULL-TIME POSTSECONDARY TEACHERS, BY LEVEL, CANADA, 1961 TO 1993

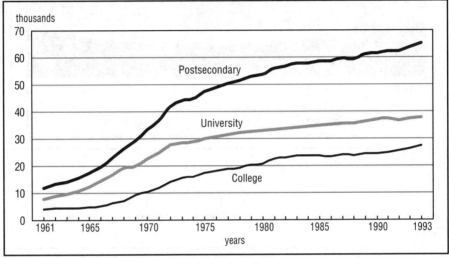

Source: Statistics Canada, Catalogue nos. 81-220, 81-568 and 81-229.

The number of postsecondary educators grew concurrently with the expansion at the elementary and secondary levels (see Figure 2.2). Indeed, growth at the postsecondary level was actually steadier than at elementary and secondary levels, principally because, as we argued earlier, student participation in higher education was not as directly susceptible to demographic booms and busts.

Changes in the number of Canadian university graduates obtaining degrees in education provide another glimpse of the stagnation and subsequent upsurge in the teaching sector. The number of graduates responded remarkably to the tighter job markets for teachers in the late 1970s (see Figure 2.3a), declining until 1984 and then rebounding to surpass the levels of the mid-1970s. These trends were largely parallel among men and women.

Another way to illustrate growth in the teaching force is to compare it with increases in the total population and with changes in the school-aged population. From 1955 to 1993, the number of elementary and secondary teachers grew by 144%, outpacing both the 79% growth in the total population and the 63% growth in the student-aged population (see Table 2.1). As a result, the student–teacher ratio (STR) shrank from 26.6:1 to 17.8:1, over the entire period.

FIGURE 2.3A

NUMBER OF WOMEN AND MEN AMONG EDUCATION GRADUATES OF CANADIAN UNIVERSITIES, 1974 TO 1993

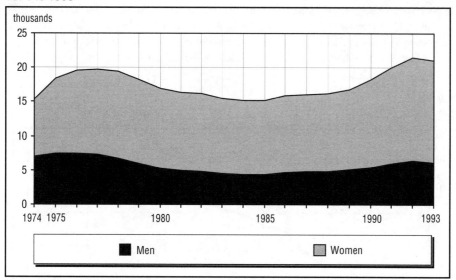

Source: Census of Canada, 1991.

FIGURE 2.3B

PROPORTION OF WOMEN AND MEN AMONG EDUCATION GRADUATES OF CANADIAN UNIVERSITIES, 1974 TO 1993

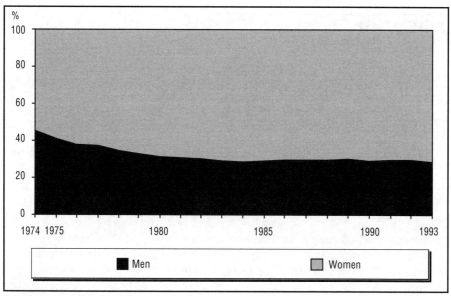

Source: Census of Canada, 1991.

Three trends are worth highlighting within this period. First, while the number of teachers greatly expanded between 1955 and 1965 (71%), the STR dropped only slightly (2.0). Hence the expanding teaching force just kept pace with the rising number of students. Second, the STR then dropped swiftly between 1965 and 1975, dipping by 4.7, from 24.6 students per teacher to 19.9 (a period coinciding with baby boomers moving beyond secondary schools). Third, the STR dropped a further 2.6 between 1975 and 1990, when the actual number of teachers reached a plateau. The teaching force thus stayed at a near-constant size during a time of fluctuating enrolments. As only a small portion of this reduction in STR can be traced to shifts in the relative mix of elementary and high school students (Easton 1988, 47), the lower class sizes served as a mechanism by which massive teacher layoffs were avoided (Lockhart 1991, 24). By way of comparison, there was no real change in the university or college STR over the period from 1960 to 1993 (see Figure 2.4).

Figure 2.4
Ratio of Full–time Students to Full-time Teachers, by Level, 1960 to 1993

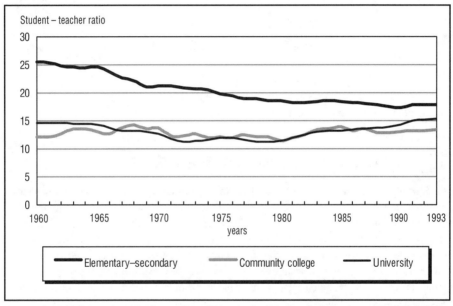

Source: Statistics Canada, *Historical Compendium of Education Statistics from Confederation to 1975,* 1978; Statistics Canada, *Advance Statistics of Education,* various years; Statistics Canada, *Education in Canada,* various years.

Another way school boards deal with mounting financial constraints and falling enrolments without laying off teachers is by converting full-time jobs into part-time and/or temporary positions. Such "silent firing" has the adverse effect of creating a two-tier membership structure that reserves security for the established, while exposing newcomers to the dictates of the market. It does, nonetheless, allow teachers more flexible hours and other work arrangements (Lockhart 1991, 25, 26). The proportion of part-time positions grew from 2.5% of all teachers in 1972 to 10.3% in 1994 (see Table 2.2).

TABLE 2.2

FULL-TIME AND PART-TIME TEACHERS IN CANADIAN ELEMENTARY AND SECONDARY SCHOOLS, 1972 TO 1994

Year	Full-time	Part-time	% part-time	Total teachers
1972–1973	190,655	4,938	2.5	195,593
1974–1975	194,542	7,104	3.5	201,646
1976–1977	199,468	9,800	4.7	209,268
1978–1979	199,455	11,736	5.6	211,191
1983–1984	270,992	19,358	6.7	290,350
1984–1985	267,598	21,810	7.5	289,408
1985–1986	267,620	23,987	8.2	291,607
1986–1987	269,899	26,203	8.8	296,102
1987–1988	276,447	25,969	8.6	302,416
1988–1989	282,201	27,184	8.8	309,385
1989–1990	289,626	29,231	9.2	318,857
1990–1991	296,271	31,731	9.7	328,002
1991–1992	303,055	33,003	9.8	336,058
1992–1993	303,272	35,040	10.4	338,312
1993–1994	306,227	34,988	10.3	341,215

Source: Data for 1972 to 1979, Statistics Canada, *Education Statistics*; data for 1983 to 1994, Statistics Canada, *Education in Canada.*

Overall, the teaching profession expanded markedly over the postwar period as Canada's growing population spent ever more time attending secondary schools and postsecondary institutions.

2.3   WHO TEACHES? THE DEMOGRAPHY OF THE PROFESSION

A traditional image of teaching is that of a young, female-dominated, humbly paid and low status occupation at its lower levels, and that of an older, male-dominated, better-remunerated profession at its higher levels. Another image of teaching is that of a vehicle of social mobility for young people (especially men) from less privileged socio-economic origins. While in some respects these images remain valid today, there have been noticeable shifts in who enters the profession, where they enter, their motives for entry, and their levels of pay. In this section we examine the composition of elementary and secondary school teachers in terms of their gender, race, age, and socio-economic origins.

TABLE 2.3
TEACHERS BY SEX, AVERAGE INCOME AND OCCUPATION, 1971 TO 1991

Teaching and Related Occupations	Number				Average income ($)			
	1971	1981	1986	1991	1970	1980	1985	1990
Total								
University Teachers	23,455	33,615	36,890	48,480	...	24,701	37,456	46,892
University Teaching and Related Occupations, n.e.c.[1]	3,030	11,075	16,645	21,360	...	8,969	13,356	17,543
Elementary and Kindergarten Teachers	146,060	173,670	189,310	208,970	...	19,205	24,348	32,284
Secondary School Teachers	111,105	137,720	131,675	142,130	...	21,915	31,413	39,429
Elementary and Secondary School Teaching and Related Occupations, n.e.c	14,595	30,275	37,375	68,110	...	15,716	10,976	16,648
Community College and Vocational School Teachers	8,975	30,315	36,300	40,680	...	20,134	28,562	35,622
Fine Arts Teachers, n.e.c.	14,505	18,680	22,445	28,000	...	9,623	12,130	18,157
Postsecondary School Teachers, n.e.c.	10,495	6,435	4,825	7,825	...	21,391	26,591	35,857
Teachers of Exceptional Students, n.e.c.	5,280	19,965	23,390	26,605	...	15,997	20,748	26,217
Instructors and Training Officers, n.e.c.	5,755	14,530	15,480	18,760	...	15,114	23,303	29,667
Other Teaching and Related Occupations, n.e.c.	6,040	12,890	13,240	18,425	...	16,013	20,480	26,558
Total Teaching and Related Occupations	349,295	489,170	527,575	629,345	...	...	...	...
Teaching and Related Occupations as a percentage of the total labour force	4	4	4	4				
Total labour force	8,813,340	12,267,075	13,141,750	14,905,395	...	12,926	18,733	24,329
Men								
University Teachers	19,540	25,365	27,045	33,625	...	31,833	43,067	53,725
University Teaching and Related Occupations, n.e.c.	2,225	6,190	9,310	11,455	...	10,659	16,302	20,121
Elementary and Kindergarten Teachers	25,900	34,045	36,835	37,875	...	22,765	33,685	41,580
Secondary School Teachers	61,645	79,605	72,715	74,320	...	25,301	35,764	44,022
Elementary and Secondary School Teaching and Related Occupations, n.e.c.	3,705	5,765	6,300	11,995	...	25,042	20,174	26,158
Community College and Vocational School Teachers	6,375	18,375	20,850	21,925	...	25,042	33,711	41,663
Fine Arts Teachers, n.e.c.	4,690	5,225	5,965	7,495	...	13,247	20,002	26,791
Postsecondary School Teachers, n.e.c.	5,585	2,420	1,280	2,555	...	25,266	32,777	41,740
Teachers of Exceptional Students, n.e.c	1,405	5,760	5,805	5,890	...	17,987	25,392	33,096
Instructors and Training Officers, n.e.c.	3,915	9,460	9,490	10,740	...	19,815	27,281	34,282
Other Teaching and Related Occupations, n.e.c.	3,180	6,015	5,830	7,330	...	21,272	27,382	33,596
Total Teaching and Related Occupations	138,165	198,225	201,425	225,205	...	...	...	...
Teaching and Related Occupations as a percentage of the total labour force	2	3	3	3				
Total labour force	5,760,245	7,266,805	7,488,470	8,105,020	...	16,988	23,231	29,847

TABLE 2.3 (CONCLUDED)

TEACHERS BY SEX, AVERAGE INCOME AND OCCUPATION, 1971 TO 1991

Teaching and Related Occupations							Average income			
Women	1971	1981	1986	1991	1970	1980	1985	1990
	Number					$		
University Teachers	3,910	8,245	9,845	14,855	∷	17,569	23,036	31,428
University Teaching and Related Occupations, n.e.c.	800	4,885	7,330	9,905	∷	7,279	9,835	14,562
Elementary and Kindergarten Teachers	120,160	139,625	152,480	171,100	∷	15,644	22,161	30,227
Secondary School Teachers	49,460	58,115	58,960	67,805	∷	18,528	26,171	34,395
Elementary and Secondary School Teaching and Related Occupations, n.e.c	10,890	24,510	31,075	56,110	∷	6,389	9,212	14,615
Community College and Vocational School Teachers	2,600	11,945	15,450	18,765	∷	15,225	21,838	28,565
Fine Arts Teachers, n.e.c.	9,815	13,460	16,475	20,500	∷	5,999	9,412	15,000
Postsecondary School teachers, n.e.c.	4,910	4,020	3,545	5,275	∷	17,516	24,410	33,003
Teachers of Exceptional Students, n.e.c	3,880	14,205	17,580	20,720	∷	14,006	19,222	24,261
Instructors and Training Officers, n.e.c.	1,840	5,065	5,990	8,015	∷	10,413	15,790	23,482
Other Teaching and Related Occupations, n.e.c.	2,855	6,870	7,415	11,100	∷	10,753	15,254	21,910
Total Teaching and Related Occupations	**211,120**	**290,945**	**326,145**	**404,150**	∷	**∷**	**∷**	**∷**
Teaching and Related Occupations as a percentage of the total labour force	**7**	**6**	**6**	**6**				
Total labour force	**3,053,100**	**5,000,270**	**5,653,275**	**6,800,375**	∷	**8,863**	**12,891**	**17,751**

1. n.e.c., not elsewhere classified

    The number of teachers for 1971 to 1986 were compiled with the *Occupational Classification Manual, 1991*. All other data were compiled with the *Standard Occupational Classification, 1980*.

∷   figures not available

...   figures not appropriate

Source: Census of Canada, various years.

2.3.1 Gender

Historically, teaching has been a female-dominated occupation, one of the more accessible professions for women. However, the profession's gender-composition over this century has followed a *u*-shaped pattern. In the 1920s, women held between 80% and 85% of all elementary and secondary school teaching jobs. As working conditions and pay levels improved, more men entered the profession. Between 1960 and 1980, men's proportion of all teachers at the elementary and secondary levels grew from 28% to 47% (see Lockhart 1991, 119). Part of this growth can be linked to an increase in secondary school teaching and administrative positions, which became more acceptable options for male university graduates during the 1960s and 1970s. Also, as opportunities for women opened in other areas, professions such as medicine and law vied with teaching as attractive occupations for women. By 1980, women's share of elementary and secondary school positions had dropped to 53%. Then, the percentage of women rebounded so that, by 1991, women held 70% of teaching positions (see Table 2.3 for changes from 1971 to 1991). In addition, since the mid-1970s the percentage of female university graduates with degrees in education rose from about 55% in 1974 to 71% in 1993, with most of the increase occurring between 1974 and 1984 (see Figure 2.3b).

What influenced this resurgence in the proportion of female teachers? To comprehend this we need to examine the proportions of men and women at different levels of teaching.

In the economy at large, women and men typically do different jobs, even within the same occupational group. Gender segregation in the work force is common, with women often occupying jobs in less-desirable niches characterized by lower pay, limited promotion opportunities, and fewer required skills (Siltanen 1994). Gender segregation in teaching parallels the gendered division of labour that occurs elsewhere, with more women teaching in elementary than in secondary schools. Furthermore, women represent 7 out of 10 elementary and secondary school teachers, but they do not occupy 70% of all types of teaching jobs.

Between 1981 and 1991, women noticeably outnumbered men in elementary and kindergarten classes, and this gap grew from 80% to 82% over the decade (see Figure 2.5). The higher concentration of women at elementary-level teaching leads to pay disparities. For example, in 1990 elementary school teachers working full year, full time earned $5,560 less on average than their secondary school colleagues.[3]

FIGURE 2.5

WOMEN AND MEN IN ELEMENTARY AND SECONDARY SCHOOL TEACHING, CANADA, 1981, 1986 AND 1991

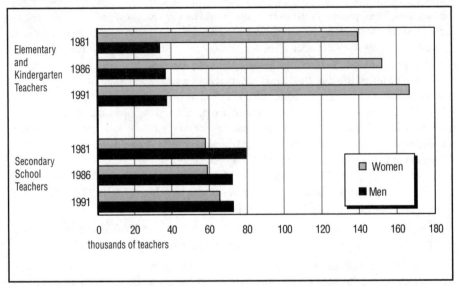

Source: Census of Canada, 1981, 1986 and 1991.

More men than women teach in secondary schools, but that gap shrank between 1981 and 1991. In 1991, women held more than 47% of secondary teaching jobs, up from 44% a decade earlier. This trend towards gender parity at the secondary level stems from two changes. First, 7,620 fewer men worked at the secondary level in 1991 than in 1981. Second, between 1981 and 1991 the number of women secondary teachers grew by 8,005. In fact, women outnumber men among younger secondary-level teachers and may soon outnumber men throughout secondary teaching as they replace older men who retire (King and Peart 1992, 21). Evidence of this scenario can be seen in the age distribution of women and men in different teaching occupations in 1991 (see Figure 2.6). Women made up about 40% of secondary teachers between the ages of 45 and 64, but constituted almost 60% of those 25 to 29 years old. In comparison, at the elementary school level, women make up 80% to 85% of every age group.

Greater numbers of younger women are taking up secondary positions, and other aspects of the gendered division of labour in education are changing as well, albeit gradually. The continued male dominance in administration and university teaching is also being altered through slow increases in female representation (Statistics Canada, *Education in Canada* 1996).

2.3.2 Age

As a group, teachers have aged, and this trend is expected to continue into the next decade (Lockhart 1991, 42). Between 1970 and 1990, the number of teachers dropped in the 15-to-24 age category and increased in the 45-to-64 group. The 25-to-44 age group held the highest concentration of teachers throughout this period (Pagliarello 1995, 15). This phenomena reflects not only the hiring boom of the 1960s and 1970s, but also the older age of newly recruited teachers. In recent years school boards have begun to hire permanent teachers from their "on-call" or "call-up" lists, rather than recent university graduates, and this results in a gradual aging of the cohort of newly hired teachers.

2.3.3 Race and ethnic origins

The classic sociological depiction of racial and ethnic stratification in Canada is John Porter's *The Vertical Mosaic* (1965). Porter argued that Canadians of British origin were over-represented in positions of power and privilege, and they oversaw "others" from non-British and non-French origins who formed a multi-layered hierarchy of advantaged and disadvantaged. Though there is controversy over the accuracy of Porter's original image, and though many sociological studies since Porter have shown that the days of British advantage have waned, his concern with disparities among ethnic groups has left a lasting impression on Canadian researchers. One instance of Porter's impact has been Lockhart's (1991) attempt to apply the *Vertical Mosaic* thesis to the teaching profession. Using data from 1983, Lockhart found some British over-representation within the profession, but also found this to be at the expense of teachers of French background. "Other" Canadians were slightly over-represented in the profession.

As noted in our introductory chapter, the conceptualization of ethnic and racial stratification in Canada has recently taken a new tone. The multi-variegated ethnic categories of the *Vertical Mosaic* have been replaced by Abella's racial dichotomy of "white"/"visible minority" (the latter term is a unique Canadianism). This adoption of Abella's categories reflects the shifting priorities of politicians, policy makers, interest groups, and academics in Canada.

Data from the 1991 Census indicate that, overall, visible minorities were under-represented in the teaching work force (see Table 2.4). They constituted roughly 8.3% of the Canadian population aged 15 and over, but only 5.4% of the full-time teaching work force. However, the data also reveal a more complex situation. Rates of representation varied widely by occupation level and by minority group. Visible minorities as a whole were under-represented at some higher levels (Administrators, School Principals) but were over-represented among others (University Professors and Teaching and Research Assistants—the latter being the professors of the future). Likewise visible minorities were over-represented in some lesser-paid areas (Other Instructors, Early Childhood Educators) and under-represented in still others (Instructors of Disabled Persons, Public School Teaching Assistants). Moreover, the levels of representation varied by particular groups (see Table 2.5). All groups except Japanese-Canadians are under-represented among elementary and secondary school teachers, but some are sharply over-represented in the postsecondary sector (Chinese, West Arabian, South Asian, Japanese).

TABLE 2.4

FULL-TIME TEACHERS, BY TEACHING OCCUPATION AND VISIBLE MINORITY STATUS, 1991[1]

Teaching occupation	Population	% visible minority	% non-visible-minority
All Teachers	568,870	5.4	94.6
Administrators in Postsecondary Educational and Vocational Training	7,045	4.5	95.5
School Principals and Administrators of Elementary and Secondary Education	28,580	2.7	97.3
University Professors	36,835	10.1	89.9
Postsecondary Teaching and Research Assistants	19,770	14.5	85.5
College and Other Vocational Instructors	67,735	6.1	93.9
Secondary School Teachers	136,005	4.3	95.7
Elementary and Kindergarten Teachers	175,965	3.5	96.6
School and Guidance Counsellors	10,865	3.9	96.1
Early Childhood Educators	46,030	10.2	89.8
Public School Teaching Assistants	22,190	3.6	96.4
Instructors and Teachers of Disabled Persons	13,600	3.0	97.0
Other Instructors	4,250	13.2	86.9
Total population 15 and over	**21,112,165**	**8.3**	**91.7**

1. Percentages may not add to 100 due to rounding.
Source: Census of Canada, 1991, special tabulations.

We can conclude that in 1991 minorities were indeed under-represented in teaching, but there were large variations among groups and levels. The social forces underlying these patterns are difficult to explain, and the data do not permit us to judge whether the patterns are caused by discrimination, recency of immigration and other supply-side factors among minorities, the recent stagnation in hiring, or particular occupational choices made by minority group members. Ethnic representation in teaching likely reflects supply-side factors as much as particular dynamics in education labour markets.

TABLE 2.5

FULL-TIME TEACHERS, BY TEACHING OCCUPATION AND DETAILED VISIBLE MINORITY STATUS, 1991

Teaching occupation	Chinese	Black	South Asian	West Arabian	Filipino	South-east Asian	Latin American	Korean	Japanese	Multiple visible minority
					%					
All Teachers	1.0	1.3	1.2	0.9	0.2	0.1	0.2	0.1	0.3	0.1
Administrators in Postsecondary Educational and Vocational Training	0.8	1.4	0.9	0.7	0.0	0.0	0.0	0.1	0.2	0.0
School Principals and Administrators of Elementary and Secondary Education	0.4	0.8	0.6	0.4	0.1	0.0	0.1	0.0	0.2	0.1
University Professors	2.0	1.1	3.2	2.3	0.1	0.4	0.2	0.2	0.5	0.1
Postsecondary Teaching and Research Assistants	5.4	1.4	3.1	2.6	0.3	0.4	0.6	0.3	0.4	0.3
College and Other Vocational Instructors	1.0	1.6	1.3	1.0	0.2	0.2	0.2	0.1	0.3	0.2
Secondary School Teachers	0.8	1.2	0.9	0.9	0.1	0.1	0.1	0.0	0.2	0.1
Elementary and Kindergarten Teachers	0.6	0.8	0.7	0.6	0.2	0.1	0.1	0.0	0.3	0.1
School and Guidance Counsellors	1.0	1.0	0.7	0.5	0.1	0.0	0.1	0.0	0.2	0.0
Early Childhood Educators	1.2	3.7	2.4	0.9	0.7	0.2	0.8	0.1	0.1	0.2
Public School Teaching Assistants	0.8	0.9	0.7	0.4	0.1	0.2	0.2	0.0	0.2	0.0
Instructors and Teachers of Disabled Persons	0.4	1.5	0.3	0.3	0.3	0.0	0.0	0.0	0.0	0.2
Other Instructors	3.5	2.5	4.8	0.8	0.0	0.5	0.5	0.0	0.0	0.4
Canada's total population 15 and over	2.2	1.6	1.6	0.9	0.6	0.4	0.4	0.2	0.2	0.4

Source: Census of Canada, 1991, special tabulations.

2.3.4 Socio-economic origins

Historically, teaching has meant different things to men than it has to women. Teaching was an avenue of upward mobility for men from rural, farming and working-class backgrounds. In contrast, teaching tended to attract women from middle- and upper-class families, as it was one of the few professions that these women could enter. Studies in Canada, the United States, and Britain have all shown this historic pattern (Lockhart 1991). Lockhart suggests, however, that these socio-economic differences between male and female teachers vanished by the 1980s. He offers two reasons: secondary-level teaching had become more attractive to male graduates from middle-class backgrounds and, as opportunities for women opened elsewhere, middle-class women especially were more likely to enter other professional occupations.

There are different ways to measure the social or family origins of teachers. We use the educational attainments of teachers' parents (see Table 2.6). Family income or parental occupations are other possible measures of social origins but these latter indicators suffer from greater inaccuracy of recall by survey respondents. Especially for mothers' paid employment, there is often a good deal of missing information.

TABLE 2.6
EDUCATIONAL ATTAINMENT OF THE PARENTS OF CURRENT TEACHERS, 1994 PERCENTAGES[1]

Current teachers	Mother's level of education					
	0–7 years of school	8–13 years school	High school graduate	Some college	Some university	Total
			%			
Women	16	27	26	19	12	100
Men	20	40	19	13	8	100

Current teachers	Father's level of education					
	0–7 years of school	8–13 years school	High school graduate	Some college	Some university	Total
			%			
Women	13	37	14	21	15	100
Men	27	32	16	7	17	100

1. Figures may not add to 100 due to rounding.
Source: Statistics Canada, General Social Survey, 1994.

More male teachers than female have less-educated parents, but the difference is small. Male teachers were more likely than their female counterparts to have mothers and fathers who had not graduated from high school (60% versus 43%, respectively for mother's education; 59% versus 50% for father's education). There is also a slight tendency for women to have parents with more postsecondary experience but again the difference is small (Chi^2 tests show no statistically significant difference). These findings tend to concur with Lockhart.

Where differences by social origin do appear, however, is with respect to movement out of the profession. In the 1990s, men who came from less educated backgrounds were more likely to train as teachers, but then shift out of the profession. More than two-thirds of men whose fathers had not graduated from high school left the profession. For women, exactly the opposite was the case: women from more educated backgrounds tended to leave teaching. More than two-thirds of women whose fathers had postsecondary experience left the profession.[4] Our data cannot help us sort out exactly why these differences arise. For men from relatively humble backgrounds, teaching still appears to be an important stepping stone to other occupations. For women whose parents were relatively well educated, mobility out of the profession may reflect their use of their parents' connections and networks to find other professional avenues of employment.

In summary, we can offer several conclusions about the demographics of teaching. While the profession has always been female-dominated, the decades following the Second World War saw an influx of men into teaching, especially at the secondary level. This pattern has shifted in recent years, with women now entering secondary and administrative positions in larger numbers. There has been no reciprocal movement of men into elementary teaching. Men continue to dominate upper hierarchies, though this is slowly changing. Teachers today are older than in previous times, and this pattern will probably not change for another decade. Visible minorities are under-represented in teaching, though their representation varies substantially by level of teaching and by the particular minority group under study. Finally, although male teachers were once more likely than their female colleagues to hail from humble socio-economic origins, today these differences have all but disappeared.

2.4   PAYING TEACHERS: TRENDS IN INCOME

Historically, most Canadian teachers have had unstable incomes that were typically below the average for the labour force. In the 1800s and early 1900s, teaching was only a temporary job or stepping stone to a more lucrative career for many young adults, especially men. The lowly status of the profession persisted until recent decades.

Canada is now depicted as a post-industrial or knowledge society (Bell 1973; Stehr 1994) in which the "knowledge professions"—occupations that are characterized by their focus on processing and disseminating ideas—are vital to societal well-being. As a corollary, the argument runs, professionals such as teachers should be highly remunerated, given the importance of their calling and given that income is a significant incentive for high performance in contemporary societies. Since the 1970s teachers have been better paid, and indeed, the profession has become one of the more desirable destinations among university graduates.

We trace trends in teachers' median salaries from 1955 to 1993 by comparing them with Canada's annual industrial aggregate wage (IAW), which is a measure of the average wage in the country. Note that the salaries of Quebec teachers are excluded from 1955 to 1983, so there is a sharp discontinuity in 1984 because the lower pay of Quebec teachers reduces the Canadian average. As recently as 1955, teachers' salaries were below the average wage (see Table 2.7). When incomes are adjusted to 1986 constant dollars, the data show that teachers earned only 89% of the IAW in 1955. Thereafter, their constant or real earnings increased over time and in relation to other earners (see Figure 2.7). Teachers' salaries rose steadily from 1955 to 1977, with each year except 1968 showing an increase over the previous year. By 1983, teachers' salaries had grown to more than $36,000, an increase of 275% over their 1955 income. This rapid increase outpaced most other occupations; the IAW over the same period increased by only 155%. Hence, teachers in 1983 were earning 1.59 times the IAW. By this standard, teachers have done well. Their 1990 earnings were substantially greater than other large occupational groupings, such as secretaries (165% greater) and janitors (213% greater). But teachers still received less than some other prominent professions, earning 33% of the income of a typical physician, 46% of the average lawyer and 68% of the average university professor (Pagliarello 1995, 11).

TABLE 2.7

ANNUAL MEDIAN SALARY OF ELEMENTARY AND SECONDARY SCHOOL TEACHERS COMPARED WITH ANNUAL INDUSTRIAL AGGREGATE WAGE, CURRENT AND 1986 CONSTANT DOLLARS, CANADA (EXCLUDING QUEBEC FROM 1955 TO 1983), 1955 TO 1993

Year	Median teacher salary ($ current)	Median teacher salary (T) ($ constant 1986)	Industrial aggregate wage ($ current)	Industrial aggregate wage (I) ($ constant 1986)	Ratio T/I
1955	2,840	13,209	3,175	14,767	0.89
1956	3,162	14,505	3,351	15,372	0.94
1957	3,470	15,422	3,532	15,698	0.98
1958	3,757	16,264	3,662	15,853	1.03
1959	4,055	17,329	3,820	16,325	1.06
1960	4,247	17,920	3,943	16,637	1.08
1961	4,414	18,469	4,068	17,021	1.09
1962	4,522	18,686	4,188	17,306	1.08
1963	4,722	19,195	4,330	17,602	1.09
1964	4,954	19,737	4,499	17,924	1.10
1965	5,215	20,292	4,733	18,416	1.10
1966	5,567	20,929	5,008	18,827	1.11
1967	6,524	23,638	5,344	19,362	1.22
1968	6,497	22,638	5,714	19,909	1.14
1969	7,124	23,747	6,117	20,390	1.16
1970	7,688	24,800	6,595	21,274	1.17
1971	8,525	26,724	7,157	22,436	1.19
1972	9,600	28,743	7,759	23,231	1.24
1973	10,500	29,167	8,344	23,178	1.26
1974	11,900	29,825	9,261	23,211	1.28
1975	14,004	31,683	10,578	23,932	1.32
1976	16,615	34,979	11,858	24,964	1.40
1977	18,408	35,883	12,997	25,335	1.42
1978	20,023	35,819	13,799	24,685	1.45
1979	22,200	36,393	14,989	24,572	1.48
1980	24,877	37,019	16,504	24,560	1.51
1981	28,845	38,205	18,475	24,470	1.56
1982	32,128	38,385	19,994	23,888	1.61
1983	32,126	36,301	20,210	22,836	1.59
1984[1]	26,651	28,843	20,701	22,404	1.29
1985	26,082	27,168	21,425	22,318	1.22
1986	27,269	27,269	22,061	22,061	1.24
1987	29,387	28,149	22,894	21,929	1.28
1988	31,797	29,279	23,907	22,014	1.33
1989	31,513	27,643	25,132	22,046	1.25
1990	32,416	27,127	26,267	21,981	1.23
1991	36,013	28,537	27,487	21,781	1.31
1992	36,487	28,483	28,445	22,205	1.28
1993	35,688	27,368	28,445	21,813	1.25

1.   Quebec is included from 1984 to 1993.

Source: Lockhart, 1991; Statistics Canada, *Earnings of Men and Women,* various years; Statistics Canada, *Employment, Earnings and Hours,* various years; *The Canadian Global Almanac,* 1995.

FIGURE 2.6

PERCENTAGE OF TEACHERS WHO ARE FEMALE, BY AGE AND TEACHING LEVEL, 1991

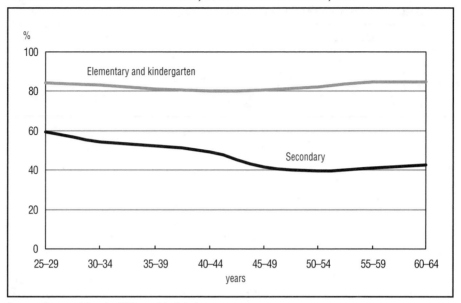

Source: Census of Canada, 1991, special tabulations.

These trends did not differ by gender (see Table 2.8). Both male and female teachers enjoyed higher pay than many of their labour force counterparts. In 1991 and 1992, the ratio of teacher salaries over the IAW for men was 1.8; for women it was 2.0. Teaching is thus a relatively lucrative occupation for women, earning them twice the wage of the average women, and this helps to explain why teaching has continued to attract large numbers of women.

A new era, both for teachers and for other Canadian workers, began in 1983. From 1983 to 1993, teachers' real earnings dropped 5% and the IAW fell 3%. Consequently, the ratio between teachers' salaries and the IAW fluctuated from 1.29 in 1984, to 1.33 in 1988, to 1.25 in 1993 (see Table 2.7).

The data suggest two distinct periods with respect to teachers' salaries: an era of rapid real increase starting in the 1950s and ending in early 1980s, followed by stagnation and a slight drop in real earnings. Increases in human capital account for part of the rise in real income during the earlier period. The collective agreements between teachers and school boards explicitly rewarded both education and experience. By the 1970s, most teachers had a university degree, a stark contrast from the profession's earlier days, and the average teacher was more experienced than in previous years (Lockhart 1991, 43; Easton 1988, 50; Pagliarello 1995, 12). Yet, salaries rose to a degree that is independent of these factors and many (see Easton 1988) conclude that much of this increase can be attributed to the effectiveness of teachers' collective bargaining units.

TABLE 2.8

ANNUAL MEDIAN SALARY OF TEACHERS COMPARED WITH ANNUAL INDUSTRIAL COMPOSITE WAGE,[1] BY SEX, CURRENT AND CONSTANT 1991 DOLLARS, 1984 TO 1992

Year	Median teacher salary ($ current)	Median teacher salary (T) ($ constant 1991)	Industrial aggregate wage ($ current)	Industrial aggregate wage (I) ($ constant 1991)	Ratio T/I[2]
Total					
1984	26,651	36,408	19,075	26,059	1.4
1985	26,082	34,273	20,062	26,363	1.3
1986	27,269	34,431	21,277	26,865	1.3
1987	29,387	35,535	22,114	26,740	1.3
1988	31,797	36,930	23,431	27,214	1.4
1989	31,513	34,898	25,056	27,748	1.3
1990	32,416	34,231	26,095	27,555	1.2
1991	36,013	36,013	27,120	27,120	1.3
1992	36,487	35,947	27,748	27,338	1.3
1993	35,688	..	..	..	..
Males					
1984	33,366	45,582	19,156	26,169	1.7
1985	35,005	45,999	20,181	26,519	1.7
1986	37,853	47,794	21,487	27,130	1.8
1987	39,130	47,316	22,474	27,175	1.7
1988	40,173	46,659	24,045	27,927	1.7
1989	40,788	45,169	25,072	27,765	1.6
1990	41,673	44,005	25,832	27,278	1.6
1991	46,192	46,192	26,115	26,115	1.8
1992	47,326	46,627	26,383	25,993	1.8
1993	45,702	..	..	..	..
Females					
1984	22,356	30,540	9,819	13,414	2.3
1985	21,516	28,273	10,350	13,601	2.1
1986	21,079	26,615	11,383	14,372	1.9
1987	23,670	28,622	11,838	14,314	2.0
1988	26,757	31,077	12,729	14,784	2.1
1989	26,101	28,905	14,164	15,685	1.8
1990	27,089	28,605	14,579	15,395	1.9
1991	30,663	30,663	15,045	15,045	2.0
1992	30,853	30,397	15,636	15,405	2.0
1993	30,073	..	..	..	..

1.   The industrial composite wage is the modern version of the industrial aggregate wage.

2.   The ratio in the teaching profession as a whole is lower than the respective ratios for men and women because of the balance of women and men in the profession.

..   figures not available

Source: Lockhart, 1991; Statistics Canada, *Earnings of Men and Women,* various years.

FIGURE 2.7

MEDIAN TEACHER SALARY (EXCLUDING QUEBEC FROM 1955 TO 1983) AND INDUSTRIAL AGGREGATE WAGE IN 1986 DOLLARS, 1955 TO 1993

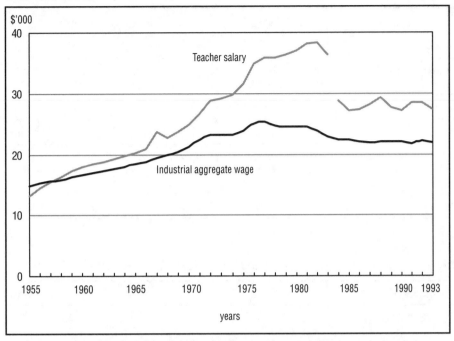

Source: Lockhart, 1991; Statistics Canada, *Earnings of Men and Women, various years;* Statistics Canada, *Employment Earnings and Hours,* (various years); *The 1995 Canadian Global Almanac,* 1995.

Historically, male and female teachers have never been remunerated at identical rates. Gender has mattered. In the 19th century, male teachers typically earned 50% more than their female counterparts (King and Peart 1992, 7). But does gender still matter? A comparison of the average employment income across teaching categories in 1980, 1985 and 1990 indicates that men earned higher salaries than women did in every year at every level (see Table 2.9). Disparities were greatest among university teachers, where females earned 75% of the male wage in all years; disparities were smallest among secondary school teachers, where females earned between 87% and 88% of the male wage over the period. Female–male earnings ratios remained relatively stable at all levels over the decade, with a slight movement towards gender equality in all levels except among elementary teachers. Since women earn less than men in each category, gender disparities cannot be attributed solely to differences in proportions of male versus female teachers at various levels.

TABLE 2.9

POPULATION 15 AND OVER WHO WORKED FULL YEAR, FULL TIME IN SELECTED TEACHING OCCUPATIONS, BY AVERAGE EMPLOYMENT INCOME AND SEX, 1980, 1985 AND 1990

Teaching Occupation	Men			Women		
	1980	1985	1990	1980	1985	1990
University Professors	$35,940 (22,340)	$51,185 (19,485)	$65,761 (22,990)	$26,565 (2,905)	$38,315 (4,340)	$49,000 (6,350)
College and Vocational Instructors	$27,430 (15,715)	$38,590 (13,665)	$47,840 (14,180)	$22,500 (6,865)	$32,775 (6,635)	$40,885 (8,020)
Secondary School Teachers	$26,635 (68,845)	$38,094 (60,795)	$47,385 (61,065)	$23,135 (39,340)	$33,220 37,160)	$41,665 (44,675)
Elementary and Kindergarten Teachers	$24,170 (28,595)	$36,381 (30,110)	$45,471 (30,500)	$20,280 (89,270)	$29,505 (91,130)	$37,695 (107,750)

RATIOS OF FEMALE[1] TO MALE INCOMES BY TEACHING LEVEL, 1980, 1985 AND 1990

Teaching Occupation	1980	1985	1990
University Professors	.74 (.12)	.75 (.18)	.75 (.22)
College and Vocational Instructors	.82 (.30)	.85 (.33)	.85 (.36)
Secondary School Teachers	.87 (.36)	.87 (.38)	.88 (.42)
Elementary and Kindergarten Teachers	.84 (.76)	.81 (.75)	.83 (.78)

1. Figures in parentheses represent the proportion of females in that category.

Note: $ = average employment income; figures in parentheses are the number of people working full time, full year and reporting an employment income.

Source: Statistics Canada, *Population, Worked in 1980: Employment Income by Occupation,* 1984, Table 1; Statistics Canada, *Employment Income by Population,* 1989, Table 1; Statistics Canada, *Employment Income by Population,* 1993.

This comparison does not consider age, however. Age is important because these income ratios remained stable during a period when women increased their numbers at all levels, but especially among younger cohorts at the secondary and university levels. Wage disparities could reflect, in part, the over-representation of women among younger teachers, who are paid less regardless of gender. Indeed, as we saw in a previous section, most younger high school teachers are women; the majority of older high school teachers are men. These younger women, now at the beginning of their careers and at the bottom of their earnings trajectory, over-represent women at lower income levels, and thus deflate the average female salary. However, as these women move through the system and earn higher incomes, female average earnings will rise. Conversely, more men are now at the height of their earnings trajectory, but as this cohort begins to retire in the next decade, there will be downward pressure on the average male salary. Both of these trends lead us to expect that male–female earnings should slowly converge—as age differences diminish so too will earnings disparities.

But how far will they converge? This depends on whether factors other than age influence gender disparity. Another way to compare male and female incomes is to use multiple regression techniques. These allow us to statistically control for factors other than age—particularly those that differ by gender such as hours and weeks worked, certification and marital status—that affect teachers' salaries (see Table 2.10). Using 1991 Census data, we apply this technique to examine the wage disparity among elementary and secondary teachers.[5]

TABLE 2.10

REGRESSION OF ELEMENTARY AND SECONDARY SCHOOL TEACHERS' EMPLOYMENT EARNINGS ON SELECTED INDEPENDENT VARIABLES

Variable name	Unstandardized regression coefficient	Standardized regression coefficient	Level of statistical significance
Sex	−8,673.93	−.214	<.0000
Age	374.18	.151	<.0000
Lives in a census metropolitan area	2,658.10	.064	<.0000
Born outside of Canada	1,070.68	.021	<.0000
Member of visible minority group	−4,231.38	−.060	<.0000
First Nations ancestry	−1,510.61	−.012	<.0000
First official language: English	832.08	.018	<.0000
Number of full-time weeks worked	462.70	.217	<.0000
Number of hours worked per week	92.23	.050	<.0000
Highest level of education (bachelor's degree is reference variable)			
Less than secondary school graduation	−9,580.74	−.206	<.0000
Secondary school graduate	−6,970.40	−.149	<.0000
Trade certificate	−6,305.92	−.113	<.0000
College diploma or certificate	−5,138.69	−.095	<.0000
University diploma, below bachelor's	−3,177.22	−.025	<.0000
Bachelor's degree plus university certificate	2,238.02	.016	<.0000
Professional degree (e.g., MD, LLB)	23,525.67	.067	<.0000
Postgraduate degree (e.g., MA, PhD)	6,289.85	.061	<.0000

Note: Provincial differences were statistically controlled in the estimation equation by using a series of dummy variables that are not reproduced here. Education was coded as a series of dummy variables, with bachelor's degree as the reference, or omitted category.

Source: Census of Canada, 1991, special tabulations.

Controlling for the variables shown in the left-most column of Table 2.10, the results show that women, on average, earn $8,674 less than men. While part of this disparity is undoubtedly due to differences in level, some disparity probably remains unattributed. For many researchers, the persistence of wage disparities after controlling for relevant human capital variables signals the existence of wage discrimination by gender. While limitations in the data do not allow us to conclude that there is evidence of such discrimination among teachers, there remains a large wage gap after key variables have been statistically controlled.

The effects of other variables in the equation are also noteworthy. As one would expect, age is positively related to income, with each additional year contributing increases of approximately $375 to employment earnings. This partly captures effects of work experience. Teachers born outside of Canada receive greater employment incomes than do teachers born in Canada. This finding *could* be a consequence of, among other things, the tendency for foreign-born teachers to work at the secondary school level or in areas such as foreign languages or sciences where demand is higher and hence salaries higher. Notice also that teachers from visible minority backgrounds and those with First Nations ancestry earn substantially less than other teachers, even after controls for age, education, sex, and hours and weeks worked. Minorities may be less likely to teach at the secondary school level, and many Aboriginals teach in outlying regions where salaries are lower. However some researchers would interpret this as evidence consistent with discrimination. Again we must caution that the census does not provide the full range of variables that would allow us to make that interpretation with any confidence.

In summary, teachers made great absolute and relative gains in their salaries during the first years of the postwar era, but since the early 1980s their salaries have stagnated in real terms. Teachers continue to earn more than the average Canadian worker does; female teachers' salaries are notably higher than those of other Canadian women. While gender inequalities remain, male and female salaries should gradually converge in future years since greater numbers of young women are entering higher levels of teaching. If women enter all facets of the profession (e.g., secondary as well as elementary, administrative positions as well as classroom teaching), then wage disparities will shrink. Furthermore, if young women remain in the profession, an issue that we turn to below, then the male–female wage gap ought to narrow in the future.

2.5 CAREER PATTERNS OF TEACHERS[6]

The idea of a teaching "career" conjures up images of young professional recruits choosing to make teaching their lifelong calling. In any profession, however, there is job turnover. Some new entrants decide, even only after a few years of service, to seek new opportunities outside their first chosen field. This has been especially the case for teachers. Historically, teaching was regarded as a stepping stone for men, and for many women an occupation held only until childbirth. Among those who qualified to be teachers, entry into the profession was relatively smooth, yet subsequent turnover rates were comparably high. This may have been due to some attributes unique to teaching and its labour market dynamics.

Compared with many other professions, teaching has less onerous job-specific preparation. Until recently, people with bachelor's degrees needed only one year of training in education to work in most jurisdictions; this still holds in some provinces at some levels, (e.g., elementary). This makes teacher training a relatively small investment that yields a good dividend. But it also encourages "no-shows"—those who train to be teachers but never enter the profession. Many university graduates, especially males, train to teach while looking for other opportunities (Lockhart 1991). Also, since teachers reach their maximum salary grade quickly compared with other professions, some argue that this flat salary gradient fails to inspire a lifelong commitment to the profession (Easton 1988, 55). Finally, education has always promoted a strong service orientation among its trainees, yet the realities of the occupation have disenchanted many teachers. For, instance, American researchers found that among teachers in the 1960s and early 1970s, those who favoured ideals of public service over money were more likely to become frustrated and leave the profession (Miech and Elder 1996).

The improvement in teaching conditions since the 1960s, as documented in the previous section, were thought by observers to reduce turnover, and make career patterns among teachers resemble those of other professions. Better pay, strong unions, more professional control, and greater prestige in the public eye have made teaching a more desirable and popular occupational goal among university graduates.

Recently, however, career patterns among the broad populace could also be shifting in important ways and this could influence teaching careers. Many labour market observers now argue that working life is shifting from a single, linear career path toward more flexible and adaptable employment trajectories. Workers of the future, it is claimed, will have multi-career work lives (Beck 1995). Beck maintains that job turnover, even among professionals, will soon be commonplace. Especially within professional fields, where heavily subsidized university-based education is an occupational prerequisite, the issue of turnover has important public policy implications. As a result, the idea of a dedicated teacher remaining true to his or her profession for a lifetime—if it was ever grounded in reality—is said to be fading.

By studying entry to, exit from, and turnover in teaching, we can develop a fuller picture of the changes in the profession. Using data from the 1994 Statistics Canada General Social Survey (GSS), we looked at two groups who were, at one point in their lives, involved in the teaching profession. One group consisted of members whose highest degrees were in education. They therefore possessed a key professional credential. The second group comprised individuals whose first jobs after completing their highest level of schooling were in elementary or secondary school teaching. We then looked at what individuals in these two groups were doing in 1994. Were they still members of the teaching profession or had they moved to other pursuits?

Among women, just less than 80% of the education graduates who found work started as elementary or secondary school teachers (see Table 2.11). Another 6% of female graduates worked in teaching-related fields at the postsecondary level or as special educators outside the formal school system. Approximately 15% of women graduating from a faculty of education program did not pursue teaching for their first job. Less than 1% of education graduates had never held a job since graduation.

TABLE 2.11

FIRST JOB AND CURRENT (1994) JOB OF WOMEN AND MEN, AGED 25 TO 64, WHOSE MAJOR FIELD OF STUDY FOR THEIR HIGHEST DEGREE WAS EDUCATION (SAMPLE ESTIMATES)

First job after completion of highest degree	Women (%)	Men (%)
In elementary or secondary teaching	79	56
In other education	6	12
Not in education	15	32
Total	**100**	**100**
Current (1994) job		
In elementary or secondary teaching	57	55
In other education	9	13
Not in education	34	32
Total	**100**	**100**
% not in 1994 labour force	15	9

Source: Statistics Canada, 1994 General Social Survey (Cycle 9), unpublished data.

Among men there is a striking difference. More than twice as many men as women (32% versus 15% respectively) pursued occupations other than teaching as their first full-time job after graduation. Even when they did find jobs in teaching, more men (12%) found careers in streams other than elementary or secondary school instruction. Whether men had more difficulty finding teaching jobs than did women or whether more men deliberately chose to pursue jobs other than teaching we cannot say. In recent years the typical route to a teaching job is for university graduates to work first in temporary, "on-call" positions, from which they are then hired into permanent posts. Men may be less willing, or less able, to work on this temporary basis for as long as women.

The evidence shows women more often than men turn their education credentials into jobs in the teaching profession. The GSS did not ask the age at which the respondent's highest degree was attained and it is possible that women graduates were older and had more valued experience than did men. Alternatively, since we know men are more likely than women to pursue secondary school teaching jobs, it could be that this labour market is more competitive and hence men have higher initial non-transition rates.[7]

As well as looking at the first jobs of education graduates, we also examine their 1994 occupations (see Table 2.11).[8] This is done in the table's second panel, where we display the "current" jobs of individuals who were between 25 and 64 in 1994 and who had chosen education as the major field of study for their highest degree. Almost the same percentages of women and men (57% and 55% respectively) were employed as elementary and secondary school teachers, and almost identical percentages (34% and 32% respectively) worked in jobs outside education. This relative parity in the career persistence of women and men is interesting given that a greater percentage of female education graduates initially enter the profession while at the same time many women tend to "stop out" to have children.

The survey responses concerning current (1994) jobs again show more men than women teaching outside elementary and secondary schools. For men, 13% held education-related jobs outside the Kindergarten to Grade 12 classroom as compared with 9% of women. Some of these men worked in postsecondary teaching but a significant number were senior administrators in public education.[9]

A second way to examine teaching careers is to look at the percentage of people who start their working lives in teaching and continue in that line of work. About two-thirds of those whose first job was in teaching are still working as classroom teachers in their current jobs (62% of women and 65% of men—see Table 2.12). In other words, about two-thirds of teachers have kept on a single career track. For individuals whose first job was in teaching, however, men were more likely than women to be in teaching streams outside elementary and secondary classrooms by 1994 (7% of women and 12% of men).

TABLE 2.12

CURRENT (1994) JOB OF WOMEN AND MEN, AGED 25 TO 64, WHOSE FIRST JOB AFTER COMPLETING THEIR HIGHEST DEGREE WAS TEACHING (SAMPLE ESTIMATES)

Current (1994) job	Women (%)	Men (%)
In elementary or secondary teaching	62	65
In other education	7	12
Not in education	33	23
Total	**100[1]**	**100**
Percentage not in 1994 labour force	17	17

1. Numbers do not add to 100 due to rounding.

Source: Statistics Canada, 1994 General Social Survey (Cycle 9), unpublished data.

The percentage of women versus men who began their employment lives as teachers and who are still in the labour market, but outside education, is 33% as opposed to 23% for men (see Table 2.12). Although more women than men make the transition from faculty of education programs to teaching, more men than women who begin their careers as teachers remain in education. Men leave the profession more often than women at the first transition, from university to a teaching job. In contrast, women are more likely than men to leave teaching, once they have begun to work as teachers.

There are several plausible reasons for this latter finding, although our data do not allow us to choose between these alternatives (and all may be at least partially true). First, women's childbearing and child-rearing experiences may make it difficult for them to re-enter teaching after having children, especially if they are out of the teaching labour force for several years. Instead, women may seek part-time jobs or employment that is less demanding than teaching. Second, men experience greater promotion opportunities in teaching and are in better-paying teaching positions. Combined, these factors enhance men's incentives to remain in the profession. Notice, however, that an identical percentage (17%) of women and men who began their careers as teachers and who are not yet 65 are now out of the labour force.

What do former teachers do when they pursue jobs outside education? One answer can be found by looking at the current occupations of people whose first jobs were as elementary or secondary school teachers. The occupational careers of former teachers differ markedly for women and men (see Table 2.13). Men who were formerly teachers and were still in the labour force in 1994 were much more likely than women to pursue careers in professional or managerial occupations (85.1% of men versus 45.1% of women). Conversely, women were almost as likely to be in clerical, sales, and service jobs (44.6%) as in professional and managerial occupations. Relatively few women and men who had once been teachers were found in "blue-collar" industrial or construction trades (10.3% and 5.5% respectively).

TABLE 2.13

CURRENT OCCUPATIONS[1] OF FORMER TEACHERS OR OF INDIVIDUALS WITH TEACHING QUALIFICATIONS (BUT WHO ARE NOT CURRENTLY TEACHING), AGES 25 TO 65, BY SEX

	Current occupation of former teachers (first job was teaching) (%)		Current occupation of individuals whose major field of study was education (%)	
	Women	Men	Women	Men
Professional/Managerial	45.1	85.1	57.7	63.6
Clerical, Sales and Service	44.6	9.4	39.4	22.2
Industrial/Construction	10.3	5.5	2.9	14.2
Total	**100.0**	**100.0**	**100.0**	**100.0**

1. Current occupations were created by collapsing the 1981 Standard Occupational Classification as follows: Professional/Managerial, codes 1111 to 2730 and 2740 to 3379; Clerical, Sales and Service, codes 4110 to 6199; Industrial/Construction, codes 7000 to 9950. Individuals whose current occupation is teaching are excluded.

Source: Statistics Canada, 1994 General Social Survey (Cycle 9), unpublished data.

The data do not definitively explain why these differences exist between women and men. We suspect that women are more likely to leave the profession for family-related reasons whereas men may leave to pursue attractive career opportunities. School boards are increasingly offering the greater flexibility in work arrangements desired by working mothers (such as job sharing and part-time work), but this is a relatively recent change in collective bargaining agreements.

A second way to examine the career paths of people who began in teaching, but have since shifted to other occupational streams, is to look at the current non-teaching jobs of individuals who attended university faculties of education. An almost equal proportion of women and men who obtained university teaching degrees but were not currently working as teachers, were employed in professional and managerial fields in 1994 (57.7% of women and 63.6% of men). Many who obtained university teaching degrees (42.3% of women and 36.4% of men) pursued jobs outside the professional and managerial fields.

Turnover among teachers is relatively high. There are many male "no-shows" and teachers of both sexes leave the field for other occupations. It is plausible that, judging by the high occupational quality of the jobs they attain, these leavers are attracted to the prospects of continued mobility in other careers.

2.6 CONCLUSION: THE ONGOING HISTORY OF CANADIAN TEACHING

Shifts in Canada's demography, economy, and governance have shaped the teaching profession. Like other occupations, teaching is in transition and may be entering a new era. As governments deal with large public debts, provincial education systems must stretch fewer dollars to meet the needs of a growing population. These fiscal straits come with heightened expectations for our education system. The result is that schools are facing a series of competing demands. They are expected to provide high-quality and accessible teaching that is also cost-efficient. They are to be simultaneously innovative, relevant and accountable, and ensure high standards. For some policy advocates, these new pressures demand an innovative organization of the teaching profession (Economic Council of Canada 1992; see also Hargreaves 1994 for a discussion). Critics have called for longer periods of initial training, continual skill upgrading, and periodic re-accreditation. But more importantly, some have called for new methods of assessing and remunerating teachers, methods that reward individuals according to their ability and effort. Monetary incentives and merit rewards have been suggested as ways to inspire teachers to improve their craft and keep it at a high level.

Whatever the virtue of these changes, the teaching labour market will likely become more volatile for newcomers. Teaching will remain a desirable occupation for recent university graduates who are experiencing keen competition for jobs, but unlike the education graduates of previous decades, many today will not find jobs easily. Public schools cannot absorb all recent graduates, and indeed, many recent education graduates were not permanently employed in any occupation two years after their graduation (Coish 1994, 21).

The data that we have presented in this chapter suggest four key periods in the development of teaching in 20th century Canada. Our general descriptions of those periods are based on broad trends in the size of the teaching work force, teacher income, demographics and equity. Note that the final period is, by necessity, speculative; it is based on projections of recent trends and by some of the policy recommendations voiced increasingly today.

2.6.1 Prewar era

- Teaching is a female-dominated occupation but men control the hierarchy's upper levels.
- The profession is a route of upward mobility for men from humble socio-economic origins.
- Pay is low and institutionalization is weak.

2.6.2 1945 to 1969: Era of growth

- The teaching force increases significantly due to the pressures of population growth (the baby boom and immigration), and the societal commitment to higher retention rates at the secondary level.

- Real income grows substantially as teachers raise their collective human capital and create effective collective bargaining units.
- Teachers start earning more than the average Canadian.
- There is an influx of men into secondary teaching.

2.6.3 1970 to 1993: Era of stagnation

- The actual number of teachers stagnates, though teacher salaries continue to grow into the early 1980s.
- The student–teacher ratio continues to fall.
- The trend of increasing male composition falters as more women enter secondary teaching.
- There is a slight move toward gender equality in pay.
- Teachers as a group are aging.
- More teachers are employed part time.
- Minorities are under-represented.
- Teaching is no longer a ladder of mobility for those from low socio-economic origins.

2.6.4 The immediate future: Retrenchment?

- As public sector retrenchment continues, demand for teachers will become increasingly volatile as multiple forces buffet the education system.
- The student–teacher ratio will increase.
- Salaries will stagnate.
- Teachers' average age will continue to rise until the turn of the century, but many teachers will retire, sparking demand for new teachers, whose human capital continues to increase.
- In response to criticism over the quality of teaching, remuneration schemes will be altered to consider merit pay and other innovations to mark career progress.
- Education's presumed economic value will become the predominant justification for its continued expansion and increases in funding levels.

From this look at the historical development and future challenges of the teaching profession, we shift our attention to the regional composition of the education system. According to the British North America Act of 1867, formal schooling comes under provincial jurisdiction. Regional variation is therefore an especially important aspect of the organization of Canadian education.

ENDNOTES

1. Our labels (e.g., Elementary School and Kindergarten Teachers) are derived directly from the 1991 Census classification of occupations. The appropriate definitions can be found in the National Occupational Classification (NOC) (Human Resources Development Canada 1993).

2. This comparison of 1986 and 1991 relies on occupational definitions from the Standard Occupational Classification (SOC) system that was used prior to the 1991 Census. In the SOC system, a "not elsewhere classified" category captured these additional teaching occupations (e.g., supply teachers). These latter groups are included under the elementary and kindergarten, or secondary school, categories in the 1991 NOC system.

3. This pay gap, derived from 1991 Census data, is due to several related factors. Secondary school teachers tend to have accumulated more years of experience and to have higher educational credentials, both of which result in higher levels of pay. Pay rates are equivalent for elementary and secondary school teaching jobs in some, but not all, jurisdictions. Income is defined here as employment earnings.

4. We should note, however, that a comparison of the social origins of teachers-in-training tells us little about the social origins of teachers, since transition rates from training to teaching jobs differ by social origin and gender (see Guppy and Davies 1996).

5. Our analysis does not control for teaching level. There is debate as to whether or not teaching level ought to be statistically controlled in this type of analysis. On one hand, teaching is teaching and controlling for teaching level would constrain the regression equation too much. Conversely, a control for teaching level would allow one to examine more closely what income differences would be like *if* men and women were equally distributed in the same teaching positions (which, of course, they are not). Also, age is an imperfect proxy for years of experience because some teachers start their careers later than others, and some drop out for short durations.

6. Some material in this section comes from Guppy and Davies (1996).

7. By "non-transition" rate we mean the percentage of people (men in this case) who have the appropriate education credentials, but who do not make the transition into the teaching work force.

8. In comparing panels in Table 2.11, or in comparing across tables, it is important to note that people who are not in the labour force are excluded from the base percentage calculations.

9. In 1991, 20,880 men held positions as school principals and administrators of elementary and secondary education while 8,775 women held such positions (70% versus 30% respectively).

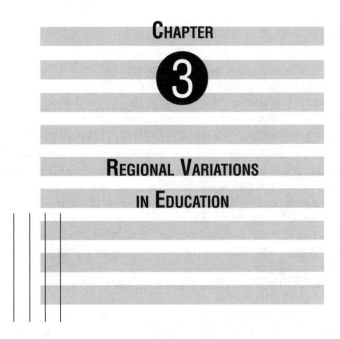

CHAPTER

3

REGIONAL VARIATIONS

IN EDUCATION

Regionalism is a recurrent theme in discussions of Canadian society. Where people live influences their likelihood of receiving Employment Insurance, of living above or below the national standard of living, or of obtaining a postsecondary diploma or degree. Social and cultural differences of this sort, when combined with the diversity of Canada's physical landscape, lead to distinctive regional communities.

This chapter centres on how, and with what consequences, populations and their associated social and cultural characteristics, and particularly their educational composition, vary by region. We stress, though, that our focus is on regional differences as opposed to regionalism, which refers to regional identities and interests as exemplified by feelings of belonging to a region (Matthews and Davis 1986). We begin by considering the definition of "region."

3.1   DEFINING THE REGION OF STUDY

Political boundaries are, in an important sense, arbitrary lines drawn around geographic regions. Physical features influence where borders are drawn but they are not the sole determinants. In other words, geographical landmarks are a good, but not a perfect, reflection of boundaries. It is even more unclear where exactly boundaries that separate social and cultural groups should be drawn.

Any regional study of Canada is thereby complicated because political boundaries, such as the border between New Brunswick and Quebec, often arbitrarily cut across social or cultural groupings. Studies of Canada often skirt this dilemma by using province or territory as the regional unit of analysis, but this approach is often one of pure convenience, since data are not available for any other areal unit. When examining regional differences in education, however, it makes sense to use the provinces and territories as "regions" of study because under the British

North America Act responsibility for schooling is organized according to these boundaries.

Educational decisions made in provinces and territories help foster a collective regional identity within those jurisdictions. Across the provinces and territories there are significant variations in the provision of schooling, which include the availability and duration of kindergarten, the number of years of high school offered, the existence and role of community colleges, and the availability of certain university faculties, such as optometry and law. Provinces also differ with respect to development and economic structure, cultural history, and so forth.

We recognize, however, that treating provinces or territories as homogeneous entities—as the only relevant regional divides in Canada—may conceal some interesting differences, such as those of a rural–urban nature. Canada's highly decentralized system of educational governance, where local school boards control crucial aspects of schooling (for example some control finances and curriculum—although always under provincial or territorial guidelines), also makes the decision to focus on provinces and territories less than perfect, but still justifiable. This chapter, therefore, will address the variations that occur within these regions.

3.2 REGIONAL DIFFERENCES IN EDUCATIONAL ATTAINMENT

In Chapter 1, we pointed out that education plays an increasingly significant role in the lives of individual Canadians. Beyond its influence on future prospects at the individual level, we suggested also that the fortunes of various regions in the world are strongly related to educational development. It is important, therefore, to understand regional differences in educational attainment. If certain regions surge ahead while others lag behind in educational endowments, this has important consequences for future cultural and economic development. As knowledge becomes an increasingly important currency in the world, regions with more-educated populations face brighter prospects than areas where educational qualifications are weaker. New forms of social inequality based on knowledge levels or educational credentials may be emerging and this trend needs examination. Beyond creating new tensions in Canada, regional disparities in education may also exacerbate existing cleavages in the country.

3.2.1 University attainment by region

How much difference is there in the educational attainment of Canadians living in different provinces and territories? As Figure 3.1 shows, in 1991 the proportion of residents aged 25 and over who had university degrees was greatest in the Yukon Territory (14.8%), Ontario (14.6%), and Alberta (13.7%). In contrast, less than 10% of the residents 25 and over in Saskatchewan, Prince Edward Island, New Brunswick, and Newfoundland were university graduates in 1991.

Provincial differences in university attainment are a popular measure of regional variations in education, and so they should be. Credentials from higher education are an important currency in the labour market because they indicate that those who possess them have certain skills and abilities. As we increasingly move toward a knowledge society, certain regions of the country are better poised to take advantage of new opportunities. Recall, however, that in 1991 only 12.8% of Canadians aged 25 and over held university degrees.

FIGURE 3.1

PERCENTAGE OF THE POPULATION 25 YEARS AND OVER WITH A UNIVERSITY DEGREE, 1991

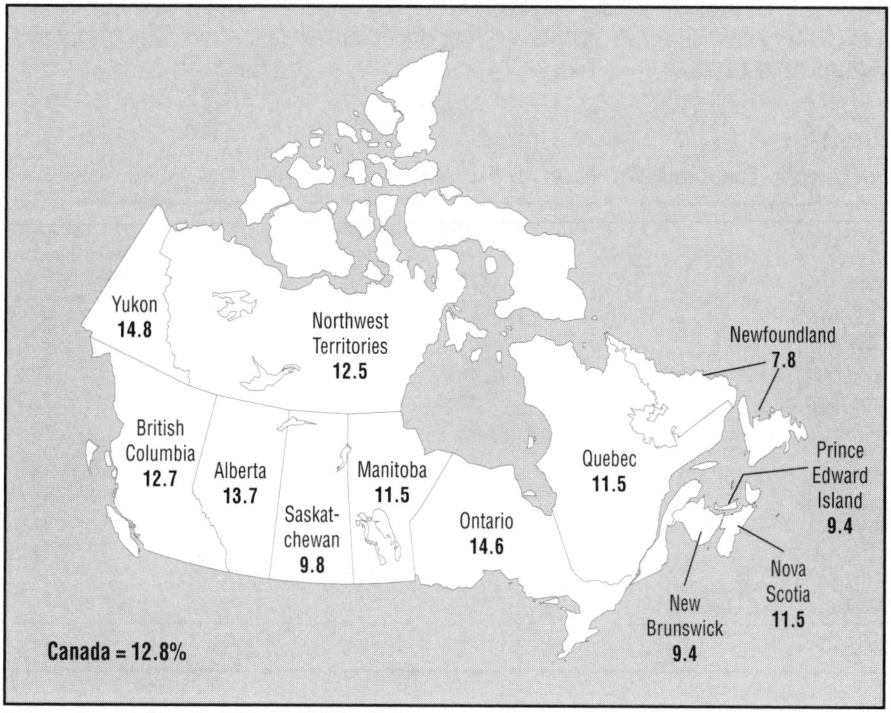

Source: Census of Canada, 1991, special tabluations.

3.2.2 Low educational attainment by region

Focussing on university graduates reveals only one side of the educational distribution. Regions with well-educated populations may also have large numbers of residents with below-average years of schooling. Examining only one end of the education distribution can therefore be deceiving. We examine the other end of the distribution, the low education end, using two separate measures: the percentage of people aged 15 to 24 in 1991 who had less than Grade 9 and the estimated 1991 provincial rate of school leavers (for 20-year-olds).

The 1991 Census counted 38,220 people between 15 and 19 who had less than Grade 9. At a time when many social commentators are stressing the importance of education, both for the individual and for the country, this is a staggeringly large number of poorly educated young Canadians. Add to this number the 53,255 people aged 20 to 24 who did not have Grade 9 and who were not attending school full time in 1991. Certainly some of these 91,475 individuals will upgrade their schooling later in life, but that will only occur at large personal and societal cost.

Regionally, the Northwest Territories has the highest proportion of less-educated people, with almost one out of every three people aged 15 to 24 having less than Grade 9 education (see Table 3.1). Here, the focus on region at least partially masks another Canadian phenomena, the low educational attainment of many First Nations people (a topic we pursue in the next chapter). Although First Nations people in the Northwest Territories have been rapidly increasing their schooling levels in recent decades, only about half of all First Nations children remain in school until Grade 12. The other half have dropped out or stopped out prior to returning (Indian and Northern Affairs 1993).

TABLE 3.1
LOW LEVELS OF EDUCATIONAL ATTAINMENT, BY PROVINCE AND TERRITORY

Region	15- to 24-year-olds with less than Grade 9 education, 1991 (%)	School-leaver rates for 20-year-olds, 1993 (%)
Newfoundland	5.6	24.0
Prince Edward Island	4.4	25.0
Nova Scotia	5.8	22.0
New Brunswick	5.4	20.0
Quebec	6.0	22.0
Ontario	2.0	17.0
Manitoba	4.8	19.0
Saskatchewan	5.4	16.0
Alberta	3.3	14.0
British Columbia	2.3	16.0
Northwest Territories	31.3	..
Yukon	4.6	..
Canada	**3.8**	**18.0**

.. not available

Source: Percentage of 15- to 24-year-olds with less than Grade 9 education taken from the Census of Canada, 1991; school-leaver rates for 20-year-olds taken from Gilbert and Devereaux 1993, Chart 2-2.

Variations between the other provinces and territories are not so dramatic, but important differences do exist. For example, the rate of low attainment—the percentage of 15- to 24-year-olds with less than Grade 9—is three times greater in Quebec (6.0%) than in Ontario (2.0%), and just over two-and-a-half times higher in Nova Scotia (5.8%) than in British Columbia (2.3%). There is evidence that low educational attainment levels are linked to poverty and unemployment (for example Corak 1990; Ross, Shillington and Lochhead 1994) so these disparities work to further concentrate social problems regionally. Low levels of schooling not only reduce the labour market prospects of individuals, they also influence regional economies.

Another way to measure regional differences in education levels is to look at the percentage of 20-year-olds who left school early. The regional differences are almost identical to those observed from the percentage of 15- to 24-year-olds with less than Grade 9. Indeed, the correlation between the two different measures reported in Table 3.1 is 0.59, signifying a high but not perfect correlation between the two indicators.

Notice that school-leaver rates were higher in the eastern provinces (averaging almost 23%) than in the western provinces (averaging about 16%). This pronounced tilt in educational outcomes is an increasingly recognized feature of the educational landscape in this country (for example Economic Council of Canada 1992). This tilt is apparent both in the map (see

Figure 3.1) in which we display the upper end of the education distribution, the attainment of university degrees, and at the lower end of the distribution, whether reflected by school leaving or by attaining less than nine years' schooling.

3.2.3 Average years of schooling

The same tilt pattern is harder to detect if we plot the average years of schooling of Canadians (see Figure 3.2). The variation among regions is noticeable but the westward tilt of the distribution is not quite so pronounced. First, the highest levels of average years of schooling occur in Quebec and Ontario.[1] Adding the Yukon, where education levels are high and the Northwest Territories where levels are low, obscures any westward tilt. Earlier pronouncements on the westward tilt of educational achievement have conveniently ignored the country's northern regions (Economic Council of Canada 1992).

FIGURE 3.2

AVERAGE YEARS OF SCHOOLING OF 25- TO 34-YEAR-OLDS, BY SEX, PROVINCES AND TERRITORIES, 1991

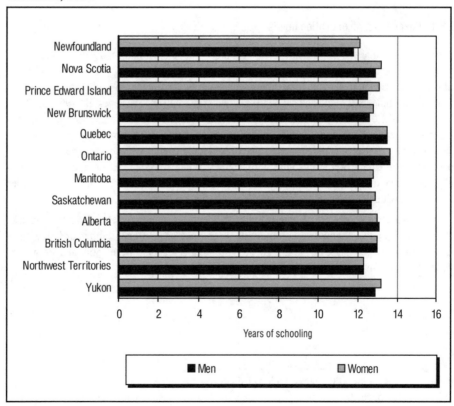

Source: Census of Canada, 1991, special tabulations.

Notice that in Figure 3.2 the differences between provinces and territories are for the most part greater than are the differences between women and men. For example, the average years of schooling varies regionally by 1.6 years, from a low of 12.0 years in Newfoundland to a high of 13.6 in Ontario. Considering all provinces and territories, the greatest discrepancy between women and men occurs in Prince Edward Island and amounts to 0.6 years. The difference between regions is a full year greater than is the difference between women and men. This provides one yardstick against which one can judge the size of the educational differences by region.

3.3   CONVERGENCE AND DIVERGENCE

As we have seen, describing regional variation in educational attainment is difficult because different indicators present slightly different pictures. To some extent, variation can be said to rest in the eye of the beholder. Nevertheless, a clear pattern of variation exists. This raises an even more interesting question, however. Are the current educational attainment differences between provinces and territories increasing or decreasing? As we move toward a "knowledge society" (Stehr 1994), the importance of education increases. Are all of Canada's regions keeping up with increasing levels of educational attainment or are the differences between regions that we have seen so far increasing?

3.3.1 Change in high education levels

One way to examine this is to see how the percentage of people with university degrees changes over time in each province or territory. In 1951, 2.3% of Canadians 25 years and over had a university degree but in Newfoundland the corresponding percentage was only 0.6. Relative to Canada as a whole, Newfoundland had fewer residents with university degrees. By 1961, 3.4% of Canadians and 1.0% of Newfoundlanders had university degrees. At first glance it is not easy to determine whether the percentage of Newfoundlanders with university degrees kept pace with the Canadian average. Not only did the percentage of Newfoundlanders with degrees increase, but so too did the percentage of all Canadians with degrees. What is needed is a method of assessing whether the rate of increase in Newfoundland is greater or lesser than the rate of increase for the country as a whole.

An easier way to measure change is to use the overall Canadian average as a benchmark (that is, 100%) and ask how far each individual province or territory is above or below this benchmark (see Table 3.2). In 1951, then, Newfoundland was below the national average, as shown by the following:

$$\frac{.6}{2.3} \times 100 = 26.1$$

The closer a province's figure is to 100, the closer that province's population is to the national average. Figures below 100 represent a lower-than-average proportion of residents with degrees while a figure above 100 reflects a population with an above-average number of residents with degrees.

TABLE 3.2

RELATIVE PROPORTION[1] OF POPULATION AGED 25 AND OVER WITH A UNIVERSITY DEGREE,[2] BY PROVINCE AND TERRITORY, 1951 TO 1991

Region	1951	1961	1971	1981	1991
Newfoundland	26.1	29.4	43.4	59.4	60.9
Prince Edward Island	43.5	50.0	62.3	74.0	73.4
Nova Scotia	65.2	79.4	83.0	88.5	89.8
New Brunswick	47.8	64.7	71.7	75.0	73.4
Quebec	100.0	100.0	98.1	88.5	89.8
Ontario	130.4	114.7	111.3	110.4	114.1
Manitoba	65.2	88.2	90.6	90.6	89.8
Saskatchewan	52.2	67.6	71.7	76.0	76.6
Alberta	69.6	102.9	115.1	122.9	107.0
British Columbia	104.3	108.8	107.5	103.1	99.2
Yukon	82.6	88.2	92.5	119.8	115.6
Northwest Territories	104.3	88.2	86.8	105.2	97.7
Canada	**100.0**	**100.0**	**100.0**	**100.0**	**100.0**
Disparity gap (highest/lowest)	5.0	3.9	2.7	2.1	1.9

1. Relative to the national average, Canada = 100.
2. In 1951, "university degree" is imputed for individuals having 17 or more years of schooling.
Source: Statistics Canada, *Educational Attainment and School Attendance*, 1993.

Since 1951, Newfoundland's percentage of residents with degrees has risen, and more importantly it has risen relative to the national average. The relative proportion has risen from 26.1 to 60.9. At the other extreme, Ontario was above average in 1951 (at 130.4) but its advantage has declined in recent decades and, while still above the national norm, is now at 114.1.

Over the decades, the provinces and territories have become more alike in the proportion of their residents with university degrees—their relative percentages are converging toward 100. A simple but revealing measure of this convergence is formed by dividing the highest relative percentage by the lowest relative percentage for each individual decade. As the bottom row of Table 3.2 reveals, this number is converging on 1, the result that would occur if all regions had identical percentages of residents with university degrees.

This pattern of convergence shows that, at least for university degree attainment, social inequalities between regions are eroding. If there are regional economic returns to university education, in the sense that higher education improves aggregate or collective economic prosperity, then we are moving toward more equalization of these returns across regions. Similarly, if higher levels of education foster active political debate and participation, then on this dimension too we are moving toward regional convergence.

3.3.2 Change in low education levels

Trends at one end of the distribution, however, do not necessarily reflect changes occurring elsewhere. An analysis of the low end of the educational attainment distribution reveals that here the pattern of convergence does not exist. Particular regions are developing higher concentrations of residents aged 15 and over with less than Grade 9 education than are other parts of the country (see Table 3.3). Scanning the magnitude of the relative percentages in 1951 and comparing these to the figures in 1991 reveals that the latter numbers exhibit far more variability. This is evidence of divergence: The provinces and territories are growing more dissimilar. The bottom row of Table 3.3 shows that over the decades the disparities between provinces and territories have grown steadily and unequivocally. Looking at specific regions it is clear that in the Northwest Territories, Quebec, New Brunswick, and Newfoundland are found the highest concentrations of residents with low educational attainment.

TABLE 3.3

RELATIVE PROPORTION OF POPULATION[1] 15 AND OVER WITH LESS THAN GRADE 9 EDUCATION, BY PROVINCE AND TERRITORY, 1951 TO 1991

Region	1951	1961	1971	1981	1991
Newfoundland	132.4	124.9	137.5	148.8	145.5
Prince Edward Island	102.3	103.2	114.2	116.4	109.8
Nova Scotia	93.6	91.6	97.5	101.0	95.1
New Brunswick	116.2	121.1	127.6	138.2	140.6
Quebec	117.9	118.1	126.6	131.4	144.1
Ontario	90.4	93.9	87.3	87.4	83.2
Manitoba	98.7	92.5	99.4	107.7	106.3
Saskatchewan	107.3	105.2	110.2	113.5	114.0
Alberta	88.4	84.1	73.7	63.8	63.6
British Columbia	75.3	71.7	70.6	66.2	63.6
Yukon	83.0	82.3	73.7	62.3	51.0
Northwest Territories	145.1	142.4	156.7	176.3	193.7
Canada	**100.0**	**100.0**	**100.0**	**100.0**	**100.0**
Disparity gap (highest/lowest)	1.9	2.0	2.2	2.8	3.8

1. Relative to the national average, Canada = 100.

Source: Statistics Canada, *Educational Attainment and School Attendance*, 1993.

It is important to make a distinction here. The message is not that a growing percentage of people in some regions have less than Grade 9 education. Rather, we are saying that, relative to the national average, the proportion of people with low levels of schooling is becoming concentrated in certain regions. Conversely, over the decades some regions, and especially the Yukon, Alberta, British Columbia, and Ontario, are experiencing decreases in the number of residents with low levels of schooling. We explore explanations for this change later in the chapter.

3.3.3 Educational inequality index

We examine one last indicator to complete our discussion of educational attainment and distribution in Canada. Comparing the two ends of the distribution—the percentage of residents in a region with less than Grade 9 versus the percentage with university degrees—gives a useful picture of the degree of educational inequality that exists in a particular region.

In 1991, 16.6% of the population aged 25 and over had less than Grade 9 education compared with 12.8% of Canadians who had a university degree. Dividing the former by the latter gives a simple educational inequality index of 1.3 for 1991. The inequality index is the greatest in Newfoundland, where more than three times as many people have less than Grade 9 education than have university degrees (see Table 3.4). At the other extreme is the Yukon, where university degree holders outnumber individuals with less than Grade 9 education by a margin of almost 2 to 1 (or 0.5 on the index).

TABLE 3.4

PERCENTAGE OF POPULATION 25 AND OVER WITH LESS THAN GRADE 9 EDUCATION, AND PERCENTAGE OF POPULATION 25 AND OVER WITH A UNIVERSITY DEGREE, BY PROVINCE AND TERRITORY, 1991

Region	Less than Grade 9 education (%) (a)	University degree holders (%) (b)	Inequality index (a/b)
Newfoundland	25.4	7.8	3.3
Prince Edward Island	18.5	9.4	2.0
Nova Scotia	15.5	11.5	1.3
New Brunswick	23.7	9.4	2.5
Quebec	23.6	11.5	2.1
Ontario	14.1	14.6	1.0
Manitoba	17.6	11.5	1.5
Saskatchewan	18.8	9.8	1.9
Alberta	10.5	13.7	0.8
British Columbia	10.4	12.7	0.8
Yukon	7.9	14.8	0.5
Northwest Territories	26.5	12.5	2.1
Canada	**16.6**	**12.8**	**1.3**

Source: Statistics Canada, *Educational Attainment and School Attendance,* 1993.

Across all provinces and territories, Table 3.4 reveals a now-familiar pattern. The Yukon, Alberta, British Columbia, and Ontario have larger proportions of people with university degrees, relative to those with less than Grade 9 education, than do other regions of the country. In Nova Scotia the education balance almost perfectly parallels the Canadian average, but in Manitoba, Saskatchewan, Prince Edward Island, Quebec, the Northwest Territories, New Brunswick, and Newfoundland, the educational balance is tipped toward those with less schooling.

The discrepancies that we note in Table 3.4 could, at least theoretically, be a function of variations in age distributions among the provinces and territories. One way to examine this is to look at educational inequality for a narrower age range. The data for the 25-to-34 age group show that the general pattern would not change much (see Table 3.5). By restricting the age range, fewer people are found in the less than Grade 9 education category, but the relative balance remains similar. In the Yukon, Ontario, Alberta, and British Columbia the index is less than or equal to the national average (less inequality), while in all other regions it is above the national average (more inequality). This disparity presumably occurs because of different economic opportunities in each region.

TABLE 3.5

PERCENTAGE OF POPULATION 25 TO 34 WITH LESS THAN GRADE 9 EDUCATION, AND PERCENTAGE OF POPULATION 25 TO 34 WITH A UNIVERSITY DEGREE, BY PROVINCE AND TERRITORY, 1991

Region	Less than Grade 9 education (%) (a)	University degree holders (%) (b)	Inequality index (a/b)
Newfoundland	11.2	10.3	1.1
Prince Edward Island	7.1	12.1	0.6
Nova Scotia	5.4	14.7	0.4
New Brunswick	7.4	11.6	0.6
Quebec	4.7	15.3	0.3
Ontario	2.6	18.7	0.1
Manitoba	5.1	14.3	0.4
Saskatchewan	4.3	12.3	0.3
Alberta	2.7	14.9	0.2
British Columbia	2.5	14.0	0.2
Yukon	2.1	15.2	0.1
Northwest Territories	15.6	12.0	1.3
Canada	**3.7**	**16.0**	**0.2**

Source: Census of Canada, 1991. Tabulations by the author.

Again, our finding underlines the point that the education balance in the country is not changing in any significant manner, at least not so far as regions are concerned. Among younger Canadians we find almost exactly the same pattern as among all Canadians, suggesting that regional economic imbalances are not being altered through differential educational attainment. The fact that in both the Northwest Territories and Newfoundland there are more 25- to 34-year-olds with less than Grade 9 education than there are with university degrees reinforces the idea that people with low educational attainment are becoming concentrated in certain areas.

There are several explanations for the different educational attainment rates between provinces and territories. As we saw earlier, regional variation in school-leaver rates accounts for some of this difference. The variation is at least in part a reflection of regional economic differences, especially where primary resource industries, which do not require much formal education of their workers, with little formal education, are strong sectors of provincial and territorial economies. Regional differences in the ways educational systems are shaped also influence levels of schooling from one province or territory to another. For example, community colleges are more established as higher education alternatives in some regions than in others (Dennison 1995).

The different age profiles of the provinces and territories also influence overall levels of schooling by region. As we saw in a previous chapter, older Canadians tend to have less formal schooling than younger generations. Age is also associated with region, since some regions of the country have younger populations on average (for example the Yukon) and other regions have older populations (for example British Columbia). The result is that regions with older populations tend to have more people with lower levels of schooling. The effect of these regional differences cannot be too large, however, since even when we restricted attention to narrow age ranges, the general patterns were maintained.

3.4 INTERNAL MIGRATION

One last factor that we have yet to investigate but which might influence regional differences in educational attainment is internal migration. Internal migration refers to geographic mobility, the movement of individuals and families from one part of the country to another (this research is reviewed in Liaw 1986; Ram, Shin, and Pouliot 1994). Such movement can occur over short or long ranges, but given our concern here with regional issues, we focus on mobility between provinces or territories in the last five years. As a first step it is important to clarify whether or not an individual's level of education is related to inter-regional mobility.

There are relatively few long-distance movers in Canada. Although Canadians move often (over a five-year interval about half of all Canadians move), only about 4% of the population moves to a different province or territory in the course of a five-year span. In Table 3.6 we compare the educational backgrounds of long-range "movers" (people who reported living in a different province or territory in 1991 as compared with 1986) versus "stayers" (people who reported living in the same province or territory in both 1986 and 1991).

TABLE 3.6

INTERPROVINCIAL MIGRATION IN CANADA, BY LEVEL OF EDUCATION, 1991

Level of education	Stayers[1]		Movers[2]	
	Number	%[3]	Number	%[3]
Less than Grade 9	2,918,640	14.2	41,265	5.0
Grades 9 to 10	2,584,370	12.6	79,260	9.7
Grades 11 to 13	2,419,085	11.8	87,625	10.7
High school graduate	3,046,090	14.8	100,255	12.2
Trade certificate	822,225	4.0	24,665	3.0
Postsecondary, non-university	4,544,945	22.2	211,255	25.8
Postsecondary, university	4,149,715	20.3	275,340	33.6
Total	**20,485,070**	**100.0**	**819,655**	**100.0**

1. Stayers are those who remained in the same province from 1986 to 1991.
2. Movers are those who moved between provinces at some time during the period 1986 to 1991.
3. Percentages may not add to 100 due to rounding.
Source: Census of Canada, 1991, special tabulations.

Canadians with less than Grade 9 education represented 5% of those who moved between regions and 14.2% of those who stayed in the same province or territory. At the other end of the educational spectrum, 33.6% of all movers had some university experience (although not necessarily a degree) compared with 20.3% of all stayers. In comparison with stayers, long-range movers were more likely to have higher education (Ram, Shin, and Pouliot 1994, 17, 18).

Looking at internal migration another way, we see that the university-educated are more than six times more likely to move than are people with less than Grade 9 education (see also Che-Alford 1992). This is hardly surprising since moving is expensive and more-educated Canadians are more likely to have the resources to fund such endeavours. The more educated are also better positioned to obtain information about opportunities elsewhere, via access to and familiarity with a range of knowledge sources. As well, they may move more if they think this will optimize their returns to education, presumably by providing a better fit between their skills and those needed by employers (see Pineo 1985).

One way to think about this regional migration is to ask which, if any, regions benefited from the 165,730 university-educated Canadians who changed region of residence between 1986 and 1991. Table 3.7 provides details relevant to this kind of comparison by contrasting the educational attainments of people moving into and out of different regions. The information provided for each province and territory is similar to that found in Table 3.6, except that another column is added to show the net educational gains or losses a region has experienced as a result of internal Canadian migration.

TABLE 3.7

PERCENTAGE OF INTERPROVINCIAL IN- AND OUT-MIGRATION BETWEEN 1986 AND 1991 FOR PROVINCES AND TERRITORIES, BY LEVEL OF EDUCATION

Province	Newfoundland			Prince Edward Island		
Level of education	In-migrants	Out-migrants	% difference	In-migrants	Out-migrants	% difference
Less than Grade 9	8.2	5.7	2.5	6.0	3.9	2.1
Grades 9 to 10	15.1	11.8	3.3	12.6	6.9	5.7
Grades 11 to 13	10.5	11.0	-0.5	11.0	9.6	1.4
High school graduate	12.4	14.5	-2.1	12.3	12.3	0.0
Trade certificate	2.7	2.3	0.4	3.9	3.6	0.3
Postsecondary, non-university	26.6	25.1	1.5	22.2	26.4	-4.2
Postsecondary, university	24.6	29.6	-5.0	33.2	37.3	-4.1
Total %	100.0	100.0	...	100.0	100.0	...
N	16,030	30,295		7,125	8,155	

Table 3.7 (CONTINUED)

Percentage of Interprovincial In- and Out-migration between 1986 and 1991 for Provinces and Territories, by Level of Education

Province	Nova Scotia			New Brunswick		
Level of education	In-migrants	Out-migrants	% difference	In-migrants	Out-migrants	% difference
Less than Grade 9	4.6	3.7	0.9	7.2	6.4	0.8
Grades 9 to 10	9.7	9.5	0.2	11.0	9.5	1.5
Grades 11 to 13	9.5	10.2	-0.7	10.0	9.2	0.8
High school graduate	11.0	11.8	-0.8	12.7	13.5	-0.8
Trade certificate	3.8	3.1	0.7	3.2	3.1	0.1
Postsecondary, non-university	25.6	24.2	1.4	23.3	22.0	1.3
Postsecondary, university	35.7	38.3	-2.6	32.5	36.2	-3.7
Total %	100.0	100.0	...	100.0	100.0	...
_N_	44,630	49,040		29,535	35,555	

Province	Quebec			Ontario		
Level of education	In-migrants	Out-migrants	% difference	In-migrants	Out-migrants	% difference
Less than Grade 9	6.7	5.4	1.3	4.6	5.3	-0.7
Grades 9 to 10	8.1	7.7	0.4	8.5	10.5	-2.0
Grades 11 to 13	7.4	8.1	-0.7	9.9	12.4	-2.5
High school graduate	13.4	12.7	0.7	12.7	12.0	0.7
Trade certificate	3.7	2.8	0.9	2.7	3.2	-0.5
Postsecondary, non-university	22.5	22.0	0.5	23.4	23.3	0.1
Postsecondary, university	38.2	41.3	-3.1	38.1	33.2	4.9
Total %	100.0	100.0	...	100.0	100.0	...
_N_	69,880	91,860		226,990	190,155	

Province	Manitoba			Saskatchewan		
Level of education	In-migrants	Out-migrants	% difference	In-migrants	Out-migrants	% difference
Less than Grade 9	5.6	5.3	0.3	6.5	4.8	1.7
Grades 9 to 10	10.6	10.5	0.1	11.9	10.6	1.3
Grades 11 to 13	12.8	12.4	0.4	11.9	12.4	-0.5
High school graduate	11.5	12.0	-0.5	10.2	11.8	-1.6
Trade certificate	2.7	3.2	-0.5	2.9	2.3	0.6
Postsecondary, non-university	24.7	23.3	1.4	26.3	26.2	0.1
Postsecondary, university	32.0	33.2	-1.2	30.3	31.9	-1.6
Total %	100.0	100.0	...	100.0	100.0	...
_N_	36,090	65,710		30,770	81,545	

TABLE 3.7 (CONCLUDED)

PERCENTAGE OF INTERPROVINCIAL IN- AND OUT-MIGRATION BETWEEN 1986 AND 1991 FOR PROVINCES AND TERRITORIES, BY LEVEL OF EDUCATION

Province	Alberta			British Columbia		
Level of education	In-migrants	Out-migrants	% difference	In-migrants	Out-migrants	% difference
Less than Grade 9	4.7	4.5	0.2	4.5	5.2	-0.7
Grades 9 to 10	11.3	9.9	1.4	9.1	10.3	-1.2
Grades 11 to 13	12.9	11.4	1.5	11.1	11.8	-0.7
High school graduate	13.1	11.6	1.5	11.3	12.5	-1.2
Trade certificate	2.7	3.3	-0.6	3.1	3.0	0.1
Postsecondary, non-university	27.5	29.3	-1.8	28.5	27.1	1.4
Postsecondary, university	27.7	30.0	-2.3	32.3	30.2	2.1
Total %	**100.0**	**100.0**	...	**100.0**	**100.0**	...
N	142,410	159,900		202,875	94,005	

Territory	Yukon			Northwest Territories		
Level of education	In-migrants	Out-migrants	% difference	In-migrants	Out-migrants	% difference
Less than Grade 9	2.9	3.9	-1.0	2.7	4.8	-2.1
Grades 9 to 10	9.2	10.8	-1.6	7.7	10.4	-2.7
Grades 11 to 13	8.4	9.7	-1.3	8.3	10.9	-2.6
High school graduate	10.2	11.5	-1.3	11.3	12.3	-1.0
Trade certificate	4.9	4.1	0.8	3.0	3.4	-0.4
Postsecondary, non-university	32.8	32.4	0.4	31.5	31.6	-0.1
Postsecondary, university	31.6	27.7	3.9	35.5	26.5	9.0
Total %	**100.0**	**100.0**	...	**100.0**	**100.0**	...
N	5,380	4,585		1,730	1,250	

...   not applicable

Note: Percentages may not add to 100 due to rounding.

Source: Census of Canada, 1991. Tabulations by the author.

For example, in Newfoundland, 24.6% of in-migrants (people moving to Newfoundland between 1986 and 1991) versus 29.6% of out-migrants (people leaving Newfoundland between 1986 and 1991) had some university credentials. On balance, Newfoundland lost 5% more people with university education than it gained (as noted in the rightmost column of Table 3.7). At the other end of the education distribution, Newfoundland experienced net gains of 2.5% for people with less than Grade 9 and 3.3% for people with Grades 9 or 10. Phrased in terms of university degree holders, the province experienced a net loss of 2,875 people with university degrees (this was composed of 2,160 in-migrants who had degrees and 5,035 out-migrants who had degrees—the raw numbers are not reported in the table).

Comparing across other provinces, a familiar pattern is apparent. Beginning in the east and moving to the west, the following regions were net losers of university-educated people: Newfoundland, Nova Scotia, Prince Edward Island, New Brunswick, Quebec, Manitoba,

Saskatchewan, and Alberta. Conversely, Ontario, British Columbia, the Yukon, and the Northwest Territories were net recipients of university-educated people. The Northwest Territories and Alberta are the anomalous regions when we compare these migration findings to the overall patterns of educational attainment by region reviewed earlier in the chapter. Alberta has one of the highest percentages of university-educated people in the country, yet it actually lost highly educated people between 1986 and 1991. At least for this time period, the data suggest that the resource-rich Alberta economy did not generate sufficient highly skilled jobs to satisfy the pool of highly skilled labour in the province. The Northwest Territories, which does not as yet have a degree-granting university of its own, experienced the greatest influx of university-trained people.

Overall the patterns in Table 3.7 show that part of the educational differences that exist between provinces are a function of regional migration. Highly educated Canadians are more likely to be geographically mobile over long distances and they are most likely to move to specific regions of the country.

Another aspect of these migratory flows is the movement of people to pursue university study in a province in which they do not permanently reside. Of all full-time university students, Butlin and Calvert (1996, 35) estimate that 8% or 37,500 undergraduate students study outside their province of permanent residence. The proportion of cross-boundary migrants is highest in Prince Edward Island (35%) and lowest in Quebec and Ontario (6%) (see Table 3.8). Overall, Nova Scotia and Ontario receive the most out-of-province students. If the net flows (in-migrants versus out-migrants) were equal these exchanges might be of little consequence, but provinces with net positive in-flows subsidize the costs of out-of-province students. Especially as federal transfer payments to support university education shrink, more of this cost is borne by provincial taxpayers. There are, of course, potential benefits to the receiving provinces and corresponding disadvantages to the provinces losing students, especially if the students who move are among the better students.

TABLE 3.8

INTERPROVINCIAL MOVEMENT OF FULL-TIME UNDERGRADUATE UNIVERSITY STUDENTS, 1993 TO 1994

Province of origin	Undergraduates studying in another province (%)	Main province of destination for out-migrants[1]
Newfoundland	26	Nova Scotia (54%)
Prince Edward Island	35	Nova Scotia (49%)
Nova Scotia	13	Other Maritime provinces (59%)
New Brunswick	20	Nova Scotia (53%)
Quebec	6	Ontario (80%)
Ontario	6	Quebec (48%)
Manitoba	9	Ontario (40%)
Saskatchewan	10	Alberta (36%)
Alberta	9	Ontario (34%)
British Columbia	13	Ontario (42%)

1. The figures in the third column refer to the percentage of students from the province of origin who are studying in the province of destination (that is, the receiving province).

Source: Butlin and Calvert, 1996.

3.5   VARIATION BETWEEN URBAN CENTRES AND REGIONS

One final feature of regional variation in education deserves attention. Although we have focussed on provinces and territories as the units of analysis, these regions are not internally homogeneous. In particular we know that urban centres house populations with higher levels of education than do rural areas. Comparing regional rates of university degree attainment with similar rates for selected cities generally shows the higher levels of formal education in urban areas (see Table 3.8; see also Looker 1992). Notice, however, that this is not always true, as Hamilton, Ont., shows. Here is a large city where average education levels fall below the provincial norm (11.9% of Hamiltonians have university degrees compared with the provincial average of 13.0%).

The data in Table 3.9 also reveal two areas where urban education levels are substantially different than the regional averages. The percentage of residents with university degrees in St. John's differs sharply with the average for all of Newfoundland and Yellowknife shows a similar disparity with the rest of the Northwest Territories. In these regions the difference between educated "city folk" and the school levels of the rest of the region is most marked.

TABLE **3.9**

PERCENTAGE OF POPULATION **15** AND OVER WITH A UNIVERSITY DEGREE, BY PROVINCE, TERRITORY AND SELECTED URBAN AREAS, **1991**

Region	% with university degree	Region	% with university degree
Newfoundland	6.6	Manitoba	10.2
St. John's	11.9	Winnipeg	13.0
Prince Edward Island	8.5	Saskatchewan	8.6
Charlottetown	12.1	Regina	13.0
		Saskatoon	14.2
Nova Scotia	10.4	Alberta	11.9
Halifax	16.8	Calgary	16.3
		Edmonton	13.2
New Brunswick	8.4	British Columbia	11.2
Saint John	8.8	Vancouver	14.4
		Victoria	14.7
Quebec	10.3	Yukon	12.5
Montréal	13.3	Whitehorse	14.6
Québec	13.8		
Ontario	13.0	Northwest Territories	9.6
Hamilton	11.9	Yellowknife	17.6
Toronto	16.6		
Canada	**11.4**		

Source: Census of Canada, 1991. Tabulations by the author.

3.6 CONCLUSION

This chapter addressed two questions. How much regional variation exists in the educational attainment of Canadians? Is the regional variation in education changing in any systematic way over time? Education has a distinctive impact on the skills of regional labour forces and it directly influences the cultural styles of regional communities. As we move toward a knowledge society, we need to understand whether the different regions of Canada are moving closer together or whether they are diverging in their educational profiles. Evidence of convergence suggests that, at least on the education dimension, regional tensions will be less taxing since skills and cultural tastes will be shared across the country. Conversely, divergence suggests that educational disparities may reinforce other regional fault lines and contribute to tensions between regions.

The actual patterns discussed above show a complicated picture. At the upper end of the educational distribution, as measured by the percentage of citizens with a university degree, the regions of Canada are becoming more alike (see Table 3.2). There are still differences between regions but the educational discrepancies are narrowing, not widening, at this end of the education spectrum.

At the lower end of the education distribution, Canadians with lower levels of schooling are becoming concentrated in certain pockets of the country (see Table 3.3). While Canadians' average levels of schooling are rising, some areas continue to experience relatively high levels of low educational achievement, most noticeably the Northwest Territories, and to lesser extents, Newfoundland, Quebec, and New Brunswick.

These patterns suggest that on the issue of social inequality based on knowledge, the regional variations across the country are mixed. University-educated people are found in relatively similar abundance everywhere in the country (see Table 3.2). However, if those with less education are increasingly shut out of opportunities in a knowledge society, then there is some cause for worry in selected regions where there tend to be concentrations of residents with low educational attainment. Education is linked to poverty, unemployment and political alienation, and the trends discussed above have the potential to balkanize the country if the immediacy of these social problems is not appreciated in all regions, especially those where education levels are relatively high.

Next, we attempt to understand how social attributes of Canadians (for example visible minority status, First Nations status, immigration status) interact with these regional differences to influence the shape of the educational distribution in this country. Who are the winners and losers in education, or, put slightly differently, who benefits the most and the least from educational opportunities?

ENDNOTES

1. Regional differences in the structure of schooling cloud easy interpretations here because Ontario, for example, has required 13 years of schooling (14 or 15 counting pre-elementary) prior to acquiring a secondary school graduation certificate as opposed to British Columbia, where only the completion of Grade 12 is necessary.

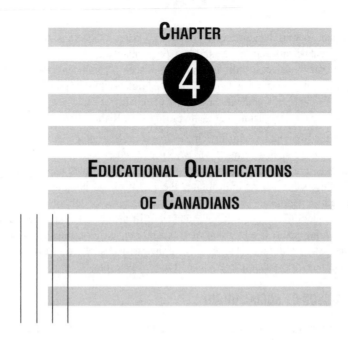

CHAPTER

4

EDUCATIONAL QUALIFICATIONS

OF CANADIANS

An individual's level of schooling is one of the best predictors of a range of life chances, from how much someone might earn to how long they might live (see Curtis, Grabb, and Guppy 1993). John Porter's prophetic remark in *The Vertical Mosaic,* that "now, more than ever, education means opportunity" (1965, 167), gains strength with every decade. Schooling alone is no passport to success, of course. It does not necessarily guarantee a fulfilling and prosperous life. Nevertheless, for the majority schooling matters a great deal.

Self-made millionaires are the exception proving the rule. Regardless of how success is defined, some extraordinary individuals can succeed in life without much schooling. Nevertheless, these individuals are rare. For most Canadians, their experience in the school system lays the foundation for, and plays a key role in, subsequent life events. This "long arm of schooling" illustrates the degree to which we have come to live in a schooled society.

Given this importance of schooling, in this chapter we look at how education is distributed throughout the population. This is an issue often addressed by politicians. Speaking in 1982 to the Council of Ministers for Education, Bette Stephenson, then Ontario's Minister of Colleges and Universities, said:

> While we have dramatically increased the number of students attending post-secondary institutions, access to post-secondary education remains far from equal across all social and economic groups in Canada. (Stephenson 1982, 250)

Stephenson's remarks illustrate the oft-repeated premise that education facilitates social mobility and equal opportunity for Canadians of all backgrounds (Anisef 1985). Various arguments are used to justify this assumption. One conception of equality of opportunity rests on the idea of social justice, wherein the educational system is seen as equalizing the life chances of children who, through no fault of their own, are born into wealth or misery. Merit is the hallmark of this idea. An equally powerful argument rests on the idea that in a modern, knowledge society, where productivity and performance are central, a society cannot afford to waste human talent. Promoting human capital—citizens' skills and training—is seen as paramount in an increasingly global economy. Efficiency is central and the best and the brightest must be promoted. Whatever the merits of these two lines of argument, the rhetoric of equality of educational opportunity is powerful. Politicians and policy planners promote the idea (see Richer 1988).

To reiterate a point from our introductory chapter, we focus here almost exclusively on how much schooling people accumulate, using this as evidence of educational opportunity. However, we recognize that exposure and experience are two different issues. Peoples' exposure to various levels of schooling gives us no direct indication of the quality of education they received. Not everyone at the same level of schooling has the same experience of schooling—they study different subjects under different conditions, such as full-time or part-time—nor have they necessarily had the same quality of education. We lack, unfortunately, measures of the quality of the schooling experience or educational process. Nevertheless, exposure is a necessary, although not sufficient, condition for the attainment of a good formal education.[1]

4.1   A COMPARISON OF SOCIAL GROUPS

In the previous chapter we explored what, if any, regional differences existed in educational attainment and showed how those patterns had changed over time. Here, instead of using geographical boundaries as the categories across which we compare educational attainments, we use a range of other social categories. However, choosing these categories presents a problem. In a federal state like Canada, which comprises so many distinct regions, social analysts have almost always used "region" as a key variable on which to compare outcomes. Other choices are not so easy to make. Given the plethora of social categories we could choose from, including anything from people's social class to their accents, how does any choice get justified?

A starting point is to list the categories that are consistently related to school attainment (see Anisef, Okihiro and James 1982; Guppy and Arai 1993; Porter, Porter, and Blishen 1979). Such a list surely includes social class, age, sex, ethnicity or ancestry, linguistic group, disability status, place of birth, and place of residence. Next, we added categories used to explain other factors that might affect an individual's opportunities in life. These are often areas where there have been calls for social intervention to right perceived wrongs. The Royal Commission on Equality in Employment is the most relevant work here, because Judge Rosalie Abella (Commission of Inquiry 1984, v) highlighted the employment prospects of four designated groups: women, Native people, disabled people, and visible minorities. These four groups were said to lag behind other groups in terms of labour force participation, occupational and income attainment, and social mobility, and were thought to more often live in poverty, be unemployed, endure inferior housing, and the like. Although Abella's task was employment-related, her categories are relevant for a study of school attainment because employment opportunities are so tightly tied to education. Finally, we chose from these lists the categories that are available in the 1991 Census, given the mandate of this monograph. Some categories had to be dropped or modified. For example, Statistics Canada collects no data on social class per se, and while there is census information on families, for most Canadians there are no data on their parents' social class backgrounds. Similarly, attributes such as an accent may affect a person's chances in the education system, but we lack the systematic data, either national or regional, necessary for addressing this question.

Based on social policy concerns, the availability of data and our understanding of the research literature, and given our mandate, we explore educational attainment across eight social categories: gender, linguistic group (francophone/anglophone), ethnicity, Aboriginal ancestry, visible minority status, immigration status, disability, and finally, socio-economic status (SES). Given that relevant data are more abundant for some categories than for others, the detail we present in each section is uneven.

4.2   GENDER DIFFERENCES

Accurate and comparable administrative records on school enrolments and attendance are unavailable for most of Canada before the turn of the 19th century. The records that do exist construct enrolment and attendance figures in ways that today seem odd. For example, Prentice (1977) reports an 1866 regulation in Upper Canada that resulted in discounting the number of girls enrolled. In effect, a girl was counted as half a boy.

After Confederation, the Census fell under the domain of the federal government, and data collection became more accurate and consistent. By 1901, the Census of Canada showed that any earlier differences in the public school enrolments of females and males that might have existed had disappeared. Although boys and girls still entered many schools through separate doors, their classes were not formally segregated by sex at the elementary and most of the secondary levels. Indeed, in contrast with the church, the Girl Guides and Boy Scouts, and the YWCA/YMCA, the education system was one of the first modern institutions to admit both boys and girls into the same building and have them share common classes. In Chapter 1 we distinguished between enrolment and regular attendance, but census records show that on both counts the schooling experiences of the sexes were similar. In fact, Harrigan (1990, 805) notes that substantial rural–urban variations in school attendance remained long after they had disappeared between boys and girls (here again is evidence of the importance of region as a persistent and salient divide in Canadian social life).

Gender differences in enrolments did appear among students of higher ages, but the pattern was mixed. At the secondary school level, girls were more likely to attend school later into their teenage years than were their brothers. For example, Harrigan (1990, 804) reports that in 1921 women made up 59% of high school enrolment, and that even as late as 1951, 55% of high school students were women. More recently, with the transition to nearly full attendance at the high school level, the gender differences among secondary school students have been reduced sharply, but not eradicated. Data from the 1991 Census show that among teenagers aged 15 to 18, females were more likely than males to attend school and to do so full time (see Table 4.1).

The census data also permit us to examine the average years of schooling attained by people in different age groups. Comparing older to younger age groups gives us an approximation of the levels of schooling attained during different time periods (see Table 4.2). People in the oldest age cohort, aged 75 and over in 1991, attained an average of 8.5 years of schooling as compared to the 25- to 29-year-olds, who attained an average of just over 13 years of schooling. In the oldest age group, women had attained slightly more schooling than had men, but in every age group from the 30-to-34 cohort to the 70-to-74 cohort, men attained more schooling than women did. For the youngest age cohort, 25- to 29-year-olds, women had slightly more schooling than did men (13.25 years versus 13.13 years respectively).

TABLE 4.1

RATES OF SCHOOL ATTENDANCE, POPULATION AGED 15 TO 18, BY SEX, 1991

Age and sex	Population	Not attending school (%)	Attending school full time (%)	Attending school part time (%)
15 years				
Female	184,140	7.7	91.7	0.6
Male	194,345	8.5	90.9	0.6
16 years				
Female	183,275	9.6	89.3	1.1
Male	196,845	10.1	88.8	1.1
17 years				
Female	178,330	12.7	85.4	1.9
Male	187,990	14.0	83.8	2.2
18 years				
Female	180,035	20.4	74.4	5.2
Male	190,600	22.2	73.1	4.7

Source: Census of Canada, 1991, special tabulations.

TABLE 4.2

AVERAGE NUMBER OF YEARS OF SCHOOLING, BY AGE GROUP AND SEX, POPULATION 25 AND OVER, NOT ATTENDING SCHOOL FULL TIME, 1991

Age group	Women		Men	
25–29	13.25	(2.7)[1]	13.13	(3.0)
30–34	13.09	(2.8)	13.19	(3.1)
35–39	12.10	(3.7)	12.60	(3.9)
40–44	12.60	(3.3)	13.16	(3.7)
45–49	12.02	(3.6)	12.66	(4.1)
50–54	11.24	(3.8)	11.69	(4.4)
55–59	10.57	(3.9)	10.93	(4.4)
60–64	10.10	(4.0)	10.41	(4.5)
65–69	9.75	(3.9)	10.00	(4.4)
70–74	9.59	(3.9)	9.81	(4.4)
75+	8.61	(4.2)	8.51	(4.6)

1. Standard deviations appear in parentheses.

Source: Census of Canada, Public Use Sample Tape, 1991; author's computations.

Table 4.3

Highest Level of Schooling, Population Aged 15 to 24, by Sex and Year, 1951 to 1991

Sex and year	Population	Less than Grade 9 (%)	Grades 9–13 (%)	Some postsecondary (%)	University degree (%)
1951					
Female	1,076,898	37.6	62.0	..	0.4
Male	1,069,715	45.6	53.4	..	1.0
1961					
Female	1,300,031	24.2	74.8	..	0.9
Male	1,316,174	30.4	68.3	..	1.3
1971					
Female	1,975,615	11.3	65.6	20.2	2.8
Male	2,006,885	13.4	63.1	19.9	3.6
1981					
Female	2,296,030	4.7	63.7	28.1	3.5
Male	2,341,975	6.3	64.7	25.9	3.1
1991					
Female	1,885,625	3.2	56.3	35.1	5.3
Male	1,947,200	4.4	62.0	29.7	3.9

.. figures not available

Source: Census of Canada, various years.

These averages describe the experiences of typical people in a cohort, but they do not tell us how much variation or spread there might be in a cohort. Thus we report the standard deviation, a measure of how dispersed people in an age group are relative to the mean. If everyone spent almost identical numbers of years in school, then the standard deviation would be lower than if the experiences of people were more diverse. The figures in parentheses in Table 4.2 show that the standard deviations have been shrinking as the average years of schooling have been increasing. This suggests that, for successive cohorts, the amount of time people spend in school is increasingly similar. Put another way, the 13.19 years of schooling for the 25-to-29 age group is a closer reflection of the experience of everyone in the group than is the 8.56 years for the oldest cohort.[2] This greater uniformity in years of schooling could mean that other factors such as level of schooling (college versus university) or field of study may start to carry more weight in terms of employment opportunities and so on. We pursue this idea in later chapters.

In the past, men's employment prospects were less tightly tied to schooling than were women's. Primary sector work such as fishing, farming, logging or mining, or secondary sector work in manufacturing and construction have always been male-dominated, and such work has historically required only modest levels of schooling. Until recently, men with little formal schooling often found steady, well-paying jobs in these occupational venues. In contrast, schooling has been more closely linked to women's job destinies, whether in teaching, clerical work, or sales. Spelling, good grammar and disciplined organizational skills were important assets for women who entered an array of jobs designated as "women's work," and these skills were honed in the school system (see Gaskell 1992a, 1992b; Siltanen 1994).

The net result was that many men left school sooner than women did. This pattern has begun to change, however. Employment prospects in traditional primary and secondary industries have stagnated compared with the massive growth of service sector employment in Canada. Many new, knowledge-intensive jobs in the service sector, such as those in finance and marketing, require more education than do primary and secondary jobs. As more men have turned to these relatively new areas for employment opportunities, their school attainment profile has begun to change.

Gender differences are evident when we compare educational attainments for males and females across five census periods, from 1951 to 1991 (see Table 4.3). The most obvious trend in the table is the rising level of attainment for both sexes. Setting that aside, however, have the educational profiles of the two sexes become more alike, stayed the same, or have they drifted apart? In 1951, 45.6% of males between the ages of 15 and 24 had not completed Grade 9, as opposed to 37.6% of females in the same age range, representing a gender difference of 8.0%. By 1991 the respective percentages had declined sharply to 4.4% and 3.2%, a difference of only 1.2%, though men were still more likely than women not to have completed Grade 9.

Another way to compare Grade 9 completion rates between males and females is to use the odds ratio for each sex. That is, what were the odds of a female completing Grade 9 in 1951 as compared with a male, and did those odds change by 1991? In 1951, the likelihood of a female completing only Grade 9 was 0.60 whereas for males it was 0.83. Put differently, for every 100 females who had completed Grade 9, approximately 60 had not. Among males, 83 did not complete Grade 9 for every 100 who did. The ratio of these odds for males versus females (known in statistics as the odds ratio), is a comparison measure, and here it works out to 0.72. Relatively speaking, in 1951 males were less likely to complete Grade 9 than were females.

In 1991, the odds of a person not going beyond Grade 9 were greatly reduced. For females the figure was 0.03 and for males it was 0.05. However, the odds ratio was still 0.70 (after rounding), almost the same in 1991 as in 1951. This means that although far more people completed Grade 9, the odds of males as compared to females completing Grade 9 had not changed. In a relative sense then, the educational profiles of males and females at this low end of educational attainment have not changed.

Where the educational distributions of females and males have changed dramatically, relative to one another, is at the other extreme—postsecondary attainment.[3] While the 15-to-24 group is useful for examining how the likelihood of completing Grade 9 has changed over time, it is not ideal for comparing trends in the attainment of university degrees. Few, if any, Canadians have ever attained a university degree by the age of 15 and some people over the age of 24 will eventually graduate from university with a degree. Nevertheless, for comparability purposes we will continue using this age range for the moment.

The figures in Table 4.3 show a clear reversal of a trend that we will later verify using other sources. Notice that in 1951, 1.0% of men, but only 0.4% of women, aged 15 to 24, had a university degree. Unlike the other extreme of the education distribution, where men were more likely to withdraw from school sooner, here men typically continued in school longer than women (see Hunter 1986, 121). The odds of a man completing a university degree were 2.5 times those of a woman.

By 1981, however, this pattern had reversed. More women than men aged 15 to 24 reported holding university degrees, and the difference grew by 1991. The gap between women and men with some postsecondary experience also grew, so that by 1991 more than 40% of young women either had some experience in higher education (35.1%) or had a university degree (5.3%). In contrast, only about 34% of men could report comparable experience (29.7% and 3.9% respectively). In that year, the odds of a man completing a university degree were 0.75 times those of a woman.

The table thus highlights two significant trends. First, at the low end of the educational distribution, men remained less likely than women to complete at least Grade 9 and this difference did not narrow over the 40-year interval. Second, at higher education levels, women have surpassed the lead that men clearly held in 1951.

A second way to illustrate changes at the upper end of the education distribution is to examine trends in postsecondary enrolment. Figure 4.1 shows men's and women's participation rates in higher education from 1961 to 1994. These rates are calculated by dividing the number of women and men enrolled in college or university by the number of Canadians between the ages of 18 and 24.[4] For women the rate climbs until 1979, when it dips for one year, before resuming its upward trend. For men, the rate declines in 1972 and continues to slump until the early 1980s. Exactly what explains this dip, and the resulting gender difference, is unclear. The late 1970s and early 1980s were the start of a Canadian recession and also a period when women's labour force participation rose. An increasing percentage of women may have found they needed postsecondary experience to compete for jobs in white-collar, semi-professional, and professional work. Recall from Chapter 1 that this is also the period in which male secondary school graduation rates leveled off. Perhaps, then, the same *percentage* of women and men continued to postsecondary levels, but the pool of secondary school graduates changed differently for women and men. Regardless of the cause, women's rate of participation in higher education surpassed that of men in 1987.

FIGURE 4.1

FIGURE 4.1

FULL-TIME POSTSECONDARY ENROLMENT AS A PERCENTAGE OF THE 18-TO-24 AGE GROUP, BY SEX, 1961 TO 1994

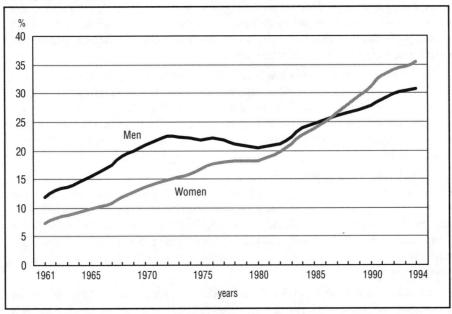

Source: Statistics Canada, *Universities: Enrolment and Degrees,* various years; Statistics Canada, *Education in Canada,* various years.

Another way to compare men's and women's educational profiles is to examine years of completed schooling by age. Restricting the cohort to 25- to 29-year-olds, a range in which most people have completed their formal education, we see that the education distributions in 1971 and 1991 are relatively similar for the two sexes (Figures 4.2 and 4.3). Both women's and men's distribution peaks at 12 years of schooling. Nevertheless, there are differences, and these are consistent with what we saw above. From the 1971 data, women stand out from men in four ways. First, women are less likely than men to leave school with only 5 to 10 years of schooling. Second, more women than men have between 11 and 13 years of schooling—the final years of secondary school. Third, more women than men report having spent between 14 and 16 years in school, the number of years needed in the 1960s to earn non-university diplomas such as nursing and teaching. Fourth, women are less likely than men to report 18, 19, and 20 years of schooling, durations that mainly represent advanced university education. By 1991 the patterns remained similar, except that the difference at the upper end had virtually vanished, with almost equal percentages of women and men reporting between 15 and 25 years of school attendance.

FIGURE 4.2

YEARS OF SCHOOLING OF MEN AND WOMEN NOT ATTENDING SCHOOL, AGED 25 TO 29, 1971

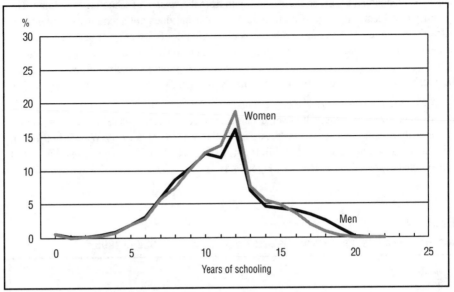

Source: Census of Canada, 1991, special tabulations.

FIGURE 4.3

YEARS OF SCHOOLING OF MEN AND WOMEN NOT ATTENDING SCHOOL, AGED 25 TO 29, 1991

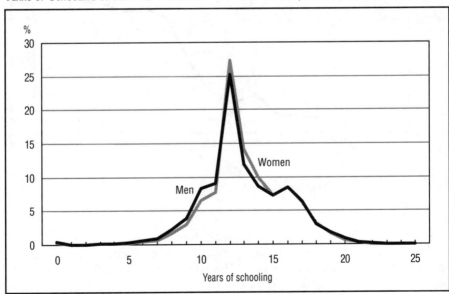

Source: Census of Canada, 1991, special tabulations.

Two points are worth stressing about the distribution of education shown in Figures 4.2 and 4.3. First, such similar patterns make it hard to imagine that male–female differences in subsequent labour market experiences could stem from the *amount* of schooling they attain. The quantity of education, as opposed to type of education, does not account for any gender differences that emerge in the labour market (see Chapter 6). Second, a person's years of schooling do not necessarily translate into credentials, at least among older cohorts. For example, men who spent as many years in school as women often found themselves at least one grade behind, because in the past males were more likely than females to fail a grade (Harrigan 1990).

A closer look at women's and men's changing educational patterns at the postsecondary level reveals some dramatic changes. It is well documented that men earned more degrees than women earlier in this century (see Anisef 1985; Andres Bellamy and Guppy 1991). What is not so well known is that women are now obtaining, annually, over 17,000 more bachelor and first professional degrees than are men (see Figure 4.4).[5]

FIGURE 4.4

BACHELOR'S AND FIRST PROFESSIONAL DEGREES AWARDED, BY SEX, 1920 TO 1995

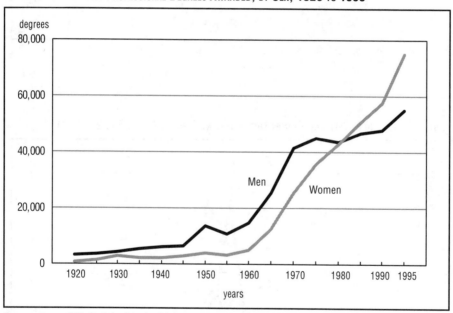

Source: Leacy 1983; Statistics Canada, *Education in Canada*, various years.

In the first part of this century, when few individuals of either sex went to university, men earned between three times and five times more degrees each year than women. This male–female disparity ballooned in the late 1940s and early 1950s as male war veterans took up the option of completing university studies (see Chapter 1). What had been an annual difference of 3,000 to 4,000 degrees mushroomed to over 10,000 degrees in 1950.

But starting in the late 1950s, the number of bachelor and first professional degrees skyrocketed for both sexes. More universities were being built and older institutions expanded. As well, governments began to spend more money on higher learning (see Cameron 1991). One result was that, year upon year, the number of degrees earned by women increased without interruption, and this growth actually accelerated in the 1990s. For men, degree attainment started leveling off in the 1970s and began to expand again only in the 1980s. Their rate of increase in the 1990s is still slower than it is for women.

A combination of factors caused men's rate of degree attainment to slow in the 1970s. First, between 1973 and 1983 the bulk of the baby boom generation passed through the 18-to-24 age range, creating a subsequent decline in the size of the age cohort that typically attains a degree. The passing of the baby boom generation seems to have affected men's but not women's absolute degree attainment. Second, male graduation rates from high school reached a plateau during this period (see Chapter 1 on transition probabilities). These two factors combined to stabilize the population of men eligible to go from secondary school to university and obtain degrees.

At the community college level, at least for career programs,[6] women had been attaining more diplomas than men for some time. Andres Bellamy and Guppy (1991, 181) report women attaining more than 60% of college diplomas in 1975–76. Unfortunately, consistent data collection covers only a short period for colleges, and even then a time series showing gender differences can only be constructed for career program diplomas. This trend—women earning more college diplomas than men—continued into the 1980s. And as with the undergraduate university figures, the gap between women and men has been widening in the 1990s (see Figure 4.5). If we total all the diplomas and undergraduate and professional degrees granted in 1993, women earned 28,000 more postsecondary credentials than did men or, conversely, men earned 42.2% of all diplomas and degrees.

FIGURE 4.5

COMMUNITY COLLEGE CAREER PROGRAM DIPLOMAS AWARDED, BY SEX, 1980 TO 1992

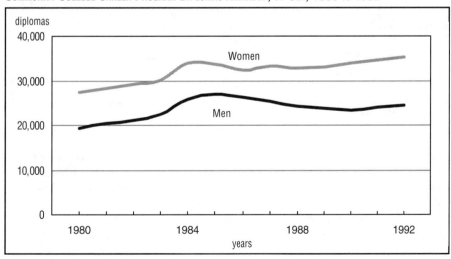

Source: Statistics Canada, *Education in Canada,* various years.

The profile is similar for master's degrees (see Figure 4.6). For both women and men the pattern for the master's level almost perfectly replicates the pattern for undergraduate and professional degrees. There are, however, two differences. First, the changes in attainment generally occurred several years later than the changes for undergraduate and professional degrees. This is to be expected, as most master's level students pursue their degrees immediately after attaining their first degree. Second, and as a result of the latter point, women have only recently begun to receive the same number of master's degrees as men. For men, the familiar spurt in degrees awarded after the Second World War occurs again, followed by a tailing off in the mid- to late-1970s. The explanations for these changes at the master's level are similar to the explanations we gave for the same changes at the undergraduate level. Between 1983 and 1993 the average annual growth rate for earning a master's degree was 2.4% for men and 5.2% for women (Statistics Canada, *Education in Canada,* various years).

FIGURE 4.6

MASTER'S DEGREES AWARDED, BY SEX, 1920 TO 1995

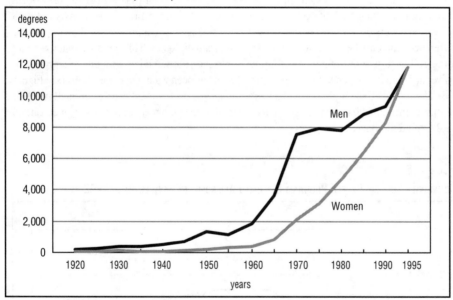

Source: Leacy 1983; Statistics Canada, *Education in Canada,* various years (1995 figures are estimates).

At the PhD level, the pattern is again familiar although the lag is much more pronounced (see Figure 4.7). Women still attain fewer doctoral degrees than do men. In 1995 women were expected to receive only 33% of all PhDs, (1,273 PhDs for women compared with 2,545 for men). Nonetheless, the number of women earning PhDs has increased almost every year since the early 1960s, with declines relative to the previous year occurring only between 1976–77 and 1981–82. By comparison, the number of PhDs earned by men year upon year has tumbled often, especially between 1975 and 1982. Put another way, between 1983 and 1993 the average annual rate of growth in PhDs for men was 4.5% as opposed to 8.0% for women.

FIGURE 4.7

PHDS AWARDED, BY SEX, 1920 TO 1995

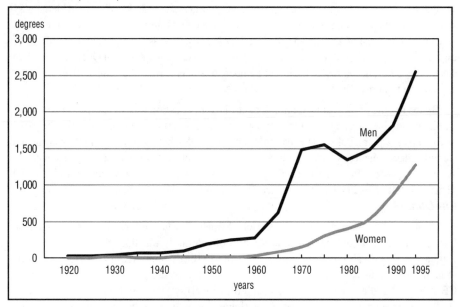

Source: Leacy 1983; Statistics Canada, *Education in Canada,* various years (1995 figures are estimates).

The authors of the Royal Commission on the Status of Women in Canada (1970, 161) claimed that "education opens the door to almost every life goal. Wherever women are denied equal access to education they cannot be said to have equality." In terms of amount of education, by the mid-1990s women's enrolment and credentials earned were equal to and often greater than men's. The sole exception was at the PhD level but even here rates for women are growing at a faster pace than for men. If current rates of PhD attainment stay constant, gender differences will vanish by the year 2015.

What explains these varying trends and shifts? Again we point to the different types of jobs that men and women traditionally enter. In particular, men have found greater opportunities in relatively lucrative and secure jobs that do not demand credentials. However, as we noted, such jobs are on the decline in the changing Canadian economy. We thus predict that male–female rates of high school diploma and bachelor degree attainment should re-equalize in the coming decades. Males have increasingly less incentive to leave high school early and eschew postsecondary schooling, so they will likely continue their schooling for longer durations, eventually catching up to their female counterparts.

4.3 FRANCOPHONE–ANGLOPHONE DIFFERENCES

Among the provinces, the structure and history of education is perhaps most different in Quebec. To some extent this is explained by the historical influence of both the Catholic and Protestant churches on education in the province. The clergy in Quebec retained control over education and teacher training longer than in most other provinces except Newfoundland. Quebec's Ministry of Education was not formed until 1964. As well, the school system was structured differently than in other provinces. In the predominantly Roman Catholic system, students began in elementary school and then moved on to classical colleges where the first four years were akin to secondary education in the rest of Canada and the last four years served as the equivalent of college or university education. Until recent decades, relatively fewer francophones in Quebec went on to advanced studies, in contrast to the larger numbers of students from the comparatively wealthy anglophone minority who had access to prestigious universities such as McGill.

By the middle of this century, church control over education was an aberration that some within the province worked to change. Perhaps the best illustration of this comes from the pages of *Cité Libre*, a journal of social comment founded in 1950 that had Pierre Elliott Trudeau and Gérard Pelletier among its former editors. *Cité Librists* wanted a modern, secularized, education system. As Quebec shifted from a rural, agrarian society to an increasingly prosperous industrial region, education became increasingly necessary for both economic and socio-political reasons. *Cité Librists* led the push to modernize the province's education system.

Change in the governance and organization of Quebec's education system came, in dramatic fashion, in the 1960s during the Quiet Revolution. Not only was this when the Ministry of Education was established, but also when the Parent Commission reported, and saw implemented, many new ideas on remaking the education system. It was at this point that the CEGEP (collège d'enseignement général et professionel) system was introduced, under which students entered college after 11 years of elementary and secondary schooling. Two-year academic programs led to university admission, while three-year technical or vocational programs linked students with the labour market. In addition to these structural differences, after the Quiet Revolution education came to be seen as "crucial to the collective project of transforming Quebec into a modern, francophone, distinctive—and for some, sovereign—society" (Fournier and Rosenberg 1997, 123). This nationalist purpose, with identity politics at the forefront, has more in common with the United States than other regions of Canada and was another factor making Quebec schooling distinctive in Canada.

These differences in the structure and to some extent the purpose of education make comparisons between Quebec and the rest of Canada difficult. Nevertheless, such comparisons are possible when done carefully. Furthermore, these comparisons suggest some reasons why *Cité Librists* and others sought to reinvigorate the education of Quebecers.

One comparison that is subject to little distortion from structural differences in school systems is an examination of the percentage of people who have only elementary levels of education (see also Baril and Mori 1991). We compare the percentages of people 25 and over, in Quebec, Ontario, and the rest of Canada (outside Quebec and Ontario) who had less than Grade 9 schooling in 1951 and 1991 (see Figure 4.8). In both years, Quebec residents were more likely than residents in Ontario or elsewhere in Canada to have less than Grade 9 education. Certainly there is evidence of massive upgrading in the stock of schooling of all Canadians, but the 1991 data give no indication that Quebec's percentage of residents with less than Grade 9 is approaching the national average (see Chapter 3).

FIGURE 4.8

PERCENTAGE OF POPULATION 25 AND OVER WITH LESS THAN GRADE 9 EDUCATION, BY SEX, QUEBEC, ONTARIO AND THE REST OF CANADA, 1951 AND 1991

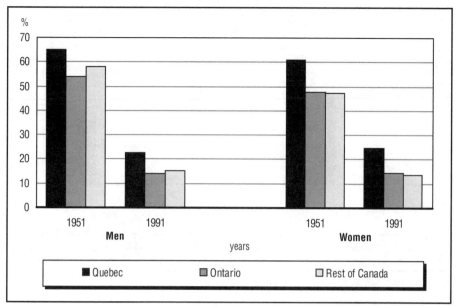

Source: Census of Canada, 1991, special tabulations.

Another indicator of educational attainment, the number of university degrees awarded, shows a different pattern. Quebec has approximately the same number of residents with degrees as does the rest of Canada. Ontario is the exception; it has more residents with degrees than the other two regions (see Figure 4.9). Patterns of change here are mixed, with regions catching up a little or sliding back a bit in different comparisons. But overall, when comparing university degree attainment, there is evidence that Quebecers have been catching up with their peers elsewhere in Canada.[7]

Including everyone over the age of 25 in these comparisons creates some ambiguity because, as we have seen earlier, older people have fewer years of formal schooling. A clearer picture of current patterns comes from examining enrolment rates for a younger cohort, since this comparison controls for differences in age distributions between provinces.

We compare the percentages of 18- to 21-year-olds in Ontario and Quebec who were enrolled in university from 1976 to 1994. In 1976 women in Ontario were almost twice as likely as their peers in Quebec to be enrolled in university (see Figure 4.10). By 1988 this difference had almost disappeared, with a gap of only 3% to 4% remaining. Quebec women now have rates of university participation similar to Ontario women. For men the story is similar. In 1976, Ontario men were almost twice as likely as their Quebec counterparts to be enrolled at university between the ages of 18 and 21, but this gap has recently narrowed considerably (see Figure 4.11).

FIGURE 4.9

PERCENTAGE OF POPULATION 25 AND OVER WITH A UNIVERSITY DEGREE, BY SEX, QUEBEC, ONTARIO AND THE REST OF CANADA, 1951 AND 1991

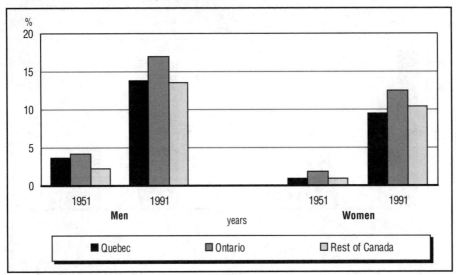

Source: Census of Canada, 1991, special tabulations.

FIGURE 4.10

UNIVERSITY UNDERGRADUATE PARTICIPATION RATE, WOMEN 18 TO 21, QUEBEC AND ONTARIO, 1976 TO 1994

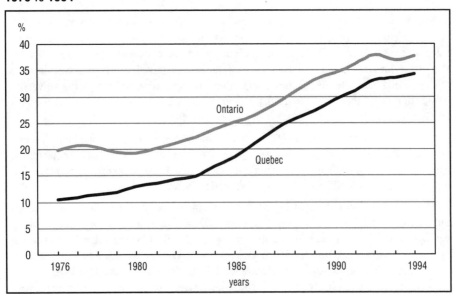

Source: Statistics Canada, *Education in Canada*, various years.

FIGURE 4.11

UNIVERSITY UNDERGRADUATE PARTICIPATION RATE, MEN 18 TO 21, QUEBEC AND ONTARIO, 1976 TO 1994

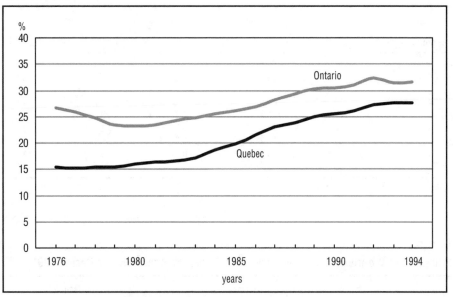

Source: Statistics Canada, *Education in Canada,* various years.

Actual educational attainment across age groups, as opposed to participation, also indicates changing levels of education. By comparing the schooling levels achieved across age cohorts, we see whether groups are becoming more alike, staying the same, or are drifting farther apart. A comparison of the percentage of Quebec residents who had less than Grade 9 education in 1991 with percentages in the rest of Canada shows some of the most compelling evidence that Quebec's educational profile is converging with those elsewhere in the country (see Table 4.4). Moving from the oldest to the youngest female age cohort, the percentage difference between Quebec and the rest of Canada has narrowed from 18% to 1%. The ratio of these percentages has shrunk from 1.4 to 1.1. This convergence is even more apparent among men: the difference has narrowed from 14% to less than 1% and the ratio of the percentages has gone from 1.3 to 1.0. Using the same type of comparison for university degrees, we see that the gap between the two regions narrows as the groups get younger (see Table 4.5) The gap narrows more over the men's groups than it does over the women's.

In combination, all of the above evidence suggests that Canadians inside and outside Quebec are becoming more and more similar in their educational profiles. This addresses differences between Quebecers and non-Quebecers, but it leaves aside questions of comparison between francophones (those whose mother tongue is French) and anglophones (those whose mother tongue is English). We study these differences in Table 4.6 (see also Harrison 1996).

Table 4.4

Percentage of Women and Men with Less than Grade 9 Education, by Region and Age Group, 1991

Age group	Women (%)		Men (%)	
	Quebec	Rest of Canada	Quebec	Rest of Canada
65+	65.5	47.2	61.4	46.8
60–64	59.0	43.2	55.5	42.4
55–59	53.3	38.4	47.9	37.1
50–54	44.5	30.4	39.7	29.8
45–49	33.2	22.2	29.3	22.0
40–44	23.7	16.3	21.5	16.2
35–39	17.2	11.9	17.1	13.5
30–34	14.1	10.9	15.3	13.7
25–29	10.5	9.5	12.7	12.2

Source: Census of Canada, 1991, special tabulations.

Table 4.5

Percentage of Women and Men with a University Degree, by Region and Age Group, 1991

Age group	Women (%)		Men (%)	
	Quebec	Rest of Canada	Quebec	Rest of Canada
65+	2.4	3.6	7.1	8.7
60–64	3.6	4.9	8.3	9.5
55–59	4.7	5.8	10.1	11.3
50–54	6.7	8.4	12.7	14.9
45–49	9.9	12.2	16.6	19.1
40–44	12.1	16.0	17.5	20.8
35–39	12.7	16.4	16.2	18.6
30–34	13.4	15.3	15.5	15.9
25–29	16.0	16.9	15.9	16.1

Source: Census of Canada, 1991, special tabulations.

Among the oldest cohort, whether for women or men, francophones were much more likely than anglophones to have less than Grade 9 education (in roughly the 65% range as compared with the 40% range, respectively). This held whether comparisons were made in the province of Quebec or elsewhere in Canada. Moving to younger age groups, the gap between francophones and anglophones has shrunk in all possible comparisons, showing that not only are regional differences in educational attainment eroding, but so too are linguistic differences. A distinctive pattern occurs for francophone men living outside Quebec. Their educational attainment falls below that of their linguistic peers within Quebec for every age group, and while their attainment is becoming more similar to anglophones in the rest of Canada, the gap is closing more slowly than it is for people living in Quebec.

TABLE 4.6

PERCENTAGE OF WOMEN AND MEN WITH LESS THAN GRADE 9 EDUCATION, BY LANGUAGE GROUP, REGION AND AGE GROUP, 1991

Age cohort	Women (%)				Men (%)			
	Quebec		Rest of Canada		Quebec		Rest of Canada	
	Franco-phone	Anglo-phone	Franco-phone	Anglo-phone	Franco-phone	Anglo-phone	Franco-phone	Anglo-phone
65+	68.9	42.3	67.2	40.5	65.1	41.0	66.8	42.6
60–64	60.1	38.1	60.1	36.3	57.9	37.4	60.6	39.1
55–59	54.5	33.6	53.2	32.2	49.6	30.9	52.4	34.3
50–54	45.1	27.9	43.3	24.9	40.6	26.2	46.6	27.3
45–49	33.3	22.2	34.1	18.5	29.9	21.4	36.9	19.9
40–44	23.4	17.1	25.6	13.4	21.6	16.2	28.7	14.6
35–39	16.9	11.5	16.8	9.8	17.3	12.1	23.2	12.1
30–34	14.1	10.3	13.5	9.5	15.6	11.1	19.1	12.7
25–29	10.4	7.7	10.1	8.5	12.9	9.5	14.8	11.2

Source: Census of Canada, 1991, special tabulations.

TABLE 4.7

PERCENTAGE OF WOMEN AND MEN WITH A UNIVERSITY DEGREE, BY LANGUAGE GROUP, REGION AND AGE GROUP, 1991

Age cohort	Women (%)				Men (%)			
	Quebec		Rest of Canada		Quebec		Rest of Canada	
	Franco-phone	Anglo-phone	Franco-phone	Anglo-phone	Franco-phone	Anglo-phone	Franco-phone	Anglo-phone
65+	2.0	4.7	3.0	3.9	6.0	12.9	4.7	9.6
60–64	2.9	9.4	3.8	5.6	6.9	17.0	5.8	10.4
55–59	4.0	10.3	5.4	6.2	8.7	18.8	7.5	11.9
50–54	5.8	13.9	7.1	8.5	11.1	23.1	8.8	15.0
45–49	8.9	17.7	10.3	12.1	14.9	27.8	12.3	19.2
40–44	10.7	20.8	12.9	15.8	15.7	27.9	14.0	20.5
35–39	11.2	22.1	13.3	16.1	14.5	25.5	13.2	17.9
30–34	12.2	21.4	13.9	14.8	13.9	24.1	11.9	15.1
25–29	14.8	23.8	17.3	16.4	14.4	25.0	13.9	15.6

Source: Census of Canada, 1991, special tabulations.

At the other end of the education distribution, the university degree attainment population, the patterns are quite different (see Table 4.7). Francophone women in Quebec over the age of 65 were less likely to have attained university degrees than were their anglophone peers. Although for both groups the percentage attaining university degrees increased dramatically in the youngest age cohort (25 to 29), anglophone women were still much more likely to have a university degree. Among men, francophones from Quebec also narrowed the gap. When compared with anglophones outside Quebec, the gap in attainment shrunk from 3.6% in the oldest cohort to 1.2% in the youngest cohort. If enrolments translate into degrees in equal proportions across the country, then enrolment trends suggest that the degree attainment rates between anglophones and francophones may continue to close (Figures 4.10 and 4.11).

For many, this is a cause for optimism, since it suggests that Quebec francophones may now be attaining education levels that are comparable to other Canadians. Michèle Fortin, commenting upon "winners" in the Canadian education system, cited "francophones, particularly Quebec francophones, who have caught up with the rest of the country overall..." (1987, 5). Fortin is certainly correct if the reference is placed between Quebec francophones and anglophones in the rest of the country.

However, a different picture emerges if we compare anglophones and francophones within Quebec only. In the youngest cohort, anglophone women were still much more likely to have a university degree (23.8%) than were francophone women (14.8%). A very similar pattern is found among men. More than twice as many anglophone men (12.9%) had university degrees in comparison with francophone men (6.0%) in the oldest cohort and, although the proportion of men holding university degrees increased in the youngest cohort (25.0% and 14.4% respectively), the linguistic difference has shrunk only modestly. There is little evidence, then, that the gap at the upper end of the educational distribution is closing in Quebec. Any convergence of the linguistic groups within that province has occurred largely at the lower end of the education spectrum.

This conclusion is more pessimistic than Fortin's, and it highlights how an assessment of equality depends on the reference group used for comparison. Comparisons of Quebec francophones to anglophones outside that province present more optimistic results than do comparisons of francophones with anglophones within Quebec. Both comparisons have their strengths and weaknesses. On the one hand, comparing the attainments of Quebecers with Canadians in other provinces is like comparing apples and oranges, because the two populations face disparate economic and social conditions, and their differently configured education systems make comparisons somewhat tentative. For instance, the college system is much more developed in Quebec than in some other provinces, such as those in the Maritimes, and so comparing university degree attainments emphasizes only one part of the postsecondary system. On the other hand, restricting comparisons to Quebec only obscures a key fact: Quebec anglophones are on average more affluent and urbanized than anglophones in the rest of the country, and thus are not representative of anglophones in Canada as a whole.

Anglophone men and women in Quebec are much more likely to have degrees than are their counterparts in the rest of the country (see Table 4.7). For Quebec males the percentage gap between anglophones and francophones did indeed increase between the older and younger cohorts—from 6.9% to 10.6%—but the gap between Quebec anglophones and anglophones in the other provinces increased by a greater amount—from 3.3% to 9.4%. Hence, one can debate which reference group is more appropriate, since anglophones in Quebec are not typical of English-speakers in Canada as a whole.

Turning to francophone Canadians living outside Quebec, Table 4.7 shows that for the older age groups, francophones were less likely than their anglophone peers to possess a university degree. This has changed, however, especially for women, so that now the linguistic gap in university degree attainment has either vanished or narrowed substantially. Nevertheless, these data continue to show a gap in the educational attainment of francophones and anglophones.

4.4   ETHNICITY, ANCESTRY, VISIBLE MINORITIES, AND IMMIGRATION STATUS

As discussed at the beginning of this chapter, two stark portraits of racial and ethnic stratification dominate the Canadian ethnic research literature and are widely held by government officials and political advocates. Porter's image of the "vertical mosaic" depicted Canadian institutions, such as education, as typified by an entrenched British hegemony that gave British-Canadians supreme privileges in all spheres of Canadian life. Standing next in the multi-layered hierarchy were descendants from Northern Europe who most resembled the British, such as Scandinavians and Germans. Porter and his many followers asserted that the Canadian education system served to block the collective mobility, generation after generation, of most other ethnic and racial groups.

The Abella model (Commission of Inquiry 1984), in contrast, depicts most social advantages and disadvantages as falling sharply along a racial dichotomy. This approach asserts that all Canadian institutions benefit whites over visible minorities (and by extension, many recent immigrants). In this section we present existing research on educational attainment and our own analysis of the 1991 Census to assess the validity of these two images (see also Alladin 1996; Dei 1996; Winn 1985).

4.4.1 METHODOLOGY

Before presenting this research, we need to raise important methodological points. First, changes in the way that Statistics Canada asks about ethnic origins, and the inclusion of both single and multiple responses, makes the interpretation of ethnicity information problematic. Some researchers attempt to make comparisons over different census years. We instead rely solely on the 1991 Census and use our now familiar strategy of comparing across age groups to obtain a proxy measure of social change. Like other researchers, we report findings for individuals who gave only a single origin in response to the question "to which ethnic or cultural group(s) did this person's ancestors belong?" Where we do report data for both single and multiple origin respondents, the patterns for each group are relatively similar.

Other aspects of the ethnicity data also require caution. We, like other researchers in this area, report data for only those ethnic groups that had sufficiently large populations in all age groups to ensure relatively robust results (small numbers among some ethnic groups in the 65+ age cohort preclude many groups from being included). Furthermore, some categories lump together a broad array of people who are only loosely connected. This is especially the case for the category of Aboriginal people, which mixes people of Inuit, Mi'kmaq, and Nisga'a descent, among many others. For Blacks too this is a problem since this category includes people born in the Caribbean, Africa, the United States, Canada, and elsewhere. Nevertheless, researchers can either exclude groups and report no information for them, or include peoples lumped into crude categories but stress the need for caution when interpreting the data patterns. We opt for the latter strategy.

Another key issue is that when assessing theories of ethnic stratification in Canadian education, it is crucial to separate the attainments of the foreign-born from the Canadian-born. Since many immigrants complete their schooling in their countries of origin, researchers should ideally focus on people who attended Canadian schools in order to assess accurately whether Canadian schools block or promote the attainments of certain groups. Otherwise, one confounds the influence of our education system with other influences. For instance, in the 1950s and 1960s, hundreds of thousands of Southern European immigrants with little formal schooling entered the country. Recent immigration policy has favoured highly educated immigrants from other continents. As a result, the average attainment of ethnic groups with large proportions of immigrants may largely reflect their schooling (or lack of schooling) elsewhere, and group disparities may reflect changing immigration policy more than how various groups fare in Canadian schools. Therefore, taking country of birth into account allows us to avoid confounding the successes and failures of our schools with those of schools in other countries. We raise this point because much existing research is limited in this regard, and because on some measures we too cannot make this distinction.

4.4.2 APPROACHES TO STUDYING ETHNICITY

Given these methodological caveats, what does existing research suggest? First, Porter does not seem to have empirically documented his original claims. Indeed, the *Vertical Mosaic* contains no direct evidence linking ethnicity and educational attainment. This is partly because the Canadian census before 1951 did not provide detailed information on educational attainment. Instead, Porter presented data from 1951 on the links between ethnicity and social class, and between social class background and schooling, and inferred that ethnicity must be thus linked to educational attainment.

Second, empirical studies over the past quarter century have offered a much more mixed, nuanced, and complex depiction of ethnic stratification in Canadian education than have either Porter or Abella. For instance, shortly before he died, Porter (1979, 51) examined 1971 Census data that mixed the foreign-born and Canadian-born and found to his surprise that his original hypothesis was unsupported. The British were far from the highest attainers in Canadian schools, and the attainments of most ethnic groups were relatively homogeneous.

Most subsequent studies of attainment present similar findings, and fail to support Abella's depiction as well. Herberg (1990, 12), using data from the 1981 Census, also mixed the foreign-born with the Canadian-born in a study that showed that five of the six top ethnic groups were visible minorities, with people of Jewish background being the sixth group. In Herberg's work there is no evidence that the British have retained any relative dominance in education. Li (1988, 78), however, separated the 1981 Census data into foreign-born and Canadian-born groupings. He reports that Canadian-born groups with the most years of schooling were, in order, Jewish, Chinese, Croatian, Czech and Slovak, Greek and Italian. The British were below the national average, ranking 12th out of 17 reported groups. Li's findings not only contradict Porter's vertical mosaic, they nearly invert it: neither the British, nor the Scandinavians nor the Germans were among the high achieving groups. Furthermore, Canadian-born youth of Greek and Italian ancestry, many of whom had immigrant parents with extremely low educational profiles, sat near the top of the new educational mosaic. Both of the visible minority groups that Li discussed,

Canadian-born Chinese and Blacks, also had above-average attainments. Far from experiencing blocked mobility, these groups have attained relatively high levels of education.

One study does declare that a rigid vertical mosaic in Canadian education has remained intact. Shamai (1992), using census data that pooled the foreign-born with the native born, claims that the British remained greatly advantaged in Canadian schools from 1941 to 1981. He notes that by 1981 the British had slipped to third spot behind Asians and Jews, yet claims that, overall, they remain advantaged, and he asserts that most ethnic groups stayed at the same rank over this 40-year interval. Though we feel Shamai's data are suspect, and that his interpretations and conclusions are faulty, we note his dissenting opinion, and attempt to see whether his claims still held in 1991.[8]

4.4.3 EDUCATION AND ETHNICITY

We turn next to our analysis of the 1991 Census, beginning with a look at the high end of the educational spectrum. For 19 ethnic groups, we rank the percentage of group members who had university degrees in 1991. Even though the data do not distinguish between foreign-born and native-born Canadians, we can infer changes in educational attainment over time by comparing two age cohorts, 25- to 34-year-olds and those 65 and over (See Tables 4.8 and 4.9).

TABLE 4.8

PERCENTAGE OF WOMEN WITH A UNIVERSITY DEGREE, BY ETHNIC ORIGIN AND AGE GROUP, 1991

Ethnic group	25–34		65+	
	Total population	% with university degree (rank)	Total population	% with university degree (rank)
Filipino	15,770	28.8 (3)	5,730	11.1 (1)
Jewish	14,865	49.9 (1)	25,670	5.8 (2)
Scottish	69,065	16.3 (9)	108,040	4.3 (3)
Irish	60,840	15.4 (10)	73,890	3.7 (4)
Hungarian	7,800	18.6 (6)	10,175	3.2 (5)
Chinese	56,800	28.9 (2)	25,825	3.0 (6)
English	302,795	11.0 (16)	367,175	2.6 (7)
Spanish	7,200	11.7 (15)	2,010	2.5 (8)
Polish	22,840	19.8 (5)	26,645	2.3 (9)
Scandinavian	11,840	14.4 (12)	22,620	2.3 (9)
German	78,875	13.8 (13)	81,165	1.9 (11)
French	561,750	12.6 (14)	380,990	1.9 (11)
Greek	11,100	21.4 (4)	6,090	1.7 (13)
Dutch	35,325	15.0 (11)	23,880	1.6 (14)
Black	19,395	9.8 (17)	5,640	1.5 (15)
Ukrainian	30,305	17.1 (8)	51,170	1.4 (16)
Italian	68,285	18.6 (6)	43,550	0.6 (17)
Aboriginal	44,000	2.6 (19)	9,980	0.4 (18)
Portuguese	22,420	6.4 (18)	7,455	0.1 (19)
Total (all groups)	2,399,275	15.7	1,666,430	3.1

Source: Census of Canada, 1991, special tabulations.

TABLE 4.9

Percentage of Men with a University Degree, by Ethnic Origin and Age Group, 1991

Ethnic group	25–34 Total population	% with university degree (rank)		65+ Total population	% with university degree (rank)	
Jewish	15,135	55.0	(1)	22,270	17.2	(1)
Filipino	10,230	20.8	(4)	3,865	15.8	(2)
Chinese	53,980	37.6	(2)	19,255	12.4	(3)
Hungarian	8,380	17.2	(7)	9,340	12.3	(4)
Scottish	80,255	15.7	(9)	84,855	9.7	(5)
Irish	67,545	14.8	(10)	58,325	8.0	(6)
Black	16,755	13.0	(12)	3,010	7.0	(7)
English	314,185	11.7	(16)	267,385	6.8	(8)
Spanish	6,865	11.5	(17)	1,375	6.6	(9)
Greek	12,300	24.0	(3)	4,985	5.9	(10)
Polish	23,845	18.4	(6)	24,670	5.8	(11)
Scandinavian	12,795	12.5	(15)	20,410	5.7	(12)
Dutch	38,205	12.9	(14)	21,225	5.4	(13)
French	559,650	13.0	(12)	269,830	5.2	(14)
German	85,505	13.5	(11)	63,635	4.9	(15)
Ukrainian	33,125	16.2	(8)	42,750	4.0	(16)
Italian	72,980	18.8	(5)	42,385	1.8	(17)
Portuguese	24,145	4.5	(18)	5,845	1.2	(18)
Aboriginal	40,035	1.9	(19)	8,525	0.4	(19)
Total (all groups)	**2,363,130**	**15.9**		**1,256,565**	**7.7**	

Source: Census of Canada, 1991, special tabulations.

One notable trend shown in the tables is that the rankings at the very top and bottom of the two age groups are fairly stable. For example, women of Filipino and Jewish ancestry were in the top three ethnic groups in both age cohorts (see Table 4.8). Chinese women moved from sixth spot among the older cohort to second place among the younger cohort. The biggest gains occurred, however, for women of Italian, Greek and Ukrainian ancestry. This latter trend corroborates Li's findings that groups that entered Canada with extremely low school attainments experienced substantial upward educational mobility. Women of British origins showed the largest drop between the age cohorts, with the English dropping nine places from 7th to 16th and the Scottish and Irish both falling six places. Women of Spanish origin also failed to keep pace with rising levels of schooling, placing 15th in the youngest cohort and eighth among the older group. Although there was a good deal of movement in the middle ranks of the table, there was also virtually no change among the groups at the bottom. This was particularly the case for Aboriginal women and women of Portuguese descent.

One immediate conclusion that we can glean from the data is that they do not correspond to the stark patterns depicted by Porter and Abella. There is little evidence of British advantage, and the attainments of racial minorities are highly variable, indicating that no clear dichotomy exists between "whites" and visible minorities. Canadians of Filipino and Chinese origin exhibit high levels of educational attainment, while Blacks and Aboriginals (the latter especially) have levels well below the Canadian average.

Putting aside the question of relative group disparities, is there evidence that the attainments of various ethnic groups are becoming generally more similar? Not really. Notice that the spread of groups around the average (the total at the bottom of Table 4.8) is relatively stable. There are exceptions to this claim. One-half of young Jewish women (25 to 34) had a university degree in 1991, three times the Canadian average. Among older Jewish women this rate was only twice the national average. So too for Chinese women, whose rate was almost equal to the national average among older women but is almost twice the national average for the younger cohort. Conversely, compared with the national norm, older Aboriginal women were about eight times less likely to attain a university degree ($3.1 / 0.4 = 7.75$), but for the younger cohort this has changed to six times less likely ($15.7 / 2.6 = 6.0$). We will discuss this slow rate of change later in the chapter.

A more formal way to compare change between the two generations is to measure the relative diversity (or variation) of degree attainment among the groups. The index of qualitative variation (IQV) is a useful statistic of variation for discrete variables (see Bohrnstedt and Knoke 1982, 76). If the percentages of degree attainment were the same for all ethnic groups, then the IQV would equal one. The further the IQV measure falls below one, the greater the spread among ethnic groups. For women in the older generation the IQV is 0.85 and it declines, although only minimally, to 0.83 among the younger generation. This change is modest at best, clearly showing little convergence among ethnic groups' receipt of university degrees.

For men the patterns are almost identical (see Table 4.9). The Jewish, Filipino, and Chinese groups dominated both age cohorts. Again, Aboriginal and Portuguese men in both cohorts fared poorly relative to other groups. Younger men of Italian, Ukrainian, and Greek ancestry improved their attainment levels relative to the older cohort while the attainments of younger men of English, Irish, Scottish and Spanish ancestry declined. As with the data for women, the IQV declines modestly (from 0.87 for the older generation to 0.84 for the younger) once more suggesting there is no strong shift toward convergence among ethnic groups in university degree attainment.[9]

Whichever cohort is studied, the data support neither Porter's nor Shamai's assertion that people of British origin have advantages in education (though we must qualify our conclusions because the tables combine data on immigrants and the native born). Furthermore, the 1991 Census data on people aged 65 and over, along with Porter's analysis of 1971 data, and Li's and Herberg's analysis of 1981 data, suggest that the patterns Porter described in *The Vertical Mosaic* have been dead for some time now, and that other groups have been attaining higher levels of education for at least 15 to 25 years.

4.4.4 VISIBLE MINORITIES

It could be argued that Abella offers a more viable description of accessibility in Canadian education, and thus we turn next to an investigation of those groups that Statistics Canada codes as visible minorities. We begin by examining a standard measure of school achievement—the acquisition of a secondary school graduation certificate—for men and women born in Canada or abroad. With these data we can isolate the population that attended school in this country, and thus more accurately examine differences in education levels.

According to the 1991 Census, between 50% and 55% of Canadians held a secondary school graduation certificate. Visible minority Canadians, whether born here or elsewhere, were more likely to have graduated from high school than were other Canadians (see Table 4.10).[10] Among those born in Canada, 69.6% of visible minority women had a secondary school graduation certificate as compared with 54.3% of other women. Among native-born men, the corresponding figures were 68.6% and 51.3%. By this one measure at least, the evidence inverts Abella's presumption that visible minorities are systematically disadvantaged in Canadian high schools.

TABLE 4.10

PERCENTAGE OF CANADIANS AGED 20 AND OVER WITH A SECONDARY SCHOOL GRADUATION CERTIFICATE, BY VISIBLE MINORITY STATUS,[1] IMMIGRATION STATUS, AND SEX, 1991

	Women (%)		Men (%)	
	Native-born	Foreign-born	Native-born	Foreign-born
All Canadians	**54.5**	**50.7**	**51.5**	**54.2**
Non-visible minority population	54.3	46.9	51.3	48.7
Visible minority population	69.6	57.7	68.6	64.5
Korean	83.3	75.0	92.5	86.1
Chinese	80.4	53.5	79.4	61.5
Filipino	78.1	77.7	73.3	79.6
South Asian	75.5	57.3	72.6	66.3
West Asian and Arab	73.2	62.5	70.8	72.3
Latin American	71.4	55.9	64.1	60.6
Japanese	69.2	69.8	69.1	72.3
Other Pacific Islanders	61.3	58.4	54.2	59.8
Blacks	57.6	55.2	55.4	60.1
South East Asian	53.3	39.5	50.0	48.6
Multiple visible minorities	73.2	65.2	70.7	66.0

1. See Endnote 10 for an explanation of visible minority status.
Source: Census of Canada, 1991, special tabulations.

However, one could argue that while minorities in aggregate are not disadvantaged, many particular visible minority groups are disadvantaged vis-à-vis the white majority. Looking at the schooling achievements for different visible minority groups born in Canada and abroad, we see that 92.5% of Canadian-born men of Korean ancestry had graduated from high school. Among Canadian-born men of Chinese ancestry, the figure was 79.4%, while for West Asian-Canadian and Arabian-Canadian men, 70.8% had a secondary school graduation certificate. The important finding is that among 11 groups of Canadian-born men, only men of South East Asian descent had lower rates of secondary school attainment than non-visible minority men did, and this difference was only 1.3%. Comparisons among foreign-born men, or among women born inside or outside Canada, reveal almost identical patterns. Finally, people with parents from different backgrounds (here classified in the "Multiple Visible Minorities" category) also had higher levels of high school graduation.[11] Altogether, men and women in 10 of 11 designated minority groups had high school graduation rates above the majority average.[12]

Yet another way to compare the educational achievements of these groups is to graph the years of schooling they have completed. Three patterns are clear when comparing Canadian-born citizens, aged 30 to 39 (the patterns are no different if we choose an even younger cohort, except that the number of high school completers is lowered slightly). First, whites are more likely than visible minorities to have completed less than 12 years of school (Figures 4.12 and 4.13). Second, whites are more likely to have stopped their schooling at 12 years (note the higher peaks). Third, visible minority Canadians are more likely to have continued in school beyond 12 years.

FIGURE 4.12

YEARS OF SCHOOLING, CANADIAN-BORN WOMEN AGED 30 TO 39, BY VISIBLE MINORITY STATUS, 1991

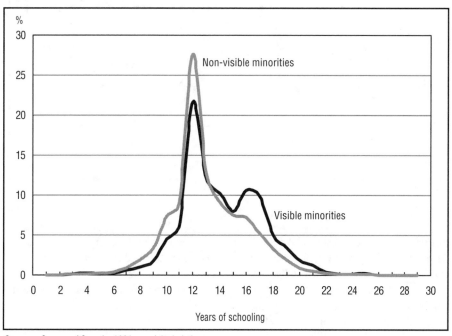

Source: Census of Canada, 1991, special tabulations.

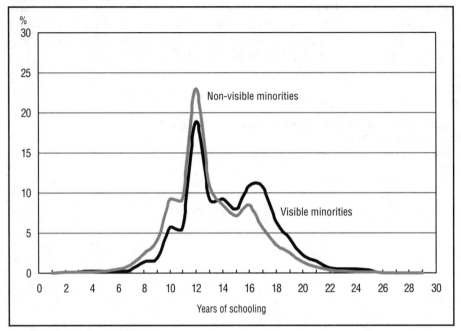

Source: Census of Canada, 1991.

This evidence does not support Abella's claim that across-the-board barriers have blocked the educational attainment of visible minorities in comparison with all other Canadians. From the data, we cannot determine exactly what role, if any, discrimination might play in the educational attainments of visible minorities. We can say, however, that some visible minority groups have achieved higher attainments than their white peers, which contradicts the notion held by many that the education system still favours whites.

4.4.5 EDUCATIONAL ATTAINMENTS OF IMMIGRANTS

Data from three separate censuses show immigrants were more likely than their Canadian-born counterparts to have less than Grade 9 education (see Table 4.11). The percentage difference between educational levels of immigrants and non-immigrants was 7.6 in 1971 but narrowed to 6.2 in 1991. Read another way, in 1971 immigrants were only about 25% more likely than the Canadian-born to have less than Grade 9, but by 1991 this gap had risen to almost a 50% difference.[13] There are a variety of explanations for why this has happened—it may depend on the number of refugees that entered the country in recent years, the countries from which immigrants came, an increase in elderly family class immigrants, and so forth. The data do not allow us to choose between the variety of possible explanations.

TABLE 4.11

PERCENTAGE OF POPULATION WITH LESS THAN GRADE 9 OR WITH A UNIVERSITY DEGREE, BY IMMIGRATION STATUS, 1971, 1981, AND 1991

Year	% with less than Grade 9			% with a university degree		
	Immigrant	Non-immigrant	% difference	Immigrant	Non-immigrant	% difference
1971	38.4	30.8	7.6	6.4	4.4	2.0
1981	25.9	18.7	7.2	10.5	7.4	3.1
1991	18.9	12.7	6.2	14.5	10.5	4.0

Source: Census of Canada, various years, special tabulations.

At the other extreme, immigrants were more likely than their native-born peers to have university degrees (see Table 4.11). Here the gap rose from 2% in 1971 to 4% in 1991. In relative terms, though, the gap shrank. In 1971, about 45% more immigrants than non-immigrants had university degrees. The difference was only 38% by 1991. The patterns, in other words, are mixed and any comparison of immigrant and non-immigrant experiences depends on exactly how educational attainment is measured, that is, whether the focus is upon average years of schooling, or on the end-points of the schooling distribution. The pattern also speaks to the history of Canadian immigration in that we have historically attracted a bipolar distribution of people from abroad, some with very high levels of education and some with relatively low levels (Porter 1965).

A different way to examine immigrant education experiences is to study school outcomes for people who were born abroad but came to Canada at a young age and went through one of our provincial education systems. Among people 20 years and over who came to Canada before age 9, 35% (37.9% of women and 32.9% of men) have no educational degree, certificate, or diploma, that is, no secondary school graduation certificate or any higher credential (see Table 4.12). People born in Africa, the United States, the Caribbean, Asia, and Central or South America are more likely than people of European descent to have some formal educational qualification.

TABLE 4.12

PERCENTAGE OF PEOPLE AGED 20 AND OVER WHO IMMIGRATED TO CANADA BETWEEN BIRTH AND AGE 9 WHO HAVE NO DEGREE, CERTIFICATE OR DIPLOMA, BY REGION OF BIRTH AND SEX, 1991

Place of birth	% with no degree, certificate or diploma	
	Women	Men
United States	25.0	24.5
Central and South America	30.9	30.0
Europe	45.2	37.6
Africa	15.9	12.0
Asia	28.7	26.8
Caribbean, Bermuda, and Jamaica	25.4	25.0
Total	**37.9**	**32.9**

Source: 1991 Census of Canada, special tabulations.

There are different ways to interpret this result. Europeans who immigrated to Canada at a young age are now likely to be older than are people from Asian backgrounds who immigrated at a young age. Because Asian immigration expanded more recently, young Asian immigrants are more likely than their European counterparts to have arrived at a time when everyone was pursuing more schooling. There is no doubt that the period of immigration likely distorts the results in Table 4.12, but the numbers of people in different cells of the table are already low and any further restriction of the age cohort would create distortions.

4.4.6 HOME LANGUAGE AND MOTHER TONGUE

We conclude this section by examining the population aged less than 15 whose home language or mother tongue was neither French nor English (see Table 4.13).[14] Provincial school systems have for many years responded to the educational needs of these children. Between 1981 and 1991, the percentage of the population with neither French or English as a home language or mother tongue increased, suggesting that the educational system will experience even greater challenges around second language instruction in the years ahead.

TABLE **4.13**

PERCENTAGE OF POPULATION LESS THAN AGE 15, WHOSE HOME LANGUAGE OR MOTHER TONGUE IS NEITHER FRENCH NOR ENGLISH, BY PROVINCE AND TERRITORY, **1981** AND **1991**

Area	Home language		Mother tongue	
	1981 (%)	1991 (%)	1981 (%)	1991 (%)
Canada	**5.5**	**7.7**	**7.3**	**9.8**
Provinces and territories				
Newfoundland	0.4	0.6	0.5	0.7
Prince Edward Island	0.4	0.4	0.4	0.5
Nova Scotia	0.9	1.3	1.3	1.7
New Brunswick	0.5	1.3	0.7	1.4
Quebec	4.1	1.1	4.9	1.5
Ontario	7.4	9.9	9.9	12.9
Manitoba	7.9	8.8	11.4	11.4
Saskatchewan	4.0	4.3	6.0	5.4
Alberta	4.7	6.8	6.7	8.9
British Columbia	6.0	9.5	8.5	12.4
Yukon	1.1	1.2	2.8	1.8
Northwest Territories	39.6	38.0	43.2	41.8
Census metropolitan areas				
Montréal	8.9	12.4	10.7	14.9
Toronto	14.6	18.4	18.9	23.8
Vancouver	9.9	16.8	13.4	21.5

Source: Census of Canada, 1991, special tabulations.

In some regions this is a more pressing issue than in others. Most notably, 4 out of 10 children in the Northwest Territories have languages other than English or French as their mother tongue. Although the percentage dropped slightly between 1981 and 1991, this pattern, in concert with the high percentage of young people with less than Grade 9 schooling, points to a major challenge for Canadian education. Many of these children speak an Aboriginal language as either their home language or mother tongue or both, yet most of the education in the Northwest Territories remains in English. The percentage of people with home languages or mother tongues other than French or English increased between 1981 and 1991 in Ontario, British Columbia, and Alberta, while the percentage declined in Quebec and remained virtually stable in other areas. The large urban census metropolitan areas of Montréal, Toronto and Vancouver showed the greatest concentrations and increases in people whose home language or mother tongue was neither official language.

4.5   MULTIVARIATE ANALYSES

Throughout the preceding discussion readers may well have been asking how our results would have differed if our comparisons could simultaneously take into account all of the factors we suggest affect educational attainment. While a full accounting of this question cannot be addressed with any existing data set in Canada, we can approximate such an analysis for a delimited number of variables.

We use four separate multiple regression models to predict the average number of years of schooling acquired by people living in Canada in 1991 (see Table 4.14). Each successive model introduces an additional set of independent variables so that, by Model 4, age, sex, ethnicity/ancestry and region are all taken into account. In Model 1, the equation estimates the impact of age (measured in single years) on years of schooling. The coefficient of –0.075 means that, for each additional year a person has lived in Canada, their schooling is likely to be 0.074 years less. So, for example, a 40-year-old person is estimated to have attained almost three-quarters of a year more schooling than a 50-year-old person (.075 * 10 = 0.75). We adjust for age so that when we begin to look at other variables, we can be confident that age effects are not distorting our interpretation.

The second model introduces three of the four equity categories that Abella used (there was no disability question in the 1991 Census). Controlling for age, sex, and First Nations ancestry, visible minorities are estimated to have had about four-tenths of a year more schooling than non-visible minorities, a finding consistent with our earlier results. Model 2 also shows that women had about a quarter of a year less schooling than men, and that people of First Nations ancestry, net of age, sex, and visible minority status, had about three and one-third fewer years of schooling than do other Canadians. These results not only confirm our earlier findings, but they also suggest that, contrary to the findings of the Abella Commission report, women and visible minorities do not seem to be disadvantaged, at least with regard to educational attainment. Our data confirm the Commission's findings on Aboriginal education levels.

TABLE 4.14

REGRESSION OF YEARS OF SCHOOLING ON AGE, SEX, VISIBLE MINORITY STATUS, FIRST NATIONS ANCESTRY, IMMIGRATION STATUS, ETHNICITY, AND PROVINCE, 1991

Variable names	Model 1	Model 2	Model 3	Model 4
Age				
(years)	− 0.075	− 0.075	− 0.078	− 0.077
Visible minority status				
Member of visible minority	...	0.408	− 0.027	0.003
Sex				
Female	...	−0.233	− 0.252	− 0.253
First Nations status				
First Nations ancestry	...	− 3.386	− 3.585	− 3.705
Immigration status				
Born in Canada	...	...	− 0.748	− 0.499
Ethnicity/ancestry				
Arabic	...	...	− 0.206	− 0.379
Asian	...	...	1.052	0.960
Balkan origin	...	...	− 1.131	− 1.306
Black/Caribbean	...	...	− 0.676	− 0.813
British, French, other	...	...	0.255	0.061
British multiple	...	...	0.888	0.772
British and French	...	...	0.065	− 0.036
British and other	...	...	0.418	0.232
Canadian	...	...	0.047	− 0.144
Chinese	...	...	− 0.677	− 0.844
Dutch	...	...	− 0.320	−0.516
Filipino	...	...	0.864	0.706
French	...	...	− 0.932	− 1.168
French and other	...	...	− 0.202	− 0.397
German	...	...	− 0.531	− 0.687
Greek	...	...	− 2.539	− 2.716
Hungarian	...	...	0.083	− 0.090
Italian	...	...	− 2.409	− 2.618
Jewish	...	...	2.050	1.824
Latin/South American	...	...	− 0.962	− 1.110
Other East and Southeast Asian	...	...	0.223	0.029
Other European	...	...	0.183	0.039
Other Asian origins	...	...	− 0.292	− 0.176
Other multiple origins	...	...	0.200	0.019
Other single origins	...	...	−0.296	− 0.406
Other Western Europeans	...	...	0.069	− 0.115
Polish	...	...	− 0.194	−0.372
Portuguese	...	...	− 4.759	− 4.909
Spanish	...	...	− 1.062	− 1.216

TABLE **4.14** (CONCLUDED)

REGRESSION OF YEARS OF SCHOOLING ON AGE, SEX, VISIBLE MINORITY STATUS, FIRST NATIONS ANCESTRY, IMMIGRATION STATUS, ETHNICITY, AND PROVINCE, 1991

Variable names	Model 1	Model 2	Model 3	Model 4
Southeast Asian	...	...	−0.694	−0.854
Ukrainian	...	...	−0.570	−0.735
Vietnamese	...	...	−2.186	−2.343
West Asian	...	...	0.102	−0.064
Place of birth				
Newfoundland	...	...	...	−2.100
Nova Scotia	...	...	...	−0.867
New Brunswick	...	...	...	−1.107
Quebec	...	...	...	−0.077
Manitoba	...	...	...	−0.337
Saskatchewan	...	...	...	−0.351
Alberta	...	...	...	−0.083
British Columbia	...	...	...	−0.139
Other regions of Canada	...	...	...	−0.681
Constant	15.274	15.422	16.481	16.606
R²	0.106	0.117	0.165	0.175

N=488,329

... figures not applicable

Source: Census of Canada, 1991, special tabulations.

Model 3 introduces immigration status and ethnicity variables to further refine our understanding of factors related to years of schooling. Canadians born in this country have about three-quarters (−0.748) of a year less schooling than do people who immigrated to this country. Controlling for all of the variables higher in the list, we compare various ethnic groups (using what are technically known as dummy variables) to the single-origin British group (which combines Scottish, Welsh, English and Irish). People of Jewish and Asian backgrounds have, on average, more years of schooling than do people from the British reference group. Southern European groups report significantly less schooling than the British: Portuguese (−4.759), Greek (−2.539), and Italians (−2.409). Also notice, that even with controls for immigration status and age, people of Vietnamese background (−2.186) have less schooling than the reference group.

The final model introduces a proxy variable for each region, controlling for province of birth (recall that immigration status is also controlled). Interpretations of this model must be made carefully, because some people will have moved from their province of birth before completing their schooling. However, we wanted to control for region when assessing French-Canadians' average level of schooling relative to others, so the assumption about province of residence seemed worth making. Do people of French ethnic backgrounds have lower levels of schooling than other Canadians? Even after controlling for province of birth and mother tongue, people of French ethnic background have about one year of schooling (−1.168) less than the reference category. This final result adds to our earlier evidence that French-Canadians have not typically stayed in school as long as other Canadians.

This regression model is based, however, on Canadians of all ages and although we have statistically controlled for age in the analysis, it is worth asking how different these four regression models might look if we restricted age to a narrower band. Table 4.15 presents the same regression equations, but for Canadians aged 25 to 34. One way to understand this table, in comparison to Table 4.14, is to look at it as a way of tracing changes in educational attainments over time. By examining a relatively young age cohort only, we focus more clearly on our most recent graduates.[15]

TABLE 4.15

REGRESSION OF YEARS OF SCHOOLING ON AGE (25 TO 34), SEX, VISIBLE MINORITY STATUS, FIRST NATIONS ANCESTRY, IMMIGRATION STATUS, ETHNICITY, AND PROVINCE, 1991

Variable names	Model 1	Model 2	Model 3	Model 4
Age				
(years)	−0.010	−0.012	−0.015	−0.015
Visible minority status				
Member of visible minority	...	0.216	−0.028	−0.078
Sex				
Female	...	0.010	−0.009	−0.006
First Nations status				
First Nations ancestry	...	−2.761	−2.410	−2.439
Immigration status				
Born in Canada	...	...	−0.123	0.106
Ethnicity/ancestry				
Arabic	...	...	1.086	0.998
Asian	...	...	0.812	0.831
Balkan origin	...	...	1.000	0.827
Black/Caribbean	...	...	0.122	0.049
British, French, other	...	...	0.641	0.502
British multiple	...	...	0.741	0.663
British and French	...	...	0.413	0.259
British and other	...	...	0.623	0.563
Canadian	...	...	0.248	0.073
Chinese	...	...	1.043	0.982
Dutch	...	...	0.474	0.322
Filipino	...	...	1.397	1.325
French	...	...	0.201	−0.261
French and other	...	...	0.428	0.247
German	...	...	0.075	0.046
Greek	...	...	0.335	0.066
Hungarian	...	...	0.872	0.738
Italian	...	...	0.875	0.582
Jewish	...	...	2.976	2.692

TABLE 4.15 (CONCLUDED)

REGRESSION OF YEARS OF SCHOOLING ON AGE (25 TO 34), SEX, VISIBLE MINORITY STATUS, FIRST NATIONS ANCESTRY, IMMIGRATION STATUS, ETHNICITY, AND PROVINCE, 1991

Variable names	Model 1	Model 2	Model 3	Model 4
Latin/South American	...	...	−0.263	−0.348
Other East and Southeast Asian	...	...	−0.006	−0.068
Other European	...	...	0.752	0.711
Other Asian origins	...	...	0.277	0.342
Other multiple origins	...	...	0.722	0.681
Other single origins	...	...	0.157	0.070
Other Western European	...	...	0.679	0.501
Polish	...	...	1.207	1.049
Portuguese	...	...	−2.085	−2.230
Spanish	...	...	0.211	0.089
Southeast Asian	...	...	0.172	0.103
Ukrainian	...	...	0.395	0.408
Vietnamese	...	...	−1.567	−1.644
West Asian	...	...	1.250	1.167
Place of birth				
Newfoundland	...	...	...	−1.579
Nova Scotia	...	...	...	−0.670
New Brunswick	...	...	...	−0.718
Quebec	...	...	...	0.205
Manitoba	...	...	...	−0.544
Saskatchewan	...	...	...	−0.615
Alberta	...	...	...	−0.397
British Columbia	...	...	...	−0.491
Other regions of Canada	...	...	...	−0.421
Constant	13.463	13.542	13.408	13.535
R²	0.0001	0.014	0.039	0.051

N=115,914

... figures not applicable

Source: Census of Canada, special tabulations.

These new estimates show that neither sex nor visible minority status has a significant effect on years of schooling. The substantial effect for people of First Nations ancestry remains, however. Immigrants have slightly higher (0.106) years of schooling than native-born Canadians. Relative to the single-origin British group, many ethnic groups have made remarkable gains in acquiring education, most notably Greeks, Italians, and Spanish, all of whom are doing far better in this recent age cohort, though people of Portuguese and Vietnamese background are still lagging behind.

The experience of the younger cohort of French origin is intriguing. Without controlling for province (Model 3), the French are doing slightly better (0.201) than are those of British background. However, when the control for province is introduced, the French slip behind (0.261). Again this is consistent with the earlier results from Tables 4.4 through 4.7. Finally, the disadvantage of the British origin group must be noted. In remarkable contrast to the presumption of many researchers, fully 28 of the 33 identified groups had more years of schooling than the British, controlling for age, sex, and immigration status.

4.6   DISABILITY

Although we have no data from the 1991 Census, there is evidence that disability also influences educational opportunities. Good measures of disability levels and educational attainment are available from the Health and Activity Limitation supplement to the 1986 Census. Of immediate consequence is the provision of schooling for children with disabilities. There were 214,030 children with disabilities between the ages of 5 and 14 living in households in April of 1986 (see Figure 4.14). Of these children, 196,575, or 91.8% were either attending school or being tutored in school subjects. Of those children who were attending school, over 80% were in regular schools, although within those schools they often attended special classes (see also Cohen 1990; Harvey and Tepperman 1990).

FIGURE 4.14

SCHOOL ATTENDANCE OF DISABLED CHILDREN, AGED 5 TO 14, RESIDING IN HOUSEHOLDS, APRIL 1986

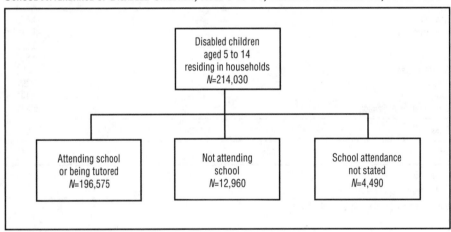

Source: Census of Canada, 1986.

Whether an attendance rate of over 90% is judged high or low is a matter of interpretation. Certainly the vast majority of non-institutionalized children with disabilities participate in formal schooling. However, among the disabled population there is a wide array of ability levels, and not all disabled children can attend regular classes on a continuing basis.

Educational attainment levels of people with disabilities lag behind levels for the non-disabled population (see Table 4.16). People with disabilities are almost twice as likely as the non-disabled not to attain a university degree. At the other end of the educational spectrum, disabled people are more than three times more likely than the non-disabled not to complete Grade 9.

A subsequent Health and Activity Limitation supplement to the census will give us a much better understanding of how these patterns are changing. The 1986 material will serve as a benchmark to show us if we are improving the educational opportunities for disabled people.

TABLE 4.16

EDUCATIONAL ATTAINMENT OF DISABLED AND NON-DISABLED ADULTS, AGED 25 TO 34, BY SEX, 1986

	Women		Men	
Highest level of schooling	Disabled	Non-disabled	Disabled	Non-disabled
Less than Grade 9 (%)	13.2	3.9	12.9	4.2
Secondary (%)	45.9	42.6	46.5	38.7
Some/completed postsecondary (%)	34.1	39.7	32.8	42.4
University degree (%)	6.8	13.8	7.8	14.7
Total (%)	100.0	100.0	100.0	100.0
Total population	139,775	2,115,135	148,925	2,046,850

Source: Census of Canada, 1986, special tabulations.

4.7 SOCIO-ECONOMIC STATUS/SOCIAL CLASS

Sociologists have long maintained that one of the key stratifying factors in modern society is social class, and that the effects of class on educational attainment are particularly acute.[16] The international research literature has offered evidence that there has been "little change in socio-economic inequality of educational opportunity" (Shavit and Blossfeld 1993, 19). This is a surprising result given that the huge expansion of the education system in the 1950s and 1960s was supposed to provide greater equality of opportunity.

In this section we present data that address whether or not a woman's likelihood of attaining some postsecondary education is influenced by the level of education her mother acquired. We also present multiple regression results from the 1994 General Social Survey (GSS) in an attempt to show the enduring link between children's educational attainment and their parents' socio-economic status (SES). But we caution that these results are tentative. While the GSS has at least some crude proxy measures for social class (unlike the 1991 Census) it lacks detail on other variables, particularly on ethnicity and ancestry.

Is a woman's likelihood of attaining some postsecondary education influenced by the level of education her mother acquired? The first set of findings (see Figure 4.15) is based on national level data collected in 1966 via an attachment to the Labour Force Survey. Lagacé (1968) shows that as mothers' levels of education increase, the percentage of daughters reporting some postsecondary education rises quite dramatically. Daughters of university- educated mothers were approximately 10 times more likely to have some postsecondary experience than daughters whose mothers stopped school at the elementary level.

The next two figures provide answers to the same question, except now the categories for mother's level of education are somewhat more detailed. Using data from Statistics Canada's 1986 General Social Survey, Creese, Guppy, and Meissner (1991) report that daughters of university-educated mothers were just more than twice as likely to have some postsecondary education than daughters whose mothers had Grade 10 or less (see Figure 4.16). There is clear evidence of inequality of opportunity but, using this admittedly crude comparison, the difference appears to have lessened. Finally, 1994 Statistics Canada survey data reported in Fournier, Butlin, and Giles (1995) suggest that daughters were now only about two times more likely to attend postsecondary school if their mothers had a university degree (see Figure 4.17) compared with daughters of the least educated mothers.

FIGURE **4.15**

DAUGHTER'S EDUCATION AS A FUNCTION OF MOTHER'S EDUCATION, **1966**

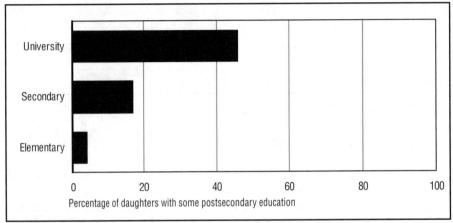

Percentage of daughters with some postsecondary education

Source: Lagacé 1968.

FIGURE **4.16**

DAUGHTER'S EDUCATION AS A FUNCTION OF MOTHER'S EDUCATION, **1986**

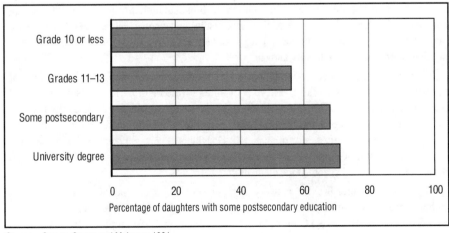

Percentage of daughters with some postsecondary education

Source: Creese, Guppy, and Meissner 1991.

FIGURE 4.17

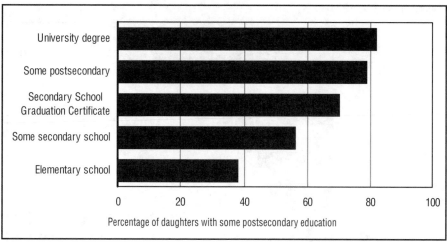

Source: Fournier, Butlin, and Giles 1995.

Richard Wanner has assembled the best longitudinal comparisons of educational attainment in Canada. In comparing evidence from survey research questionnaires for 1973, 1986, and 1994, he concludes that the effect of mothers' education on daughters' level of school attainment "distinctly declines" (1996, 14). In keeping with the analysis reported above, it is important to note that although the effect of mothers' education on daughters' schooling is reduced, it is not eliminated. His analyses in 1996 and 1986 (Wanner 1986) suggest that the same effect does not apply to men. Indeed, he argues that the effects of fathers' status, as measured either by occupation or education, have not declined. He does not speculate why these differences exist. His results, along with ours, show that social class, as measured by either occupation or education of parents, still matters.

We can assess the effect of SES (or social class) another way by using data from the 1994 General Social Survey. As a measure of educational attainment we use the highest level of schooling a person reports achieving. For simplicity we consider this in the form of a dichotomy—whether someone has, or has not, studied at the university level. Figure 4.18 shows the percentage of men and women aged 25 to 34 in 1994 who report having studied at university, by father's occupation. Father's occupation is collapsed into the following five categories: professional and senior managerial, supervisory (generally middle management and supervisors), skilled (including semi-skilled workers), unskilled, and farming. Only about one-third of 1994 GSS respondents reported studying at the university level, but the majority of those whose fathers were in professional or managerial jobs had some university experience (62% of men and 58% of women). People whose fathers were in either unskilled or farming jobs were much less likely to report studying at the university level. These differences suggest that a father's occupation has a significant bearing on the likelihood of his children studying at the university level. These differences far outweigh any effects of sex or ethnicity that we have seen above.

FIGURE 4.18

PERCENTGE OF 25- TO 34- YEAR-OLDS WITH UNIVERSITY-LEVEL EDUCATION, BY FATHER'S OCCUPATION AND SEX, 1994

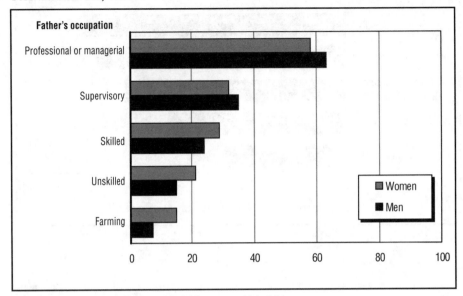

Source: Statistics Canada, 1994 General Social Survey, unpublished data.

Finally, we want to know if the results of Figure 4.18 remain firm if we simultaneously examine the effects of a range of other variables on educational attainment. To examine this, we again use data from the 1994 GSS (see Table 4.17). First we construct a measure of years of schooling and then calculate the effect of a range of variables on this measure. We estimated years of schooling from several questions asking respondents about the number of years they spent in elementary and secondary school ("How many years of elementary and high school education have you successfully completed?") and their highest level of schooling ("What is the highest level of education that you have attained?"). As independent variables we used age (measured in years), sex, location of schooling (measured by the question: "In which province or territory did you attend most of your elementary and high school studies/schooling?"), mother's place of birth, number of siblings and birth order position, father's occupation, and both mother's and father's education. Unlike the 1991 Census data that we presented earlier in this chapter, there is no measure on the GSS of ethnicity and so we opted for mother's place of birth. This is far from ideal but there is no national data in Canada where good measures of both social class and ethnicity are available. The GSS has several measures of family background, none of which are available from the census.

TABLE 4.17

REGRESSION OF YEARS OF SCHOOLING ON AGE, SEX, PROVINCE OF SCHOOLING, PLACE OF BIRTH, FATHER'S OCCUPATION, FATHER'S EDUCATION, MOTHER'S EDUCATION, BIRTH ORDER, AND NUMBER OF SIBLINGS, 1994

Variable names	Model 1	Model 2	Model 3	Model 4
Age				
(years)	−0.082[1]	−0.081[1]	−0.068[1]	−0.052[1]
Sex				
Female	...	−0.135	−0.118	−0.071
Location of schooling				
Newfoundland	...	−2.129[1]	−1.413[1]	−1.396[1]
Prince Edward Island	...	−0.895	−0.451	−0.210
Nova Scotia	...	−0.807[1]	−0.502[1]	−0.450
New Brunswick	...	−1.196[1]	−0.681[1]	−0.500[1]
Quebec	...	−1.277[1]	−0.838[1]	−0.636[1]
Manitoba	...	−0.716[1]	−0.636[1]	−0.427[1]
Saskatchewan	...	−0.506[1]	−0.335	−0.008
Alberta	...	−0.156	−0.037	0.013
British Columbia	...	−0.467[1]	−0.526[1]	−0.697[1]
Outside Canada	...	−0.512[1]	−0.350[1]	−0.377[1]
Mother's birthplace				
Canada	...	−0.939[1]	−0.671[1]	−0.502[1]
Other European country	...	−1.073[1]	−0.904	−0.488[1]
Asia	...	0.639[1]	1.070[1]	0.942[1]
Elsewhere in world	...	−0.050	0.329	0.196
Family of origin				
Number of siblings	...	...	−0.276[1]	−0.195[1]
Birth order (first versus other)	...	...	0.282[1]	0.153
Family socio-economic status				
Father in professional occupation	...	...	...	0.843[1]
Father in supervisory occupation	...	...	...	0.574[1]
Father in unskilled occupation	...	...	...	−0.374[1]
Father in farming occupation	...	...	...	−0.674[1]
Father's education	...	...	...	0.586[1]
Mother's education	...	...	...	0.650[1]
Constant	15.958	17.366	17.314	15.389
R^2	0.135	0.186	0.240	0.327

N=4,629

...   figures not applicable

1.   Statistically significant, $p < .05$.

Source: Statistics Canada, 1994 General Social Survey.

Parallel with the multiple regression results from the 1991 Census (see Table 4.14), the GSS results also show that age is negatively related to years of schooling and the effect of sex is minor. We also find similar results between the two data sets for location of schooling, although the measures differ slightly and hence the results are not perfectly parallel. Mother's birthplace is unique to the GSS and so we cannot compare it directly to earlier census results, but notice that people whose mothers were born in Asia have almost a year more schooling than people in the reference category (whose mothers were born in the United Kingdom).

With the GSS data we introduce variables to measure the effects of siblings and birth order. People in larger families tend to attain fewer years of schooling than those in smaller families (0.276 without SES controlled and –0.195 with SES controlled). This disparity occurs partly because poorer families tend to be larger, but even with SES controlled the number of siblings still affects educational attainment. Our interpretation is that larger families lack the financial and time resources necessary to see all of their children through as much schooling as smaller families. Being first-born is significantly related to attaining more schooling than other children in the family when SES is not controlled. But once such controls are introduced in Model 4, the birth order effect is not statistically significant, suggesting that the birth order effects in Model 3 result, in part, because wealthier families more often have only one child.

Most importantly, for present purposes, the three measures of family SES all prove to have statistically significant effects. People whose fathers are in either professional or supervisory occupations are more likely to attain more schooling than people whose fathers are in skilled occupations. People whose fathers are in either unskilled or farming occupations are less likely to attain as much schooling as people whose fathers are in skilled occupations (corroborating the evidence presented in Figure 4.18). Also, people whose parents have high levels of educational attainment are more likely to attain higher levels themselves. Finally, the increment in R^2, from 0.240 in Model 3 to 0.327 in Model 4 (where SES is first introduced) suggests that, net of all the other factors in the equation, SES continues to have an important and significant effect on the number of years of schooling people are likely to attain.

4.8 CONCLUSION

Have the educational qualifications of different groups of Canadians changed over time? The answer depends on which groups are being examined, which measures of schooling are being used, and whether there are historical data that permit reliable comparisons over time. Nevertheless, we can offer a number of conclusions.

First, differences have certainly eased among women and men. Women now have outcomes superior to men on many measures of educational attainment, though, as we discuss in a later chapter, disparities remain in types of education and fields of study.

Second, there are educational disparities between disabled and non-disabled Canadians, though whether these disparities are easing or intensifying we cannot say until better longitudinal data become available. But as educational budgets tighten, resources for the disabled, even though their needs are high, may face greater pressure because the number of disabled students is relatively low.

Third, the educational profiles of francophone Canadians in and outside of Quebec have begun to catch up with those of anglophones in other provinces, though with regard to educational attainment Canadians of French ancestry do not rank highly among ethnic groups in this country, and francophones within Quebec lag behind anglophones in that province.

Fourth, patterns of ethnic group disparities in recent decades do not correspond with either the "British hegemony" model or Abella's racial dichotomy. Detecting change is difficult since consistent data—especially ethnicity data—from earlier censuses is hard to find, but it appears that the relative educational attainments of people of British heritage have noticeably declined since 1951, while the educational attainments of visible minorities, particularly Asians, along with Southern and Eastern Europeans have risen sharply. There is no evidence of blocked mobility in education for any of these groups. This pattern, detectable in data as far back as 1971, is still not widely acknowledged in Canadian society.[17]

Fifth, it should be noted that at the individual level, race and ethnic background are not strong predictors of educational attainment. Indeed, the multiple regression model in Table 4.15, which consists of dozens of ethnic categories, along with gender and region, explains only 5% of the variation in attained years of education. This suggests that for most Canadians, ethnicity or race are not powerful determinants of their school attainment, at least compared with other factors.

Sixth, however, particular groups face stubborn and unyielding problems. The sharpest and most entrenched inequities are experienced by the First Nations peoples and people of Portuguese ancestry. While both groups have improved their educational levels, the rate of improvement is significantly behind all other groups in the country. If education is one of the key factors in promoting both individual and collective prosperity (emotional and financial), then we must more actively improve educational opportunities (and related issues) for these two groups.

Finally, another persistent source of educational disadvantage is class or SES (which likely explains the low attainments of Aboriginal and Portuguese youth). Though children from all class and socio-economic backgrounds have raised their attainments since the Second World War, the relative disparities among class groups have only slightly diminished. Unlike the changing situations that we described in the realms of gender and ethnicity, class background seems to be the far more enduring source of educational inequality.

How, then, has the distribution of education changed in Canada? Our findings suggest that the huge postwar expansion of publicly funded education, on the whole, has opened opportunities for all Canadians. Every group, broadly defined, has gone to school longer, and has acquired more credentials. The real question thus becomes one of the relative competition between groups. Our data suggest that our mass system, with its principle of universalism, has fostered equal opportunity among *most* Canadians.

This statement needs to be placed in historical context. To talk about the opening-up of a system implies that it was once closed to many groups. That presumption is true, but it must be qualified, and here we offer an important, but seldom made, point. Few individuals from either gender or from any ethnic background went to university before the 1950s. While most university students in the pre-1950s era were male and of white, British origin, they represented only a small segment of that group. In other words, it is difficult to argue that men or people of British origin enjoyed advantages *as a group*. Only a small elite benefited from education, and the system was small, fragmented and poorly funded. Now that we have a truly mass system, it cannot be said that any one group dominates. We believe, therefore, that more attention ought to be placed on identifying the losers in the current system as opposed to its winners.

As we have shown, access to education has changed greatly, except for working-class, Aboriginal and Portuguese-Canadian students. The question looms regarding where the future of educational equality is headed, for as we argued in the introduction to this chapter, the new economy is not hospitable for young people who lack sufficient skills and credentials. We believe, unfortunately, that as tighter education budgets and identity politics (described in our introductory chapter) continue to dominate educational politics, there is less and less chance that those remaining inequalities will diminish in the near future. Rising tuition, for instance, can only make things worse for poorer students. And while school boards and universities and colleges have adopted a flood of policies to deal with issues of "difference" and "diversity," the latter seem to be understood solely in terms of gender and race, to the neglect of class. Despite the persistence of class-related disparities, for instance, it seems that we hear less and less about this issue every year. In many ways, education policy is not being directed to where it is most urgently needed.

ENDNOTES

1. Just how much the quality of schooling varies in Canada is difficult to judge. Provincial ministries of education are under intense pressure from many quarters, including their political masters, parents, and teachers, to ensure that schooling at all levels is of comparable quality to other provinces. The quality of teacher preparation and the financial resources devoted to education are input measures often used to compare across provinces. Output measures such as standardized test results are often used to show how provinces fare relative to one another (see Economic Council of Canada 1992).

2. Note that women's durations of schooling have always been more similar than have men's. This reflects men's propensity to either drop out sooner or pursue advanced degrees.

3. The 1951 and 1961 Census questions do not allow for precise measurement of the category "some postsecondary" and so it is omitted in Table 4.3. This makes comparisons between 1951 and 1991 problematic for both "Grades 9 to 13" and for "Some postsecondary."

4. The participation rate is a crude but useful measure of college and university participation. It is *not* the percentage of 18- to 24-year-olds in higher education. Instead, it is calculated as the full-time college and university undergraduate enrolment divided by the number of Canadians in that age cohort. It is a crude rate because some college and university students are younger than 18 and some are older than 24. Furthermore, the enrolment figures include foreign students (who are excluded from the age cohort figures), ignore part-time study, and miss Canadian students who study abroad. Until recently data on the actual ages of college and university students were not routinely collected and so this crude rate was useful to measure the approximate proportion of young people in postsecondary education (see Darling 1980; Vanderkamp 1984).

5. In the following section we used the most recent available data reported in *Education in Canada* or "Education at a Glance" in *Education Quarterly Review*.

6. Career programs are vocationally oriented fields of study in community colleges or institutes of technology (for example, computer systems analysis and hotel management). In 1992, *Education in Canada* records the awarding of 85,286 community college diplomas, of which 59,772 were in career programs. By way of comparison, there were 120,745 bachelor and first professional degrees awarded in 1992.

7. Compare these results to Table 3.2 to obtain a subtler analysis where provincial differences are highlighted.

8. It is doubtful that Herberg, Li, and Shamai are all correct, particularly since they all used census data. The fact that each researcher used different census samples, different measures of schooling, and different measures of ethnicity may account for part of the discrepancy. But Shamai's findings are so dissimilar, so contradictory, that it is unlikely that these methodological differences can fully account for the contrasting results. After careful inspection of each study, we doubt Shamai's conclusions. Shamai fails to discuss methodological issues, fails to report sample sizes, and pools the results for the foreign-born and the native-born. The latter tactic allows him to conclude, for instance, that the slow, gradual increases in attainment for Italians and Greeks are evidence of blocked mobility. However, Li clearly shows that the average attainments of these groups are greatly lowered by the larger numbers of original, now-older immigrants who entered Canada with few years of schooling. Their Canadian-born offspring, as Li shows, and as we will show with our own data from 1991, are well above the Canadian average. Shamai's claim that British advantage remains strong is also highly suspect. He categorizes 10 ethnic groups based on their mean years of schooling, as "above average," "intermediate," or "below average" and places the British in the "above average" category in each of four census years. But he ignores groups that ranked higher than the British in Li's study—the Czechs and Slovaks, Hungarians, and Blacks. Furthermore, Shamai's tables reveal that in 1981 the difference between the third-ranked British and the Scandinavians, whom he places in the "intermediate" category, is a mere 0.01 years, which amounts to less than a week of schooling. This placement ignores the fact that the British mean is closer to all of the "intermediate" means than to the "above average" mean. The British attained 0.75 more years of schooling than the Poles (the lowest ranked "intermediate" group) but attained 2.34 years less than Jews and 0.81 years less than Asians, the other "above average" groups.

9. As an aside it is interesting to consider the results in light of the earlier discussion of anglophone/francophone differences. Notice that for both women and men, Canadians noting their ancestry as French were toward the bottom third of the rankings in both generations.

10. Visible minority status is coded in accordance with the federal government's Employment Equity Act of 1986. The 1991 Census asked no questions about race or colour. Visible minority status was derived, by Statistics Canada, from responses to ethnic origin, language, place of birth, and religion questions. Ethnic categories have been collapsed so that, for example, Black includes people of African, Caribbean, American, and Canadian descent, while Southeast Asian includes people of Vietnamese, Thai, Laotian, Cambodian, and Indonesian descent. Black was explicitly identified on the 1991 Census questionnaire, while Southeast Asian responses required people to write in information in a "please specify" section.

11. One other aspect of Table 4.10 deserves comment. Among women, foreign-born Canadians are less likely than are native-born Canadians to have a secondary school graduation certificate. For men, the case is exactly the reverse. In large measure, this difference is a function of the Canadian immigration point system, whereby men are typically the family members awarded points toward entrance to Canada (Boyd 1990).

12. The exception is Southeast Asians, which may indicate that many refugees from that region, especially women, lack the educational credentials that other visible minority groups possess.

13. In 1991, among people aged 65 and over, almost an equal percentage of immigrants and non-immigrants had less than Grade 9 education (40.2% for immigrants and 39.3% for non-immigrants). Among people aged 25 to 44 the gap was much wider, with 8.1% of immigrants but only 4.5% of non-immigrants having less than Grade 9.

14. Home language refers to the language now spoken most often at home while mother tongue refers to the first language learned at home and still understood.

15. Here again we control for age, but given that age only varies between 25 and 34, its effect is very modest.

16. No consensus exists in the North American research literature about how social class or socio-economic status ought to be measured. Unlike European researchers, North American social scientists often understand class in terms of socio-economic status rather than by identifying clear boundaries between working and ownership classes (or other classes). We use parental education and father's occupation as crude proxy measures for social class or socio-economic differences (see Davies 1995 for a discussion of the rise and fall debate and research on class-based inequality of educational opportunity).

17. Indeed, some researchers have been dumbfounded by the continuing popularity of the *Vertical Mosaic* thesis despite the growing gap between that theory and empirical research findings. See Ogmundson (1990) and the ensuing debate in the *Canadian Journal of Sociology*.

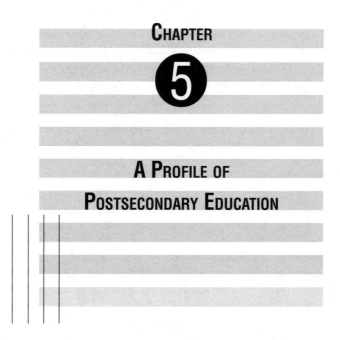

CHAPTER

5

A PROFILE OF
POSTSECONDARY EDUCATION

Institutions of higher education figure prominently in the post-industrial and knowledge societies described by such writers as Daniel Bell (1973) and Clark Kerr (1991), who portray universities and colleges as increasingly vital to society. With information as the burgeoning factor of production, postsecondary institutions—a key locus of knowledge in the modern world—will emerge as the motors of the post-industrial economy. This expanded role for higher education would, they argue, forever change its form and structure. An expansive network of massive but specialized "multiversities" would replace the old, small, general liberal arts colleges and universities. A complex division of labour would emerge between large, internally differentiated research universities, general undergraduate schools offering a plethora of specialties, and an assortment of polytechnical colleges.

Such a system would have to suit the diverse needs of swelling numbers of students and meet the demands for specialized knowledge in the high technology economy. Fields such as computer science, physics and engineering, which develop and use advanced technology, would attract the most students and become the centres of power in the university. Socially, this new mass system would promote meritocracy. It would offer more flexible programs to accommodate the rising numbers of students with diverse lifestyles and social backgrounds. Achievement would increasingly prevail over ascription. More students would be liberated from the constraints of traditional roles, particularly those roles based on gender.

This type of rhetoric shapes much of the policy debate on higher education reform. In this context, the term "higher education" describes education levels beyond secondary schooling. However, some, apparently uncomfortable with this label, have begun more recently to use the term "postsecondary schooling." Usage here is not innocent. Higher education typically refers to university education and the phrase carries with it a certain elitism that bothers some and is promoted by others. In contrast, the terms "postsecondary" or "tertiary sector" refer to an amorphous collection of institutions. Clarifying what qualifies as postsecondary education is not simple, but Gregor offers the following definition based on Statistics Canada's operational procedures for collecting national education data:

> [Postsecondary] encompasses all education programs and research activities of universities, as well as certain programs in non-university (college level) institutions, such as community or regional colleges, CEGEPs, technical institutes, and hospital and regional schools of nursing. To be included as post-secondary, programs in college-level institutions must meet certain criteria, essentially that they require high school graduation for admission, last at least one school year, lead to a certificate or diploma, and are not classified as trade/vocational (Gregor and Jasmin 1992, 7).

As the definition explicitly says, the postsecondary system consists of the university stream and the college stream. The distinction between the two is presumably the same distinction behind the term "higher education." The fact that college programs must meet specific criteria to be considered postsecondary, but university programs and activities do not, is evidence that this distinction is still in effect. This bifurcation in the postsecondary sphere affects labour market outcomes, as we discuss in Chapter 6 (see also Anisef, Ashbury, and Turrittin 1992).

National data collection on education is complicated by the fact that various educational programs are not included in our national accounts of education. Campbell (1984), writing about universities, discusses what he calls the "new majority," the almost invisible students who enrol in continuing education courses. Many adult training programs, whether job-related or language-related, are also left out of discussions of education. This diversity in types of schooling, within and across provinces and territories, makes it difficult, if not impossible, for a national body like Statistics Canada to capture fully all of the education and training occurring in the country. Schooling is "everywhere" in a schooled society, increasingly prevalent in informal or shadow systems of schooling. It would be unfeasible to quantify all of these forms of schooling.

We begin this chapter with this definitional excursus, not because we can do anything to alter the way in which our national statistics have been collected, but to alert readers to the idea that much of what occurs as education in this country cannot be included in a book like this focusing upon national-level data. An array of education programs, from cultural heritage, swimming and music classes, to career training, are not included in our data (and the task of trying to collect such information would be immense). Much of this occurs in the guise of life-long learning, and for many is "post" schooling, even if the schooling occurs in the interstitial niches of businesses (for example as job retraining or performance enhancing) or colleges and universities (for example as continuing education or adult education programs).

5.1   THE GROWTH OF THE POSTSECONDARY SYSTEM

One crude measure of the size of the postsecondary system (as of 1994–95) is a comparison of the number of elementary and secondary schools (15,926) with the number of postsecondary institutions (286).[1] Many will find such a comparison odd, if not absurd, but it effectively underscores differences in size between the institutions of the postsecondary system in comparison with earlier levels of schooling. A comparison of the number of full-time teachers shows this imbalance. Of the 338,377 full-time teachers in 1994–95, 304,002 or 89.8% taught at the elementary and secondary level. That same year, 98.2% of all schools were found at the elementary and secondary level. Measured by full-time student enrolment, the postsecondary system is again dwarfed by elementary and secondary schooling (Figure 5.1 shows full-time Canadian students by level of study). Nevertheless, since 1951 the postsecondary system has expanded significantly in comparison to elementary and secondary schooling. At the beginning of the 1950s approximately 3% of Canadian full-time students attended colleges and universities, but by the middle of the 1990s this had increased to more than 15%.

FIGURE 5.1

FULL-TIME ENROLMENT, BY LEVEL OF STUDY, 1951 TO 1994

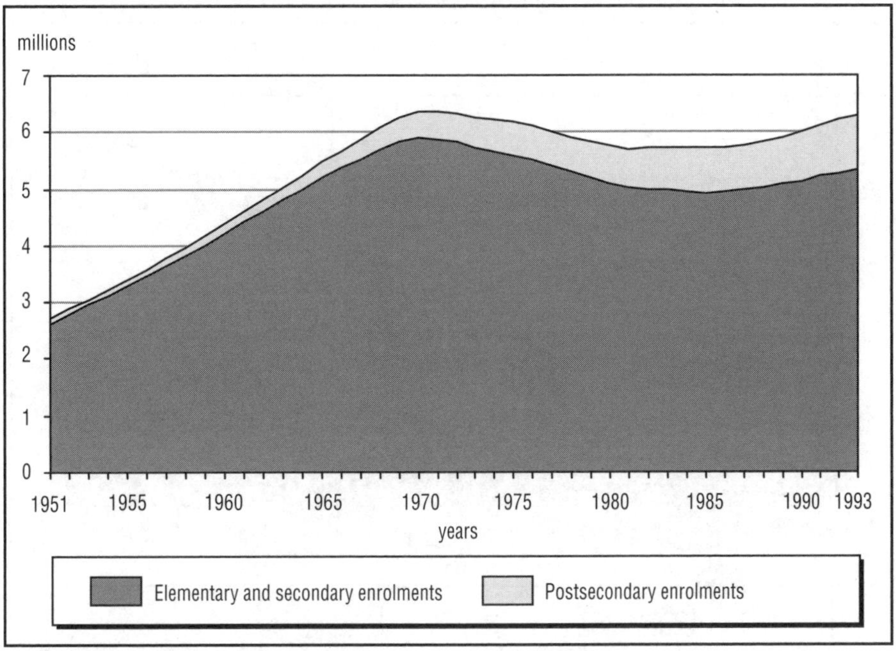

Source: Leacy 1983; Statistics Canada, *Education in Canada,* various years.

Elementary and junior level secondary attendance is mandated by the compulsory minimum school-leaving age and so the growth in voluntary participation at the postsecondary level must be considered with that significant proviso in mind. Additionally, elementary and secondary school enrolment is almost exclusively full-time, whereas the size of the postsecondary sector would be even larger if part-time students were also included in Figure 5.1.

Full-time enrolments at postsecondary institutions have increased annually, although the growth was small (0.3%) between 1977 and 1978 (see Figure 5.2). At the university level, full-time enrolments have increased in every decade since Confederation. Only in 1977 and 1978 did the number of full-time students decline (Lynd 1994, 12), but growth occurred thereafter. This continued until 1995 when preliminary figures showed 2,200 fewer full-time students than in the previous year. Whether this recent decline is the start of a trend, or once again a single year blip, is impossible to tell, although preliminary 1996 enrolment figures surpassed the previous peak year of 1994. College enrolments started to increase noticeably in the late 1960s, almost a decade after the upward surge in university enrolments. For much of the 1980s, college enrolments stagnated before again picking up steam in the early 1990s. From approximately 1976 to 1995, the relative shares of the full-time postsecondary student population have been 60:40 in favour of universities. Nevertheless, while recent data suggest full-time university enrolments are falling, community college enrolments appear to be rising, by more than 2% between 1994–95 and 1996–97.[2]

FIGURE 5.2

TOTAL FULL-TIME UNIVERSITY AND COMMUNITY COLLEGE ENROLMENT, 1951 TO 1995

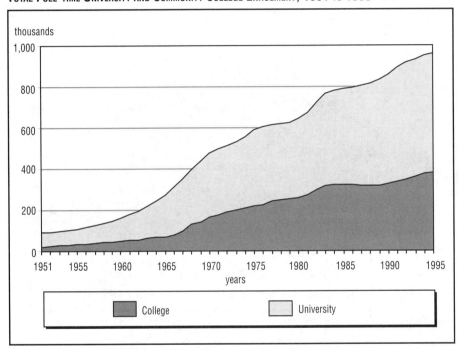

Source: Leacy 1983; Statistics Canada, *Education in Canada*, various years.

5.2   REGIONAL DIFFERENCES IN POSTSECONDARY EDUCATION

The differentiation of the postsecondary system is complicated further by the availability, or not, of college and university programs in each separate province and community (see Figure 5.3).[3] For example, in the Yukon and Northwest Territories there are no universities and so the college system, though it is small, dominates postsecondary education (except for distance education, an area for which enrolment figures are unavailable). Focusing on full-time enrolment, Quebec is the only province in which more students attend college than attend university. British Columbia is the only other province with a percentage of college students above the national average. The important message here, however, is that these different structures of postsecondary education cloud comparisons between provinces and territories.

FIGURE 5.3

PERCENTAGE OF FULL-TIME POSTSECONDARY STUDENTS IN COLLEGES AND UNIVERSITIES, 1993 TO 1994

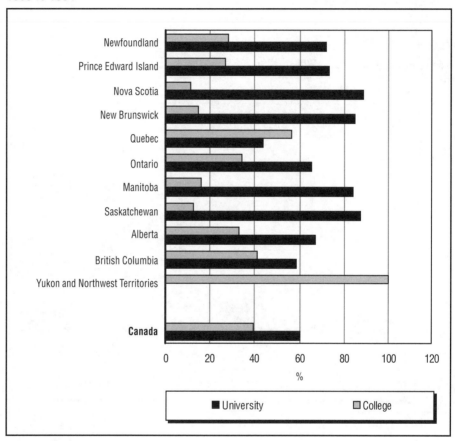

Source: Statistics Canada, *Education in Canada,* 1995.

5.3   UNIVERSITY ENROLMENTS BY PROGRAM TYPE

Differentiation occurs not only between colleges and universities, but also within each of these systems. In universities, full-time enrolment is often divided between undergraduate, master's, and PhD students. Graduate students (master's and PhD) now account for about 13% of all university students. However, since their programs are of different lengths than are undergraduate programs (master's programs are typically shorter and PhD programs are often longer), enrolment figures can be deceiving.

A look at the actual number of degrees awarded at each level between 1920 and 1996 shows precipitous growth of the university system at the undergraduate level (see Figure 5.4). The sharp increase in bachelor's and first professional degrees is not matched by similar gains for master's degrees or PhDs, which have shown only modest growth. Although discussion within universities often focuses on the expansion of graduate programs, the bread and butter of university education remains the undergraduate level.

FIGURE 5.4

DEGREES AWARDED, BY LEVEL, 1920 TO 1996

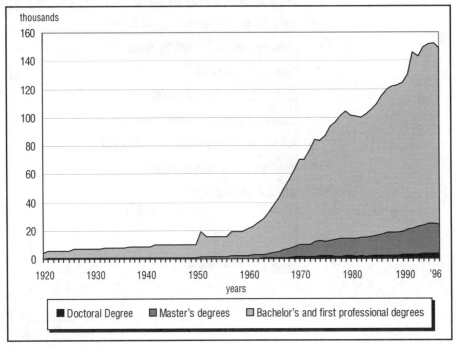

Source: Leacy 1983; Statistics Canada, *Education in Canada,* various years.

The population of 18- to 24-year-olds, the typical clientele for university programs, shrank from the early 1980s through to the early 1990s. Despite this drop, both university enrolments and the number of graduates continued to climb until the mid-1990s. Part of this increase is due to the greater numbers of women attending university. The increase occurred not so much because universities started to offer new courses geared toward women (although that happened to a modest degree, for example, with women's studies programs), but because more women started entering programs in which they had previously not enrolled. This point is worth reinforcing since it is unlikely that women's enrolment and degree attainment will continue at this pace (current indications are that some decline has recently begun already).

Figure 5.5 presents the contrasting experiences of men's and women's degree attainment from 1958 to 1996. The regression coefficient, shown as b, reflects the annual linear increase in the number of degrees earned by women and men respectively. Women received an average of 1,923.0 more degrees each year than they did the year before. For men the corresponding figure is 989.7, meaning that while men increased their degree attainment year upon year, on average they received 1,000 fewer additional degrees per year than did women. The net result of this process is that annually women now are earning over 19,000 more bachelor's and first professional degrees than men are (and, if the growth of the last three decades were to continue, women would add a further 1,000 degrees every year to the gap).

FIGURE 5.5

BACHELOR'S AND FIRST PROFESSIONAL DEGREES AWARDED, BY SEX, SINGLE YEARS, 1958 TO 1996

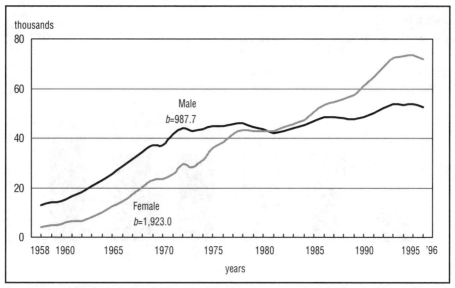

Source: Leacy 1983; Statistics Canada, *Education in Canada,* various years; Statistics Canada, *Education Quarterly Review,* various years.

There is, of course, evidence that women are not reaping the same economic rewards from higher education credentials as men. But if labour markets are stratified by sex and women often compete against each other for work, then having university degrees is still an economic asset for women (see Chapter 6; also Andres Bellamy and Guppy 1991). We think, however, this constant increase in women's university degree attainment will not continue unchecked. At some point, the economic rewards women accrue from degrees will lessen. The advantages of staying in school and completing a university degree will decrease, particularly because of rising tuition in most provinces. Some might argue that women may be more likely than men to pursue higher education credentials for non-economic reasons, but this explanation is less plausible when the recent surge of women into economically rewarding fields of study is considered (see below).

5.4 COLLEGE ENROLMENTS BY PROGRAM TYPE

As with the universities, internal divisions exist at the community college level. Most full-time college students are enrolled in an array of career programs, ranging from management and administration (with 9,026 diplomas awarded in 1991–92) to nursing (6,900 diplomas) to transportation technologies (219 diplomas). In the 1993–94 academic year, more than 250,000 full-time students were enrolled in career programs, with a further 125,000 in university transfer programs (see Figure 5.6). In 1970 the university transfer enrolments composed 37% of full-time college enrolments.[4] This figure dropped to 28% in 1994. In absolute numbers the size of university transfer programs has expanded, but as a proportion of the college enrolment, full-time university transfer enrolments represent a smaller part of the college system.

FIGURE 5.6

FULL-TIME COLLEGE ENROLMENT, BY PROGRAM TYPE, 1970 TO 1994

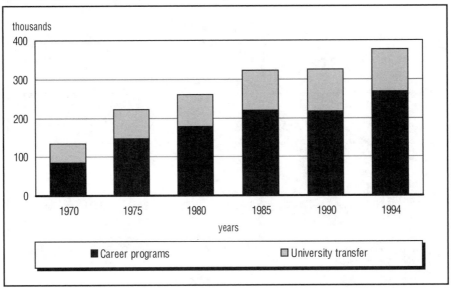

Source: Statistics Canada, Education in Canada, various years.

5.5 FULL-TIME AND PART-TIME ENROLMENTS

To this point we have examined several features that crosscut postsecondary study: college versus university enrolments, types of degree or diploma programs, and provincial variations. A further differentiation occurs between full- and part-time students. Here we look at the relative proportions of part-time and full-time students in colleges and universities and we examine how these proportions change over time.

The ratios of full- to part-time students attending colleges and universities remained nearly constant from 1983–84 to 1993–94. Counting both full-time and part-time students, the ratio of university to college enrolments remained 60:40 (see Figure 5.7). There was also little change in the proportions of students studying full- or part-time either at college or university. Over the decade, the percentages at the college level stayed virtually identical in both the full- and part-time track. At the university level, there was a slight rise in full-time students (up just over 2%) and a corresponding decline in part-time students. Also of note, college students were less likely to study part-time than were university students. In 1983–84 the ratio of full-time to part-time students at universities was 1.6 to 1.0, while for college students it was approximately 2.2 to 1.0. This spread remained in 1993–94.

FIGURE 5.7

POSTSECONDARY ENROLMENT, BY TYPE OF INSTITUTION, CANADA, 1983–84 AND 1993–94

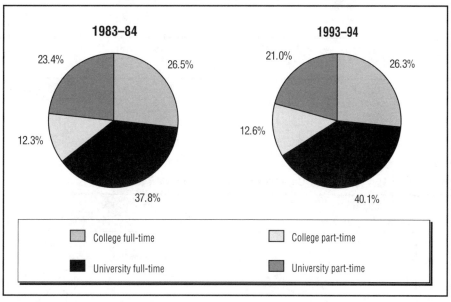

Source: Statistics Canada, Catalogue no. 81-229.

The apparent trend toward more full-time study at university, hinted at in Figure 5.7, is confined to that recent 10-year interval (see Figure 5.8). Contrasting full-time with part-time university enrolments from 1962 to 1996, the absolute gap grew almost continuously, except in the late 1970s when full-time enrolment stalled but part-time enrolment kept increasing. Of the 185,000 university students in 1962, 23% were studying part-time. By 1996, 30% of the 820,410 students enrolled at university were studying part-time. A look at the ratio of part-time versus full-time enrolments over this period shows relative changes more directly (see Figure 5.9). In 1962, part-time enrolments were only about 30% of full-time enrolments. Part-timers increased among the ranks of university students until 1982, when their numbers began to fall.

FIGURE 5.8

UNIVERSITY ENROLMENT, 1962 TO 1996

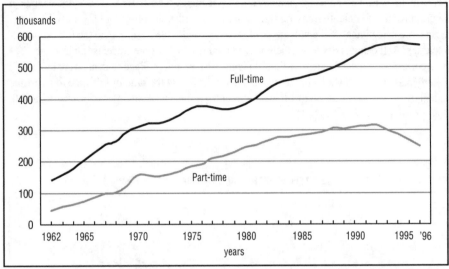

Source: Statistics Canada, *Historical Compendium of Education Statistics from Confederation to 1975,* 1978; Statistics Canada, *Education in Canada,* various years; Statistics Canada, *Education Quarterly Review,* various years.

FIGURE 5.9

RATIO OF PART-TIME TO FULL-TIME UNIVERSITY ENROLMENT, 1962 TO 1996

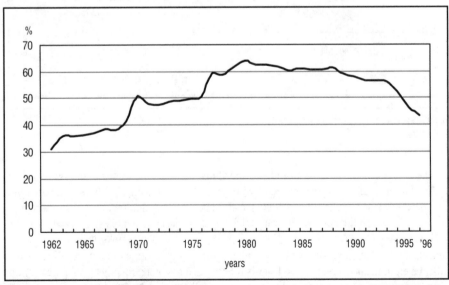

Source: Statistics Canada, *Historical Compendium of Education Statistics from Confederation to 1975,* 1978; Statistics Canada, *Education in Canada,* various years.

There are several possible explanations for why students study part time (see also Bélanger and Omiecinski 1987). As the cost of university increases (for example tuition, books, accommodation) more students are combining paid work and study, and this is easier to do by attending school part time. Additionally, many students who find steady, reliable jobs, or even the prospects of such, hold on to them while they are in school, perhaps for fear they will have no job prospects if they attend school full time. For women especially, raising children in combination with full-time studies is very difficult and so many single parents who are upgrading their education find that studying part time while raising a family is the best option.

Headcount enrolment obscures another pattern that is changing the postsecondary system. Over time students' course loads have changed (Lynd 1994). More full-time students are taking courses year-round, rather than just in the typical September to April academic year. Students often have less than the five courses that universities consider necessary for full-time status, but they are nevertheless classified as full-time students. Furthermore, many students switch between full-time and part-time studies throughout the year, a process that universities have inadvertently encouraged by increasingly offering single term or semester courses. This makes it, for example, much easier to be a full-time student for four months and a part-time student for the remaining eight. As well, as the cost of university study escalates, many students rely on student loans. To qualify for loans, students must carry the equivalent of a full-time course load (but the definition of this is not necessarily what any individual university would consider to be a full-time load).

Over the last three decades, the number of women studying part-time has increased substantially compared with men (see Figure 5.10). Now 1 out of 3 female university students is part-time (33%) while 1 out of 4 male students is part-time (25%). This represents a reversal from the early 1960s when more men than women studied part time at university. At the college level, there are also more women than men among part-time students.

FIGURE 5.10

TOTAL PART-TIME UNIVERSITY ENROLMENT, BY SEX, 1962 TO 1993

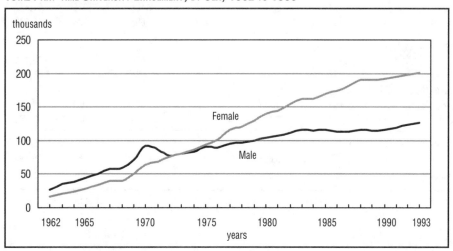

Source: Statistics Canada, *Historical Compendium of Education Statistics from Confederation to 1975,* 1978; Statistics Canada, *Education in Canada,* various years.

5.6 TEACHING STAFF

Yet another way in which colleges and universities differ is with respect to their teaching staffs. Colleges have historically focused more attention on teaching and less attention on research than have universities. One indicator of this is the ratio of full-time students to full-time faculty. At the college level the ratio in 1993–94 was 13.9 full-time students for every full-time faculty member. At the university level the corresponding ratio was 15.5 (see Renner and Mwenifumbo 1995).

University teaching staff is divided by rank, from full professors to ranks below assistant professors (for example instructors). In 1960–61, 25% of university teachers were full professors, but by 1994–95 the percentage had risen to 41.3, indicating that the professoriate is aging. The number of women among university faculty has also changed dramatically since 1960–61 (see Table 5.1). In that year, 11.4% of full-time university teachers were women, but by 1994–95 the share had increased to 22.7% (see also Hollands 1988). Comparable information for colleges is unavailable.

TABLE 5.1
FULL-TIME UNIVERSITY TEACHERS, BY RANK, SEX AND YEAR

	Full professor	Associate professor	Assistant professor	Rank below assistant professor	Other	All ranks
1960–1961						
Men	1,554	1,319	1,740	901	205	**5,719**
Women	68	143	233	290	2	**736**
1970–1971						
Men	4,677	5,948	7,736	2,181	930	**21,472**
Women	166	522	1,241	888	323	**3,140**
1980–1981						
Men	9,328	10,950	5,594	1,029	1,229	**28,130**
Women	476	1,600	1,773	668	652	**5,169**
1990–1991						
Men	12,693	10,215	5,329	672	949	**29,858**
Women	1,047	2,488	2,675	659	694	**7,563**
1994–1995						
Men	13,266	9,653	4,477	430	268	**28,094**
Women	1,582	3,101	2,810	466	308	**8,267**

Source: Statistics Canada, *Education in Canada*, Catalogue no. 81-229-XPB, various years; Statistics Canada, unpublished data.

5.7   FIELDS OF STUDY

Theorists of social change, whether using the rhetoric of the knowledge society, the postmodern world order or some other image, suggest that Western nations are in a state of significant social transformation. Some advocates of these ideas see this period of change as similar to the radical shift in social structures that occurred at the peak of the Industrial Revolution. How well do such ideas reflect the changes occurring in Canadian universities? One way to answer this question is by examining how the fields of study from which students are graduating have changed over the past two decades.

The only substantial growth occurred in the social sciences, which had 31.2% of all university graduates in 1975 and 39.8% in 1993. Education was the only field that experienced a significant decline, with 25.5% of all graduates in 1975 dropping to 17.6% in 1993. In the other major fields of study—agriculture and biological sciences, engineering and applied sciences, health professions, humanities, and mathematics and physical sciences—the proportion of graduates in 1993 is almost identical to 1975 (see Figure 5.11).

FIGURE 5.11

DISTRIBUTION OF BACHELOR'S AND FIRST PROFESSIONAL DEGREES, BY FIELD OF STUDY, 1975 TO 1993

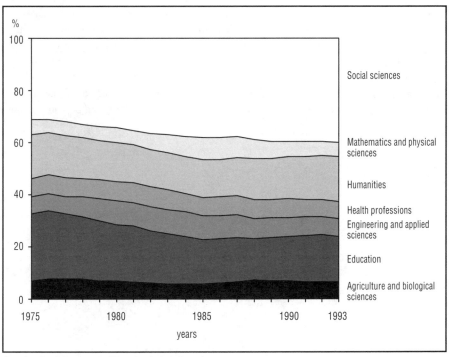

Source: Statistics Canada, *Education in Canada,* various years.

Exactly how to interpret this change, or lack of it, is not easy. Perhaps the time period is too short and significant change has occurred previously. Alternatively, perhaps the change that the prophets are perceiving is not so radical after all (see Gordon 1988 for such a view). Or, perhaps the universities are just out of sync. Educational institutions are often described as exceedingly bureaucratic and perhaps the excessive formality and rigidity of universities has impeded change (for example Lawton 1995; Marchak 1996).

5.7.1 Gender distribution across fields of study

Although we saw above that women are attaining a greater number of degrees, especially at the undergraduate level, there remain many fields in which men still dominate. This segregation is consequential for many reasons. First, some fields of study lead more directly than others to labour market opportunities (for example medicine or social work versus humanities or social science). Second, the jobs offered in different fields vary in terms of earning potential and stability (for example medicine versus social work). Third, men and women have traditionally clustered in specific fields, which has affected labour market outcomes of both sexes via supply and demand factors. Specifically, one reason why women earn less may be that they compete with each other in a limited number of fields. A sex-segregated labour market with a narrow set of jobs seen as "women's work" can lead to an excess supply of women looking for work in certain fields, which limits their power to bargain for higher wages.

Sex segregation by field of study in higher education is a precursor to similar segregation in the labour market. Table 5.2 shows the percentage of women attaining undergraduate degrees by detailed field of study in 1982 and 1993. Overall, as the bottom row of the table shows, women attained more degrees than men in both years. In many fields the gender balance was highly skewed, with the greatest disparities occurring in female-dominated disciplines, namely nursing, household science, and rehabilitation medicine. Although there have been modest swings in each field toward greater gender balance, few men are choosing to move into female-dominated fields. Furthermore, notice that in several fields, including sociology, social work, and psychology, the gender imbalance is growing.[5]

TABLE 5.2

PERCENTAGE OF UNDERGRADUATE DEGREES RECEIVED BY WOMEN, BY FIELD OF STUDY, CANADA, 1982 AND 1993

	1982	1993
Engineering	7.2	14.3
Physics	11.6	16.8
Dental studies and research	20.5	38.0
Forestry	20.7	19.5
Architecture	20.7	33.8
Geology	25.0	27.5
Computer science	26.4	19.6
Economics	28.5	35.1
Chemistry	29.3	41.9
Business and commerce	34.2	46.9
Mathematics	35.7	40.7
Geography	36.2	41.6
Medical studies and research	36.7	44.0
Political science	37.5	44.5
Agriculture	37.6	50.3
Law	37.7	51.2
Zoology	41.7	52.5
Veterinary medicine	44.6	57.3
History	46.8	48.7
Landscape architecture	47.1	57.0
Biology	47.4	55.3
Physical education	54.4	53.3
Fine and applied arts	63.7	66.4
Pharmacy	65.1	61.1
Sociology	68.6	74.6
Psychology	73.2	77.5
Education	74.3	74.7
Languages	76.0	75.0
Social work	77.8	84.2
Rehabilitation medicine	90.1	84.9
Household science	97.0	90.5
Nursing	97.2	95.2
Total undergraduate degrees received by women (%)	**51**	**57.2**

Source: Statistics Canada, *Education in Canada*, various years.

At the other extreme, engineering, physics, and forestry remain male-dominated fields of study and in computer science the percentage of women degree recipients actually fell from 26.4% to 19.6%. Smaller decreases in female enrolment occurred in forestry, physical education, pharmacy, and languages.

Examining changes in the gender distribution across 32 fields is difficult to do. One way to summarize change is to calculate an index of dissimilarity. This is a measure of the degree to which two groups, here men and women, are unevenly distributed over a set of categories. The interpretation of the index of dissimilarity is straightforward. It shows what percentage of men (or women) would have to change fields of study in order to make the distributions equal to the proportions of degrees awarded to women and men in any specific year. In the early 1980s, over 40% of men (or women) would have had to change fields of study to balance the gender distribution in all fields of study (see Figure 5.12). By the early 1990s, the percentage who would have had to change places went down to about 37, but overall there was little change.

When examining fields of study at the master's level (see Table 5.3), the available data restrict our examination to eight general fields of study, but also extend the series to cover 1970 to 1992. Mainly because the categories are much cruder, the extent of gender imbalance is not as marked as in Table 5.2. Engineering is the most unbalanced field, but there has been slow movement toward a more even distribution.

Figure 5.12

Index of Dissimilarity Scores for Undergraduate Degree Attainment, by Field of Study, 1982 to 1993

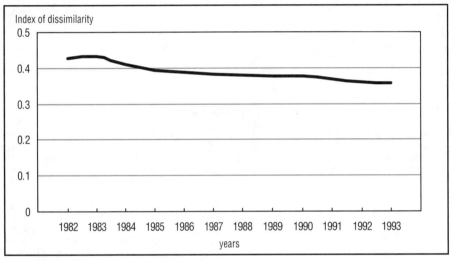

Source: Statistics Canada, *Education in Canada,* various years.

Table 5.3

Percentage of Master's Degrees Received by Women, by Field of Study, Canada, 1970, 1981 and 1992

Field of study	Year		
	1970	1981	1992
Agriculture and biological sciences	20	38	48
Education	24	49	68
Engineering and applied sciences	2	8	16
Fine and applied arts	62	53	59
Health professions	34	61	69
Humanities	36	55	56
Mathematics and physical sciences	10	16	25
Social sciences	26	33	44
Total	**26**	**39**	**48**

Source: Statistics Canada, *Education in Canada,* Catalogue no. 81-229-XPB, various years.

Over time, as Figure 5.13 reveals, the gender balance across fields of study has been relatively stable, with little systematic change in any direction. There was fluctuation year to year (the line is more jagged than in Figure 5.12) but this instability occurred mainly because fewer master's degrees than undergraduate degrees were awarded. Even though women have attained an almost equal share of master's degrees in the recent past, the gender distributions across and within fields of study at the master's level have remained stable.

FIGURE 5.13

INDEX OF DISSIMILARITY SCORES FOR MASTER'S DEGREE ATTAINMENT, BY FIELD OF STUDY, 1970 TO 1992

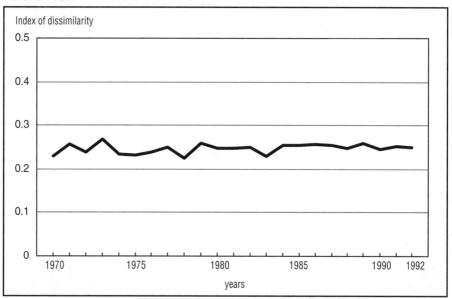

Source: Statistics Canada, *Education in Canada,* various years.

Women have increased their PhD attainment in recent decades (discussed in Chapter 6) but they still receive only about one-third of all PhDs awarded annually (see Table 5.4). Again, engineering is the field with the greatest gender imbalance. Some fields show strong evidence of movement toward gender balance, but in others, such as education and health, the representation of women has actually increased well above women's overall attainment rate at the PhD level.

FIGURE 5.14

INDEX OF DISSIMILARITY SCORES FOR PHD ATTAINMENT, BY FIELD OF STUDY, 1970 TO 1992

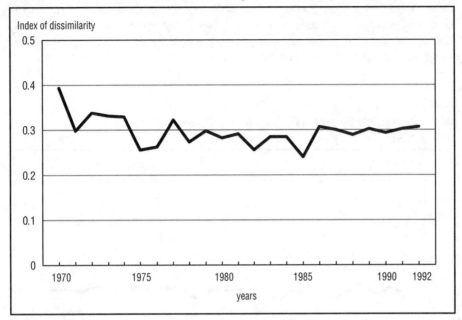

Source: Census of Canada, 1991.

TABLE 5.4

PERCENTAGE OF PHDS RECEIVED BY WOMEN, BY FIELD OF STUDY, CANADA, 1970, 1981 AND 1992

Field of study	Year		
	1970	1981	1992
Agriculture and biological sciences	9	23	28
Education	10	43	54
Engineering and applied sciences	0	4	11
Fine and applied arts	33	71	48
Health professions	8	29	41
Humanities	27	37	38
Mathematics and physical sciences	4	10	17
Social sciences	14	30	44
Total	**9**	**24**	**32**

Source: Statistics Canada, *Education in Canada,* Catalogue no. 81-229-XPB, various years.

These shifts both toward and away from gender balance suggest that between 1970 and 1992 there was little overall change in the evenness of the gender distributions (see Figure 5.14). In the early 1970s the index of dissimilarity was around 0.3, indicating that 30% of women or men would have had to change places to achieve gender equity. By the early 1990s the figure was almost identical.

5.8   SUMMARY

The vision of postsecondary schooling held by the post-industrialists has not, in many respects, yet been borne out. Computer science and other high tech fields have expanded in recent decades, but they have been outpaced by enrolments in business and related fields (see Chapter 6). Women have moved into predominately male fields, but much gender segregation remains. Perhaps most significantly, the phenomenon of continually rising enrolments has now stalled. The era of growth in postsecondary schooling, which gave many observers a sense of unlimited possibilities, has come to a close.

Yet, one major aspect of post-industrialism has come to fruition. As exemplified in the shift of the term "higher education" to "postsecondary education," the underlying organization of schooling beyond the secondary level has undergone a process of greater differentiation over the last four decades. More and more students are entering the postsecondary system, finding before them a greater variety of paths to travel.

Postsecondary education increasingly has the character of a vertical mosaic, a richly differentiated tapestry of institutions and programs. This growing variety is reflected in publications such as the *Maclean's* survey of universities or various guides to university life in Canada. Besides this inter-institutional differentiation there is a remarkable stratification within institutions. Institutions are internally layered with a hierarchy of fields of study. Higher education is organized primarily by discipline, and these disciplines are unequal with respect to power, prestige, and economic payoffs (Davies and Guppy 1997a; Allen 1996). As we show in Chapter 6, this stratification has consequences for labour market outcomes.

Beyond this differentiation among the institutions in which students study, there are key distinctions among the ways in which students choose to study. Chief among these is the decision to pursue full-time or part-time study. Since the early 1980s there has been a growing tendency for students, particularly in universities, to choose full-time studies over part-time studies.

From this profile of higher education, we turn to the issue of income and employment outcomes, focusing on the experiences of graduates from different fields of study. As tuition fees rise and as the prospects of attaining good jobs tighten, questions about the value of postsecondary education have risen.

ENDNOTES

1. Reviews of the postsecondary system include Association of Universities and Colleges of Canada 1996; Clark 1991; Gilbert 1991; McDowell 1991; Pike 1970; Committee of Presidents of Universities 1971; Smith 1991; West 1988, 1993.

2. Statistics Canada recently published preliminary figures showing full-time enrolments going down in 1995 and up in 1996, but very modestly. Part-time university enrolments continue to fall (Statistics Canada, *Education Quarterly Review* 1996, 3, 3: 64). See also Statistics Canada, *The Daily*, January 8, 1996 and December 4, 1996.

3. In this chapter we use the term *differentiation,* common in the research literature on organizations, to highlight variability among types of postsecondary institutions (for example colleges and universities, but also research-intensive universities versus undergraduate liberal arts universities). Various programs and study streams (for example full-time versus part-time) further differentiate the system.

4. The term university transfer is potentially confusing. While students in this stream take many courses that could be transferred to university, a great number of students never make the transition, and indeed, never intended to make the transition. University transfer programs offer diplomas in a variety of fields, including criminology, social work, and applied arts.

5. Discussion of gender imbalances in higher education centre almost exclusively on shifting more women into traditional male streams (Beauchamp and Feldberg 1991; Canadian Committee on Women in Engineering 1992; Gaskell and McLaren 1991; Gilbert and Pomfret 1991; Industry, Science and Technology Canada 1991, Volume 1, and 1992, Volume 2).

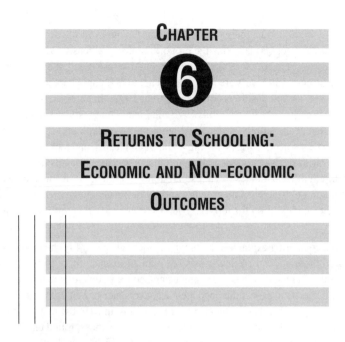

CHAPTER

6

RETURNS TO SCHOOLING: ECONOMIC AND NON-ECONOMIC OUTCOMES

As more Canadians obtain higher levels of formal education, and as our economy changes, does schooling increasingly determine people's income and employment status? Does an individual's involvement in democratic or political issues in the modern world vary by level of education? In this chapter we examine the connections of this type between education, labour market outcomes, and civic participation. We begin with economic issues and turn to non-economic issues toward the end of the chapter.

6.1 ECONOMIC RETURNS TO SCHOOLING

In previous chapters we argued that earlier this century formal schooling played less of a role in securing steady, well-paying employment. Especially for men, jobs that did not require substantial formal schooling were plentiful in the forestry, mining, and manufacturing sectors. But economic changes over recent decades are leading many to suspect that formal education is becoming more of a prerequisite for individual prosperity, and that inequalities among Canadians of different educational backgrounds may be growing. As knowledge work becomes more central to many forms of economic activity, and as jobs shift proportionately out of manufacturing and into the service sector, opportunities for workers without advanced credentials may be increasingly limited. The new service occupations, according to many observers, are polarized between "good jobs" in professional, managerial and technological areas, and "bad jobs" in retail sales, service work, and the like (Krahn and Lowe 1990; Myles 1993). The "good" occupations require people with educational qualifications, while those who lack credentials are left with low-paying jobs and extended bouts of unemployment. According to this view, education sorts young workers into increasingly diverging career paths, which vary widely in terms of income potential and opportunities for promotion (Betcherman and Morissette 1994; Bowlby 1996).

The reasons why highly educated workers would be favoured in the new economy are disputed. Human capital theorists claim that the proportion of skill-intensive jobs is rising, and since better educated workers are more skilled and productive (as signalled by their degrees, diplomas, and certificates), employers are increasingly apt to hire applicants with credentials, especially for the better paying positions (Blau and Ferber 1992). In contrast, proponents of a credentialist explanation (for example Collins 1979) maintain that most marketable skills are learned on the job, but as the supply of educated labour grows, employers increasingly use credentials as convenient sorting devices. Facing a glut of applicants, and lacking the time and knowledge to make hiring decisions, credential requirements become a socially accepted device to limit the pool of eligible candidates. As a result, employers select more educated workers, whatever the skill content of a job. The growing supply of postsecondary school graduates coupled with the keen competition for jobs only serves to intensify this process (Hunter and Leiper 1993).

Despite offering competing explanations for why credentials pay off in the labour market, both human capital theorists and credentialists see education as an increasingly powerful determinant of employment and income. A counter-perspective points to other changes in the economy that would lead us to expect the opposite—a convergence of labour market outcomes among workers of varying levels of education. In the 1960s and 1970s, many if not most university graduates, especially from the humanities and social sciences, found employment in the expanding public sector in areas such as education, social services, health, and government administration (Novek 1985). However, three subsequent economic shifts may have altered how education is rewarded in the labour market (Morissette, Myles and Picot 1993).

First, over the past 15 years, the public sector's share of all full-time jobs has declined. Most newly created jobs are in business and retail services. This trend raises uncertainties for many postsecondary graduates, since their qualifications are more consistently rewarded in public sector jobs than in the market-driven private sector. School credentials might, in aggregate, now command a smaller premium than in the past. Second, the proportion of part-time employment has risen. This too affects the education–income link because part-time jobs tend to reward school credentials at lower rates. Third, there is now greater age stratification in the labour market. As the educational qualifications of younger job-seekers outstrip those of older workers, the humbler opportunities facing young people may counteract those forces that inflate returns to higher education.

Two trends tend to further complicate our assessment of economic returns to schooling. First, approximately 55% of current postsecondary graduates are female. Though women are continually moving into higher levels of schooling and non-traditional fields of study, women in aggregate continue to earn less than men. This may be due to a combination of factors: domestic duties hindering women from accumulating continual years of employment experience; women's segregation into occupations with limited career opportunities; and employer discrimination. Whatever the cause, the possibility of lower returns to schooling among women causes us to reconsider the connections between school credentials and job market success.

A second issue complicating our assessment of economic returns to schooling is that students' labour market outcomes vary substantially within each education level. Averages mask significant variations about the mean. For instance, university graduates fare better than high school graduates on average, as we will see below, but neither group is at all monolithic. It appears that labour market outcomes among university graduates, for instance, are becoming increasingly variable (Davies, Mosher and O'Grady 1996). One major source of variation is field of study. Not all fields offer the same economic payoffs and, consequently, a clear hierarchy occurs among fields (Davies and Guppy 1997a). Degrees from professional faculties, engineering, and business typically provide superior economic prospects and, not surprisingly, these fields are much more sought after than the humanities or social sciences (McNaughton and Thorp 1992).

These factors lead us to expect that education may be an increasingly important determinant of an individual's labour market prospects, but the link between schooling and job success is likely complicated by economic shifts, gender, and differences between fields of study.[1] In the following sections we examine these connections. Our data consist of time series that pool individuals of all ages, cross-sectional data from the 1991 Census and comparisons of successive cohorts of 25- to 29- and 35- to 39-year-olds.[2]

6.1.1 A more educated labour force

The Canadian labour force has become increasingly educated (see Table 6.1). Younger workers have more postsecondary education than those in older age groups. Women show the most dramatic difference—a 10% increase from the 50-year-old group to the 30-year-old group. Older workers are more likely to have no school credentials—compared with the youngest age group, 8.6% more men and 15.2% more women had no credentials. The lower number of workers without a high school diploma in recent cohorts shows Canada is moving ahead with an ever-more educated populace. University graduates, as discussed in Chapter 5, are shifting their fields of study to business subjects and away from the humanities and education (see Table 6.2). University graduates are increasingly business-trained and bound for the private sector.

TABLE 6.1

PERCENTAGE DISTRIBUTION OF WORKERS BY EDUCATION LEVEL, BY AGE AND SEX, 1991

Highest level of education	Men			Women		
	Age 30	Age 40	Age 50	Age 30	Age 40	Age 50
No degree, certificate or diploma	23.7	23.0	32.3	16.7	21.6	31.9
Secondary school graduation certificate	24.2	21.7	17.4	27.8	29.0	23.7
Trades certificate or diploma	18.0	18.5	18.6	10.6	9.4	9.4
College certificate or diploma	16.1	13.9	10.4	23.0	18.2	16.4
University[1]	15.5	17.2	14.0	19.7	18.2	15.3
Professional degree	0.3	0.5	0.5	0.2	0.2	0.1
Master's, doctorate	2.3	5.1	6.7	2.0	3.5	3.2
Total postsecondary	34.1	36.8	31.7	44.9	40.0	35.0

1.   Includes categories "university below BA," "BA," "university above BA."
Source: Census of Canada, 1991.

TABLE 6.2

PERCENTAGE DISTRIBUTION OF UNIVERSITY-EDUCATED WORKERS BY FIELD OF STUDY, BY AGE AND SEX, 1991

Field of study	Men			Women		
	Age 30	Age 40	Age 50	Age 30	Age 40	Age 50
Education	8.5	13.5	18.9	20.2	32.6	43.7
Humanities[1]	8.5	11.7	12.3	14.9	17.8	17.6
Social Sciences	18.1	19.2	15.5	22.1	18.7	14.0
Commerce[2]	24.5	18.9	16.0	18.1	9.2	6.4
Agriculture and Biology	3.8	4.6	3.4	5.2	4.6	3.2
Engineering	20.9	19.0	21.4	3.1	1.3	0.6
Nursing	0.2	0.4	0.2	5.1	7.0	7.6
Other Health Professions	1.7	1.5	2.0	4.7	3.5	3.4
Mathematics and Physical Sciences	13.7	11.2	10.1	6.5	5.2	3.6

1. Includes Fine Arts categories.
2. Includes Secretarial.
   Table excludes "other" fields; these fields do not exceed 0.4% in any column.
Source: Census of Canada, 1991.

6.1.2 Diminishing returns to education at all levels

As successive age cohorts attain more schooling, are the economic benefits of education diminishing? Table 6.3 shows labour market outcomes for successive cohorts of high school and university graduates, aged 25 to 29, from 1979 to 1993. We distinguish full-time, full-year employees from all workers to indirectly compare disparities among earners in "good jobs" versus those working in more marginal positions. This table shows that all groups, except female university graduates, experienced declining real incomes and employment rates. For instance, among full-time, full-year workers, men's real income dropped either $6,250 (see the high school column) or $8,750 (see the university column), a decline of roughly 25% over four cohorts. The real income of female high school graduates fell more than 10%, though female university graduates who worked full time, full year actually saw a small increase. This last trend likely illustrates the movement of women into higher-paying fields such as law, medicine and commerce. We turn to the disparity figures in the tables a little later.

All groups suffered a net increase in unemployment rates between 1979 and 1993, despite employment fluctuations caused by business cycles (see Table 6.4). This declining economic situation was experienced by workers of all education levels, reflecting the stagnation of the economy as a whole.

TABLE 6.3

DISPARITY IN EARNINGS, COMPARING HIGH SCHOOL GRADUATES AND UNIVERSITY GRADUATES BY SEX ACROSS COHORTS, 1993 CONSTANT DOLLARS

	High school		University		Disparity	
	All workers	Full-time/ full-year workers	All workers	Full-time/ full-year workers	All workers	Full-time/ full-year workers
Aged 25–29						
Men						
Cohort 1 (1979)	32,000	35,250	37,750	45,000	5,750 (.85)	9,750 (0.78)
Cohort 2 (1984)	27,250	33,000	32,000	40,500	4,750 (.85)	7,500 (0.81)
Cohort 3 (1989)	27,500	31,750	30,250	36,750	2,750 (.91)	5,000 (0.86)
Cohort 4 (1993)	23,250	29,000	29,250	36,750	6,000 (.79)	7,750 (0.79)
Women						
Cohort 1 (1979)	18,250	24,750	25,000	32,000	6,750 (.73)	7,250 (0.77)
Cohort 2 (1984)	17,000	23,500	25,500	32,750	8,500 (.67)	9,250 (0.72)
Cohort 3 (1989)	17,000	21,750	25,000	32,250	8,000 (.68)	10,500 (0.67)
Cohort 4 (1993)	16,000	21,500	24,750	33,000	8,750 (.65)	11,500 (0.65)
One decade later						
Men						
Cohort 1 (1989)	35,250	38,500	53,500	57,000	22,500 (.66)	19,500 (0.68)
Cohort 2 (1993)	32,500	37,250	46,500	52,000	19,500 (.70)	14,750 (0.72)
Women						
Cohort 1 (1989)	20,500	26,000	35,500	42,000	15,000 (.58)	16,000 (0.62)
Cohort 2 (1993)	18,500	24,500	32,250	41,250	13,750 (.57)	16,000 (0.59)

Source: Crompton, 1995.

TABLE 6.4

UNEMPLOYMENT RATES, COMPARING HIGH SCHOOL GRADUATES AND UNIVERSITY GRADUATES ACROSS COHORTS

	Men (%)			Women (%)		
	High school	University	Difference	High school	University	Difference
Cohort aged 25–29						
1979	6.5	4.1	2.4	9.4	5.7	3.7
1984	12.6	6.1	6.5	12.6	7.5	5.1
1989	8.5	4.1	4.4	10.3	5.1	5.2
1993	15.0	6.8	8.2	13.9	7.1	6.8
Cohort aged 35–39						
1989	6.4	3.0	3.4	7.5	4.3	3.2
1993	10.9	5.5	5.4	10.5	6.2	4.3

Source: Crompton, 1995.

6.1.3 Comparing education levels in 1991: Does school pay?

In light of diminishing returns to schooling, do highly educated workers nevertheless earn greater incomes compared with their less-educated peers? An examination of 1991 Census data showing average 1990 annual earnings by education level shows a linear relation between income and education (see Table 6.5). We use the mean income for bachelor's graduates as a base for comparisons. Canadians with no credentials (high school drop-outs) earned the least, only two-thirds of the base income. Each group thereafter approached the base, and groups with education levels above the bachelor's degree earned more. Those with professional degrees, such as doctors and lawyers, enjoyed the highest incomes, earning 1.6 times the income of bachelor's graduates and 2.4 times the income of high school drop-outs. The immediate lesson is that credentials pay off incrementally with each step up the educational hierarchy.

TABLE 6.5

MEAN INCOMES, BY EDUCATION LEVEL (USING BACHELOR OF ARTS AS REFERENCE), 1990

	Mean income ($)	Disparity from Bachelor of Arts degree mean ($)	Net disparity[1] ($)
No degree, certificate or diploma	27,253.2	−13,757.5	−9,580.7
Secondary school graduation certificate	29,151.5	−11,859.2	−6,970.4
Trades certificate or diploma	31,726.0	−9,284.7	−6,305.9
College certificate or diploma	32,394.3	−8,616.4	−5,138.7
University certificate below bachelor level	36,007.5	−5,003.2	−3,177.2
Bachelor's degree	41,010.7	0	0
University certificate above bachelor level	44,819.5	3,808.8	22,238.0
Professional degree	65,107.0	24,096.3	23,525.7
Master's and doctorate	51,709.1	10,698.4	6,289.9

1. Figures derived from multiple regression coefficients; see text for explanation.
Source: Census of Canada, 1991.

This conclusion needs to be qualified, however, since these differing payoffs might partly reflect the different social compositions of workers with various credentials. As we saw in previous chapters, different types of people graduate from different education levels and fields of study. For instance, workers with professional degrees or PhDs are more likely to be older and male than are workers with bachelor's degrees. High school drop-outs tend to be older, to work in industries that pay less and offer more part-time and seasonal employment, and to hail from regions such as the Atlantic provinces. Since women earn less than men, younger workers earn less than older workers and those from the Atlantic provinces earn less than people in Ontario and British Columbia, portions of the income disparities between levels of education may be attributable to gender, age, region, and/or industry. We are thus interested in the "net effect" of education, that is, the pure returns to school controlling for these differences in social composition.

To determine education's net effect, we calculated a multiple regression equation for income, with education levels as our main independent variables (bachelor's graduates serve as the reference category). We are interested in the partial coefficients for education controlling for age, gender, region, ethnicity, number of hours and weeks worked, industry and occupation. In the right-hand column of Table 6.5, we present estimated net returns to education level, in the form of partial regression coefficients, which represent the disparities for each educational category from the average income of the bachelor's degree category. We compare these figures with the "total disparity"—the middle column of figures—calculated with no controls.

While all of the net disparities are smaller than the total disparities, the differences between education levels continue to be substantial, and the ranking of education levels remains intact. For instance, the net disparity between bachelor's graduates and high school drop-outs is almost $10,000. High school graduates earn almost $7,000 less, and college graduates earn $5,000 less than the base. The advantage of having a professional degree remains striking, as professionals earn almost $24,000 more than bachelor's graduates, net of other factors. Overall, these calculations suggest that credentials pay large "pure returns" in the labour market, regardless of the different types of people who attain these credentials and the broad types of occupations and industries they enter.

6.1.4 Comparing education levels over time: Widening disparities?

Given these pronounced income disparities between levels of education, is there evidence that these inequalities have grown over time? To address this question we return to the cohort data on university and high school graduates.

Between 1979 and 1993, income disparities fluctuated for male university and high school graduates aged 25 to 29 (see last two columns of Table 6.3 for constant dollar disparities and income ratios). Dollar-figure differences changed little among men in either category. Among women in the "all workers" category, the disparity grew between 1979 and 1984 only, and remained roughly constant thereafter. For women working full time and full year, the disparity widened steadily over the four cohorts, increasing by $4,250 in total. In this category, the income ratio of high school graduates to university graduates fell from 0.77 in 1979 to 0.65 in 1993. These data offer some evidence that income disparities between university and high school graduates are growing among women.[3]

Comparing income levels of college graduates to those of university graduates can also help us assess education's economic returns (see Figure 6.1). Between 1971 and 1992, university graduates earned more in all years, but the ratio of college graduates' median income to university graduates' median income fluctuated with little discernible trend. When the ratios for men and women are separated (see Figure 6.2) there is still no discernible pattern. Despite much fluctuation, the ratios for both men and women in 1994 are nearly identical to those in 1971. The male ratio is higher than the female ratio in most years, especially between 1987 and 1994, showing that disparities between university educated and college educated workers are greater among women (on the male–female wage gap see also Guppy 1989; Wannell 1990; Wannell and Caron 1995).

FIGURE 6.1

RATIO OF COMMUNITY COLLEGE GRADUATES' MEDIAN INCOME TO UNIVERSITY GRADUATES',
1971 TO 1992

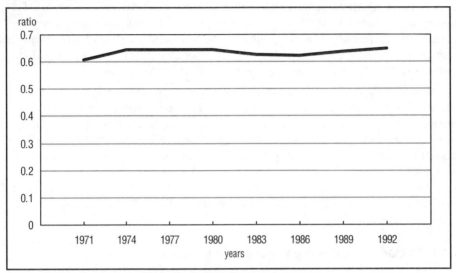

Source: Statistics Canada, *Income Distributions by Size in Canada,* various years.

FIGURE 6.2

RATIO OF COMMUNITY COLLEGE GRADUATES' MEDIAN INCOME TO UNIVERSITY GRADUATES',
BY SEX, 1971 TO 1994

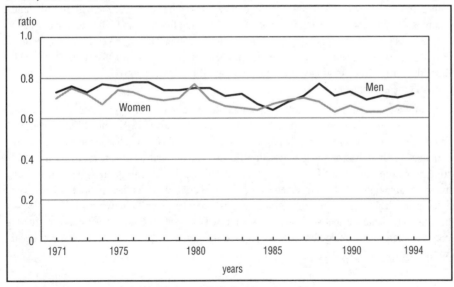

Source: Statistics Canada, *Income Distributions by Size in Canada,* various years.

We are also interested in whether unemployment is related to education level, and whether there are any trends over time. From 1975 to 1995, university-educated people had consistently lower unemployment rates than people with elementary school education (see Figure 6.3). This pattern was especially true in the 1990s. When comparing unemployment rates of high school, college, and university graduates, both male and female university graduates had the lowest unemployment rates in all years. High school graduates had the highest rates (Figures 6.4 and 6.5). Employment differences by educational level have been smaller since the peak of the recession in the early 1980s, and rates for high school graduates have drawn closer to college and university graduates, though the gap between college and university has widened somewhat since 1990. It appears, then, that the recession in the early 1990s negatively affected college graduates the most.

FIGURE 6.3

UNEMPLOYMENT RATES, BY LEVEL OF EDUCATION, 1975 TO 1994

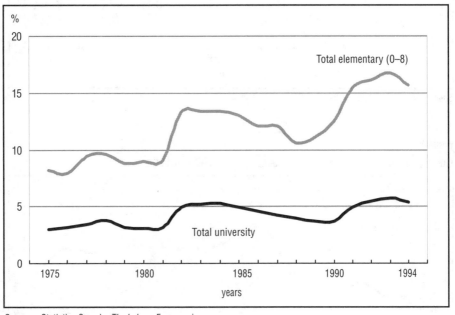

Source: Statistics Canada, *The Labour Force,* various years.

Cohort comparisons of high school and university graduates offer another way to approach the question of unemployment and education level. Data on unemployment rates for four cohorts aged 25 to 29 and two cohorts aged 35 to 39 show that, given fluctuations and net increases of unemployment rates, disparities between high school and university graduates clearly increased for both men and women across all cohorts (see Table 6.4). The table's "difference" columns show that even though disparities fluctuate, the net result is that, from 1979 to 1993, unemployment rates for high school graduates rose at higher rates than for university graduates.

FIGURE 6.4

UNEMPLOYMENT RATES, WOMEN, BY LEVEL OF EDUCATION, 1975 TO 1994

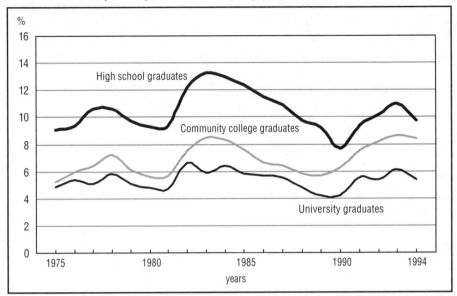

Source: Statistics Canada, *The Labour Force,* various years.

FIGURE 6.5

UNEMPLOYMENT RATES, MEN, BY LEVEL OF EDUCATION, 1975 TO 1994

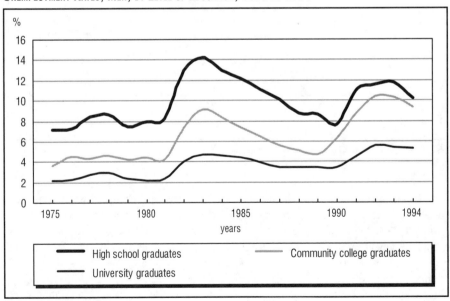

Source: Statistics Canada, *The Labour Force,* various years.

6.1.5 Returns to education over a lifetime

Experience pays in the job market. As workers age and accumulate experience, their incomes typically rise. But what are the effects of education? Do disparities between Canadians of different educational backgrounds grow or shrink over their careers? Does schooling shape one's earning trajectory over a lifetime? To explore the impact of education on earning profiles, we use two data sources: a 10-year follow-up of two recent cohorts of high school and university graduates, and the 1990 earnings of workers with different educational attainments across three age groups.

All groups in the 10-year follow-up study enjoyed rises in real income over the study period (see Table 6.3). However, disparities between high school graduates and university graduates in the first cohort, aged 25 to 29 in 1979, increased sharply by the time the cohort reached ages 35 to 39 in 1989. Among men who worked full time and full year (comparing panels in Table 6.3), disparities increased from $9,750 in 1979 to $19,500 in 1989. As a result, the ratio of high school graduates' income to university graduates' was 0.78 in 1979, but only 0.68 a decade later. Among female full-time, full-year workers (comparing panels again in Table 6.3), the disparity increased from $7,250 to $16,000 over 10 years, dropping the ratio from 0.77 to 0.62.

The second cohort in Table 6.3 (aged 25 to 29 in 1984, and 34 to 38 in 1993) shows similar trends: wider disparities and smaller earning ratios over time, among all groups. Disparities were, however, somewhat smaller in this cohort, especially among men working full time and full year. The disparity here widened by $7,250, and the ratio fell by 0.09, from 0.81 to 0.72. Among women working full time and full year, the disparity grew from $9,250 to $16,000, dropping the ratio from 0.72 to 0.59. Overall, these cohort data indicate that university graduates receive larger wage increases between ages 25 and 29 and ages 34 and 38 than do high school graduates.

Next we return to the 1991 Census to contrast the 1990 incomes of workers with a greater range of educational attainments across three broad age groups. These data indirectly illustrate the effects of education on the age–income relationship and provide a sketch of the lifetime earning profiles that accrue from various credentials. We use the average annual income of bachelor's degree-holders as a base against which we compare the incomes of workers with other educational backgrounds (Tables 6.6 and 6.7). We find that the same monotonic relation holds in nearly every age category for both men and women. At all ages, workers with higher levels of education earn higher incomes. The range of income ratios was more extreme among women, indicating that their incomes are more differentiated by schooling. This is especially apparent when one compares, for instance, the incomes of female drop-outs with those of professionals. Of greater significance is the more pronounced income hierarchy that exists among the older groups.[4] In the 25-to-34 age category, the distribution of wages is relatively compressed, likely owing much to the fact that the more-educated have had relatively few years in the job market, hence their education has not yet paid sizable dividends. But among older Canadians, the income ratios of the less-educated fall, while ratios for the more-educated rise, indicating that the effect of education levels on income increases over time.

TABLE 6.6

AVERAGE ANNUAL FULL-TIME EARNINGS FOR MEN, BY EDUCATION LEVEL AND AGE GROUP, ADDING RATIOS USING BACHELOR OF ARTS AS BASE (100%), 1990

	Age groups					
	25–34		35–44		45–54	
Highest level of schooling	($)	%	($)	%	($)	%
No degree, certificate or diploma	25,420	68	30,900	62	32,890	58
Secondary school graduation certificate	29,180	78	37,160	74	41,360	73
Trades certificate or diploma	31,080	83	36,865	74	40,020	70
College certificate or diploma	33,000	88	41,560	83	45,745	80
University certificate below bachelor level	33,625	90	42,965	86	50,435	89
Bachelor's degree	**37,332**	**100**	**50,135**	**100**	**56,860**	**100**
University certificate above bachelor level	38,725	104	51,460	103	57,680	101
Professional degree (MD, LLB)	50,540	135	70,490	141	86,010	151
Master's degree	42,175	113	55,995	112	61,200	108
Earned doctorate	42,160	113	54,390	108	68,020	120
Grand mean	**30,830**	**83**	**39,495**	**79**	**42,530**	**75**

Source: Census of Canada, 1991

TABLE 6.7

AVERAGE ANNUAL FULL-TIME EARNINGS FOR WOMEN, BY LEVEL OF EDUCATION AND AGE GROUP, ADDING RATIOS USING BACHELOR OF ARTS AS BASE (100%), 1990

	Age groups					
	25–34		35–44		45–54	
Highest level of schooling	($)	%	($)	%	($)	%
No degree, certificate or diploma	17,350	58	19,405	52	19,725	50
Secondary school graduation certificate	21,140	71	23,950	64	24,475	62
Trades certificate or diploma	19,965	67	22,905	61	23,840	61
College certificate or diploma	24,340	82	27,575	73	27,980	71
University certificate below bachelor level	26,515	89	31,195	83	32,560	83
Bachelor's degree	**29,790**	**100**	**37,545**	**100**	**39,295**	**100**
University certificate above bachelor level	32,210	108	41,265	110	44,090	112
Professional degree (MD, LLB)	44,180	148	60,630	161	63,025	160
Master's degree	34,005	114	44,535	119	47,865	122
Earned doctorate	37,200	125	48,550	129	52,855	135
Grand mean	**23,115**	**78**	**26,665**	**71**	**26,335**	**67**

Source: Census of Canada, 1991.

6.1.6 Fields of study: Variations in returns to a university degree

Failing to distinguish whether graduates hail from business, law, or the general arts can mask huge differences in school-to-work transitions. In this section we use the same 1991 Census data to examine variations among bachelor's degree holders by field of study, using the bachelor's degree average income as our point of reference.

There are clear disparities among fields of study, though these are not as great as the disparities between levels of education. Across all age groups, for men and women, graduates from generalist areas (humanities, social sciences, and non-specialized sciences) earn below the average, while graduates in specialized programs (such as engineering, medicine, and law) earn more than the average (see Tables 6.8 and 6.9).

TABLE 6.8

AVERAGE ANNUAL FULL-TIME EARNINGS FOR MEN, BY FIELD OF STUDY AND AGE GROUP, ADDING RATIOS USING BACHELOR OF ARTS AS BASE (100%), 1990

| | Age groups | | | | | |
| | 25–34 | | 35–44 | | 45–54 | |
Highest level of schooling	($)	%	($)	%	($)	%
Bachelor's degree	**37,332**	**100**	**50,135**	**100**	**56,860**	**100**
Education	32,200	86	44,195	88	47,495	84
Fine and Applied Arts	24,885	67	36,325	72	49,880	88
Humanities	30,800	83	43,675	87	50,390	89
Social Sciences	36,140	97	50,625	101	59,310	104
Commerce	37,965	102	52,820	105	61,140	108
Agriculture and Biology	33,600	90	44,065	88	47,885	84
Engineering	42,275	113	55,900	111	65,890	116
Nursing	..	...	40,210	80	..	...
Other health professions	39,465	106	46,050	92	54,575	96
Mathematics and Physical Sciences	39,320	105	53,710	107	57,245	101
Professional degree (MD, LLB)	**50,540**	**135**	**70,490**	**141**	**86,010**	**151**

..   not available

...   not applicable

Source: Census of Canada, 1991.

TABLE 6.9

AVERAGE ANNUAL FULL-TIME EARNINGS FOR WOMEN, BY FIELD OF STUDY AND AGE GROUP, ADDING RATIOS USING BACHELOR OF ARTS DEGREE AS BASE (100%), 1990

	Age groups					
	25–34		35–44		45–54	
Highest level of schooling	($)	%	($)	%	($)	%
Bachelor's degree	**29,790**	**100**	**37,545**	**100**	**39,295**	**100**
Education	29,200	98	37,560	100	39,135	100
Fine and Applied Arts	23,660	79	33,215	88	35,385	90
Humanities	26,180	88	36,720	98	38,060	97
Social Science	27,845	93	38,050	101	41,290	105
Commerce	32,460	109	38,445	102	38,765	99
Agriculture and Biology	28,220	95	32,405	86	36,860	94
Engineering	35,180	118	40,585	108	...	...
Nursing	32,735	110	38,005	101	40,955	104
Other health professions	33,140	111	39,770	106	44,710	114
Mathematics and Physical Science	34,630	116	42,225	112	35,585	91
Professional degree (MD, LLB)	**44,180**	**148**	**60,630**	**161**	**63,025**	**160**

... not applicable

Source: Census of Canada, 1991.

These disparities, however, do not grow with age; in fact, the trend is largely opposite to that among levels of schooling. In older age groups, for both men and women, disparities across fields tend to shrink. Humanities and social science graduates, for instance, fare better and improve their relative position with age. These graduates are below the average in the 25-to-34 age group, but are near or above the average in the 45-to-54 age group. The exceptions to this broad trend are those with professional degrees (that is MD, LLB), whose relative incomes are enhanced over time. But, bracketing out this group, the income structure across fields tends to contract in the older age categories. Among women, for instance, the difference between highest and lowest fields is approximately $11,500 in the youngest category; in the oldest group the disparity is about $9,300. Among men, the difference between the highest and lowest fields, excluding professional degrees, stays roughly the same across the age groups in dollar terms, from approximately $17,400 in the youngest grouping to about $18,400 in the oldest. But the ratio of lowest to highest incomes changed across age groups over this period, from 59% to 72%, indicating that the income gap shrinks with age.

The data suggest that many Canadians with generalist degrees begin their careers in lower-paying positions, but over time they partially catch up to, and sometimes surpass, graduates from other fields.[5] This pattern highlights the differences in the labour markets entered by generalists and specialists. Generalists are not trained for particular jobs and lack the occupational networks offered by such professions as law and engineering. Consequently, generalists require more time to gather experience and hunt for good jobs that suit their skills and interests. Once they find such a match, they begin to narrow the income gap.[6]

6.1.7 Returns to education: Gender differences

In our introductory chapter we made a key distinction between "exposure" to education and the actual benefits that accrue from schooling. This issue is most salient in discussions of gender and monetary earnings. Historically, women have earned far less than men, yet as we saw in previous chapters, women have now in many respects surpassed men in terms of educational attainment. Despite this, men on average continue to earn significantly more than women. Controlling for hours worked, women earn 75% to 85% of the average male wage. Much of this gap can be attributed to women's relatively flat earning trajectories over their life course, which cause gender disparities to widen with age (Gunderson and Riddell 1991). In this section we explore how education influences male and female wages. Is the gender gap larger or smaller among Canadians with more or less education? How does education shape the earning trajectories of men compared with women?

A broad method of examining gender differences in returns to education is to see whether a wage gap persists after the amount of education, age, and other relevant variables are taken into account. We regressed 1990 income on a variety of variables, including gender and levels of education to examine the size of the partial coefficient for gender, controlling for education level and other relevant variables (calculations are not shown). We estimate that on average Canadian women in 1990 earned almost $8,700 less than Canadian men, controlling for these key variables. At a general level, then, gender is obviously an important determinant of income independent of education. For a closer look at each gender's returns to education, we turn next to income comparisons within education levels.

Returning to the cohort data used earlier, we see that among recent cohorts of high school graduates and university graduates, aged 25 to 29, men clearly earn more than women (see Table 6.10). When examining the trend across time, we see the wage gap shrinking, especially between male and female university graduates. For instance, in 1979, university educated women earned only 71% of male earnings, which translated into a substantial gap of $13,000. This figure subsequently shrank across each successive cohort. By 1993, women were earning 90% of the male wage, and the wage gap was down to $3,750. Much of this trend is likely due to the on-going movement of women into non-traditional studies such as business, as illustrated in Table 6.2. This narrowing of the male–female wage gap among recent university graduates echoes the findings of the National Graduates Survey (see Davies, Mosher and O'Grady 1996).

Given the smaller wage disparities among younger cohorts, does it appear that education interacts with age to produce different earnings trajectories for men and women? To address this issue we calculated male–female disparities using the data in Tables 6.6 and 6.7. We find that the mean disparity across all education levels increases as one moves from the 25-to-34 age group to the 35-to-44 and 45-to-54 categories. The average disparity of male over female earnings rises from approximately $7,700 to $12,800 to $16,200. This clearly indicates that the wage gap increases with age. Moreover, as Table 6.7 shows, this widening wage gap can be attributed to the fact that women's income profiles are relatively flat. Their grand mean income does not increase from the 35-to-44 group to the 45-to-54 group (in fact there is a slight decrease). In contrast, men's mean income clearly increases across each age category (see Table 6.6).

TABLE 6.10

DISPARITY OF MALE OVER FEMALE EARNINGS FOR FULL-TIME, FULL-YEAR WORKERS, IN 1993 CONSTANT DOLLARS, BY EDUCATION LEVEL AND ACROSS COHORTS

	High school graduates	University graduates
Aged 25–29		
Cohort 1 (1979)	10,500 (0.70)	13,000 (0.71)
Cohort 2 (1984)	9,500 (0.71)	7,750 (0.81)
Cohort 3 (1989)	10,000 (0.69)	4,500 (0.88)
Cohort 4 (1993)	7,500 (0.74)	3,750 (0.90)
One decade later		
Cohort 1 (1989)	12,500 (0.68)	15,000 (0.74)
Cohort 2 (1993)	12,750 (0.66)	10,750 (0.79)

Note: Numbers in parentheses show income ratio of high school graduates to university graduates.
Source: Crompton, 1995.

How do earning profiles interact with education? The data show that postsecondary-educated women have steeper profiles than less-educated women (see Table 6.7). For instance, incomes increased consistently from the youngest age group to the oldest: by $2,400 for women with no credentials, by $3,300 for women with high school diplomas and by $3,900 for women with trade certificates. But for each of these education levels there is little rise in income between the 35-to-44 group and the 45-to-54 group. For women with university degrees, there is a far different story. Earnings increased steadily from the youngest to oldest group, ranging from an increase of about $9,500 for women with bachelor's degrees to an increase of almost $18,800 for women with professional degrees. Further, all the university-level groups showed significant increases moving from the middle to oldest age category.

The immediate lesson is that women's income profiles, both in terms of amounts of income and the increments across age groups, vary greatly by education. Women without postsecondary credentials have smaller incomes that do not rise greatly over their lifetimes. Among the university-educated, women's income patterns tend to more closely resemble those of men, both in terms of relative amounts of income and rises over time.

We can examine this issue in more detail by returning to the data from the 10-year follow-up study of two cohorts of high school and university graduates (see Table 6.10). The data show that the male–female wage gap increased in both cohorts and in both educational categories. Thus, even among more recent cohorts there is evidence that men experience steeper income profiles. Nonetheless, a key finding is that the smallest wage gap was found among the latter cohort of university graduates.

Overall, men continue to earn more than women regardless of their education level, disparities tend to be somewhat smaller among recent cohorts, and university educated women have earning profiles that tend to resemble those of men.

These findings beg the question: Why do gender wage gaps persist even within educational categories? While there are many reasons, one obvious cause of the wage gap is likely fields of study. Men and women do not enrol in the same fields; men are more likely to pursue lucrative fields such as engineering, while women are over-represented in less remunerative areas such as the humanities, education and nursing (see Table 6.2). Analysts of the National Graduates Survey of 1990 graduates found that, controlling for fields of study and other relevant variables, there was no gender income disparity two years after graduation (cited in Davies, Mosher and O'Grady 1996). While this does not preclude the possibility that a disparity may yet emerge with subsequent years in the labour market, it reinforces our findings that gender inequalities among recent university graduates are becoming smaller.

In terms of unemployment, men and women experienced similar fluctuations between 1975 and 1994, but women had higher unemployment rates and smaller differences between educational levels (Figures 6.4 and 6.5). Disparities between male high school and university graduates ranged from 4% to 9%; among women they ranged from 3% to 8%.

6.2   NON-ECONOMIC RETURNS TO SCHOOLING

There are also non-economic returns that flow to individuals with more schooling, including greater social status and prestige, lower rates of morbidity and mortality, and greater opportunities to pursue different, more varied educational routes (although some of these are undoubtedly linked with economic benefits). These specific forms of individual enrichment are harder to quantify than the economic returns because we lack measures that are equivalent to incomes or employment rates. However, benefits that are more societal in value are easier to calculate. For example, higher levels of education are associated with a better-informed electorate.

In this section we investigate some non-economic benefits flowing from greater amounts of schooling. Day and Devlin (1996) argue that not only does the propensity to volunteer increase with education level, but also, once engaged in volunteer work, the more-educated tend to devote more volunteer hours. In addition, this relationship between higher education and greater volunteer activity holds even after statistically controlling for marital status, sex, children, place of residence, health status, religion, language, and income. Volunteer work, whether in the community (for example coaching minor league sport), in the workplace (for example United Way representatives), in the church (for example religious teachers), or elsewhere, contributes enormously to Canadian life. While such volunteer activity is personally rewarding (although measuring this subjective benefit is difficult), it is the larger society that benefits most. The civic culture of modern Canada rests primarily upon this volunteer base and as the welfare state shrinks in the face of fiscal restraint, volunteer work becomes more important. Education's contribution to this voluntary sector of Canadian society is both impressive and important.

In our introductory chapter we claimed that "meaningful democracy" demands an educated citizenry. Is it the case, as this claim implies, that education promotes greater participation in the democratic process? We test this claim with data from the 1993 Canadian National Election Study (CNES).[7] Five separate surveys were done for the CNES but we use data only from the random sample of 3,340 Canadians collected via telephone interview between October 27 and November 21, 1993 (Northrup and Oram 1994). As measures of political engagement, we use three indicators: whether or not someone voted, an individual's attention to political issues, and a person's participation in political activity. The first measure is calculated using responses to a question about whether or not someone cast a ballot. Attention to politics is measured by people's self-reported consumption of political news via television, newspapers, and radio. Political activity is measured by people's responses to two questions about working for a political party during the 1993 campaign or discussing political issues with others during the campaign. With three separate measures of political engagement, we think we have a meaningful indication of three aspects of political participation.

The key question for us is whether or not education affects political participation, net of other factors that might influence political engagement. We calculate three separate regression equations using our political measures as the dependent variables regressed on age, sex, employment status, country of birth, mother tongue, and the presence of children in the home (see Table 6.11). On each of the three tests, education has a statistically significant effect on the dependent variable, meaning that the effect of education on political engagement is unlikely to be due to chance. Notice as well, that education is the only variable that has a statistically significant effect in all three of the tests. This suggests to us that the relationship between education and politics is clear, namely that more educated Canadians are more politically engaged.

TABLE 6.11

REGRESSION OF THREE MEASURES OF POLITICAL PARTICIPATION ON AGE, SEX, EMPLOYMENT STATUS, MOTHER TONGUE, COUNTRY OF BIRTH AND THE PRESENCE OF CHILDREN IN THE HOME, 1993, UNSTANDARDIZED COEFFICIENTS

Independent variables	Dependent variables		
	Vote[1]	Attention to politics[2]	Political participation[3]
Education	.008[4]	.039[4]	.037[4]
Age (in years)	.004[4]	.001	.006[4]
Employment status (1=paid work)	−.016	−.029	−.019
Country of birth (1=native born)	.011	−.034	−.038
Mother tongue (1=French)	.018	−.155[4]	−.042
Presence of children (1=children < 18 at home)	.020	.047	.075[4]
Sex (1=male)	−.007	.003	.095[4]
Income (in dollars, '000s)	.008[4]	.007[4]	.006
Constant	.545	.392	1.03
R^2	.042	.057	.067
Number of cases	**1,495**	**1,494**	**1,495**

1. Vote is measured as a dichotomy (0=did not vote, 1=vote). The ordinary least-square results reported here hold using logistic regression as an alternative statistical model.

2. Attention to politics is the sum of three questions asking about the consumption of media accounts of the campaign (that is, television, newspaper and radio). High values signal higher levels of attention.

3. Political participation is measured as the sum of responses to questions about helping in the campaign and discussing campaign issues with others. High values signal higher levels of participation.

4. Statistically significant ($p < .05$).

Source: Canadian National Election Study, 1993.

In summary, on two separate but significant aspects of Canadian life, volunteer activity and political engagement, we show that education has an important and independent effect. These non-economic benefits of education clearly provide value to Canada as a whole, enhancing our national community. More generally, and here we are moving well beyond the data we have presented, as social movements have galvanized around such issues as the environment and peace, and as women have come to the fore in modern life, the effects of education have become more and more evident in society. Almost invariably, the leaders in these movements are among the more educated members of society. To the extent that social movements have come to rival social classes as driving forces for change in the modern world (Giddens 1990), then education too must have become more important.

6.3   CONCLUSION

Does it pay to stay in school? We answer this question with an unequivocal "yes." Schooling can lead to numerous economic benefits, including higher annual and lifetime earnings, greater employment and income security, and a wider range of opportunities for advancement. While we cannot untangle trends over time and over the life course, our data suggest that Canadians with greater amounts of education are sorted into superior career tracks, with better opportunities and promotional chances. Further, education's role in labour market success seems to be growing. Men continue to earn more than women across all education levels, but these gaps are shrinking among younger Canadians, especially among university graduates. University educated women, unlike their less-educated peers, have income profiles that increasingly resemble those of men. Our findings indicate that relative to other options, a university education is a key route toward gender equality. Yet, as we become a more schooled society, Canadians with a high school education or less are increasingly left with meagre incomes and high unemployment rates. More and more, it seems, one needs to attend school at the postsecondary level to reap benefits in our evolving labour market.

Although we have discussed economic benefits largely in the context of individual earnings (for example personal income), there is little doubt that there is an aggregate benefit for most people in society (Stager 1996, 6; Vaillancourt 1995). Beyond this aggregation of individual benefits, other societal profits accrue in the form of better leadership, more creativity, and enhanced technological progress. As well, the better management and organizational efficiencies of those with higher levels of education indirectly enrich everyone's productivity (Stager 1996). Schooling also provides non-economic benefits for individuals and for the wider community, since the more-educated tend to be more involved in politics and civic life.

ENDNOTES

1. Reviews of this school-to-work transition can be found in Akyeampong 1990; Ashton, Green, and Lowe 1992; Andres Bellamy 1993; Clark 1991; Krahn and Lowe 1991; Mandell 1993.

2. Each of these data sets has strengths and limitations. Pooling workers of widely varying ages can confound period effects, such as the effects of entering the labour market in economically strong or weak years, or having more postsecondary graduates in later periods. Cross-sectional data only indirectly capture the returns to education over a lifetime, since not all workers complete their education at a relatively young age. Data on recent cohorts of workers help to correct for these problems, but lack a long historical profile.

3. Disparities between education levels are even more striking when it is remembered that most university degree holders in their late twenties have fewer years of work experience than high school graduates of the same age. When work experience is held constant (that is, both groups are compared two years after graduation), earnings disparities are larger (Allen 1996, 19). Also, these earning figures understate the value of a bachelor's degree since that degree allows entry into postgraduate and professional programs with further earning potential.

4. This finding could be interpreted as illustrating a period effect. It is possible that differential returns to education were greater in previous decades. However, this interpretation is not generally supported by the data presented in the previous section.

5. We should reiterate that our data do not untangle life course effects from period effects. A hypothetical example of the latter would be that in previous decades, field of study mattered less because there were greater opportunities for generalists; but in more recent years, with greater numbers of graduates, generalists are less able to find suitable employment.

6. Follow-up data for two particular fields—sociology and anthropology—found evidence of this process as well (Davies, Mosher and O'Grady 1992).

7. These data come from the Institute for Social Research, York University. The survey was funded by the Social Sciences and Humanities Research Council in grants awarded to Richard Johnston, André Blais, Henry Brady, Elisabeth Gidengil, and Neil Nevitte. None of these organizations or individuals is responsible for the analyses and interpretations presented here.

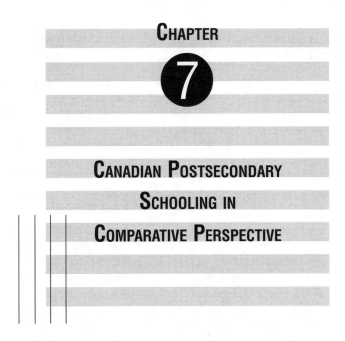

CHAPTER

7

CANADIAN POSTSECONDARY SCHOOLING IN COMPARATIVE PERSPECTIVE

Canada has always been intimately connected with foreign nations, first as a British colony and now as the northern neighbour to the world's richest nation. Globalization, the increasing interconnectedness of nation–states, has always featured prominently in our national fabric. Even so, the foundation of Canada's wealth has been its resource base, its "staples economy," as historian and political economist Harold Innis called it. This is starting to change. Our stocks of natural resources are disappearing (for example the cod fishery, the Douglas Fir forests) and other regions of the world are fast becoming rival providers of natural resources (for example South America). These challenges have prompted Canada and other nations to examine the notion of the post-industrial society, the idea that work based on brains, not brawn, will be the source of future prosperity. Education features prominently in these discussions, as we remarked in the opening chapter (see Economic Council of Canada 1992).

With this in mind, we will briefly compare Canadian educational attainments with those in other countries, paying particular attention to comparisons with the United States (for studies on the United States see Kominski and Sutterlin 1992; Roberts 1993; Waggoner 1991). Transnational developments in commerce, migration, and communications have meant that accomplishments in any single country need to be placed in international context. Under the rubric of globalization we examine how well Canada has done in comparison with other nations. Have the absolute level of schooling and the relative rate of growth of educational attainment in Canada kept pace with our international peers?

7.1 COMPARING EDUCATIONAL ATTAINMENTS BETWEEN CANADA AND THE UNITED STATES

When comparing Canada with the United States, Frank Whittingham claimed in 1965 that the education gap "has grown in favour of the United States throughout the greatest part of this century" (p. 18). Citing this widening gap, the Economic Council of Canada highlighted the relatively poor performance of the Canadian school system in relation to the United States, our largest trading partner. One consequence of this, it believed, was that "differences in the average educational attainments appear to be an important element in the difference in living standards between Canada and the United States" (1965, 74–75). John Porter (1965) echoed these sentiments in his comparative sociology of Canada and the United States (see also Bertram 1966; Steering Group on Prosperity 1992; Human Resource Development Committee 1991).

Earlier this century, Canada attempted to rectify this gap by recruiting many highly skilled individuals from abroad. Opening immigration spots for engineers, physicians, accountants, and scores of other highly trained people meant that for most of this century the educational attainments of foreign-born Canadians were equal to or greater than those of people born in Canada. Draining off educational talent from other countries was thought to be a short-term solution at best, since it caused our own educational system to languish (Porter 1965). After the Second World War, the belief that Canada needed a sophisticated and effective school system in order to become a major world power gained strength.

Given our proximity to the United States, American education has often been the standard against which Canadian accomplishments, or lack thereof, have been measured. A comparison of the educational attainments of Americans and Canadians aged 35 to 44 shows that Whittingham's findings still held true in the early 1990s (see Table 7.1). Canadians still have lower levels of schooling than Americans do. For example, while 27.1% of Americans had a bachelor's degree or higher, only 17.2% of Canadians in the same age bracket had attained similar degrees. At the other extreme, while more than one-quarter (25.7%) of Canadians between 35 and 44 were not high school graduates, just more than 1 in 10 (11.5%) Americans had not attained a high school graduation certificate. We restrict this comparison to people aged 35 to 44 to ensure that age is not a confounding variable in the interpretation of the data. This cohort has likely finished most of its schooling and it is still relatively young, thus providing the most recent comparison available.[1]

TABLE 7.1

HIGHEST LEVEL OF SCHOOLING IN CANADA (1991) AND THE UNITED STATES (1990), POPULATION AGED 35 TO 44

Highest level of schooling	Canada		United States	
	Number	%[1]	Number	%[1]
Not high school graduate	1,120,000	25.7	4,332,000	11.5
High school graduate	910,000	20.9	12,655,000	33.6
Some postsecondary	1,613,000	37.0	10,506,000	27.9
Bachelor's degree or more	747,000	17.2	10,214,000	27.1
Total population	4,354,000	100.0	37,707,000	100.0

1. Percentages may not add to 100 due to rounding.

Source: Computed by authors from Statistics Canada, *Educational Attainment and School Attendance*, 1993, 24–25; American schooling information from Kominski and Sutterlin 1992, 13.

The concern of Whittingham and the Economic Council of Canada was not just that Canadians had lower levels of schooling, but that relative to the United States the gap was widening. We present two procedures to examine whether the growing educational gap through the first part of the century has continued in the later part of the century. First, we use data from the 1991 Census of Canada and 1990 U.S. Census to show the percentage of people with university degrees in six different age groups (see Table 7.2). If the education gap between the two countries has continued to widen then the expectation is that the largest gap will occur in the youngest age group. Considering first the population aged 65 and over, more than twice as many Americans (11.0%) as compared with Canadians (5.0%) had university degrees, a ratio of 2.2:1. The ratio then shrinks as we move through the age groups. For the 55-to-64 age group, the ratio is 2.0:1, while for the 45-to-54 and 35-to-44 age groups, it is 1.6:1. The ratio shrinks further, to 1.4:1 for the youngest age group (25-to-34), but differences between the two countries in school completion ages make this last comparison unstable (and notice that a smaller percentage of people in this younger age group have degrees, mainly because some people in both countries are still in school). Nevertheless, this evidence contradicts the premise that the gap between the two countries is widening. At least on this test the gap, if anything, appears to be narrowing.

TABLE 7.2

NUMBER AND PERCENTAGE OF POPULATION WITH A UNIVERSITY DEGREE IN CANADA (1991) AND THE UNITED STATES (1990), BY AGE GROUP

Age group	Canada			United States		
	Population in age group	Population with university degree	Percentage of population with university degree	Population in age group	Population with university degree	Percentage of population with university degree
25–34	4,840,000	774,000	16.0	43,245,000	9,657,000	22.3
35–44	4,354,000	747,000	17.2	37,708,000	10,214,000	27.1
45–54	2,960,000	395,000	13.3	35,489,000	5,355,000	15.1
55–64	2,385,000	180,000	7.5	21,228,000	3,250,000	15.3
65+	2,932,000	148,000	5.0	29,776,000	3,280,000	11.0
25+	17,471,000	2,244,000	12.8	167,446,000	31,757,000	19.0

Source: Canadian data from Statistics Canada, Educational Attainment and School Attendance, 1993, 24–25; American data from Kominski and Sutterlin 1992, 13.

A second way to examine the change in the educational gap is by comparing the two countries on a broader measure of educational attainment. We use national data from Lagacé (1968) to show the percentage of the population in 1966 that had some university education (see Figure 7.1). The age groups used are comparable to those in Table 7.2 but it should be noted that, unlike the table, these data include people who may have not actually attained a degree. According to Lagacé's data, the education gap for younger age groups in 1966 was apparently about as wide, and possibly even a little wider, than it was for older groups. Among 25- to 34-year-olds, 25.8% of Americans as opposed to 12.2% of Canadians (a ratio of 2.1:1) had university experience. Compare this to the 65-and-over age group where the respective percentages are 10.9 and 5.6, for a ratio of 1.9:1. The 1966 data suggest that Whittingham's earlier concern about a growing gap might have been alarmist, but there is no denying that a substantial gap in educational attainments existed between the two countries (a gap that was often attributed to Canada's focus on resource extraction). This profile, in comparison with our findings from Table 7.2, suggests that the American postsecondary education system expanded earlier than the Canadian, but over the last few decades we have kept pace with U.S. expansion, and perhaps even surpassed U.S. growth rates in recent educational attainment.

FIGURE **7.1**

PERCENTAGE OF THE POPULATION WITH SOME UNIVERSITY EDUCATION, BY AGE GROUP, CANADA AND THE UNITED STATES, **1966**

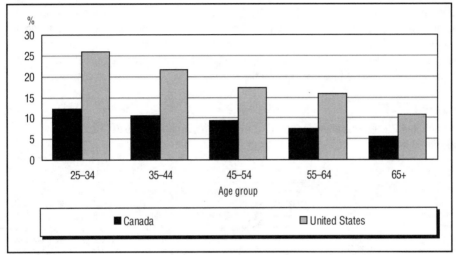

Source: Lagacé 1968, 39–40.

7.2 COMPARISONS WITH OECD COUNTRIES

Given their proximity, comparisons between Canada and the United States have a certain logic. Both countries, however, stand out when their current educational profiles are contrasted with those of other Western industrial nations. We compare percentages of university degree-holders (in 1991) and percentages of 18- to 21-year-olds enrolled in university (in 1991) for selected countries belonging to the Organisation for Economic Co-operation and Development (OECD) (see Table 7.3). The United States has the greatest percentage of 25- to 64-year-olds with university degrees (24%). Canada, at 17%, falls almost midway between the United States and the other nations. The enrolment data show more recent patterns. Here, the earlier finding that Canadian schooling levels are catching up with the United States receives additional support. The United States has a greater percentage of people aged 18 to 21 enrolled in university than Canada has (22.8% and 21.6%, respectively), but this gap is much smaller than it was earlier in the century. On this indicator as well, both the United States and Canada have greater proportions of their 18- to 21-year-old populations enrolled at university than the other nations, although at 18.5%, France is some distance above the other OECD member countries.

TABLE 7.3

PERCENTAGE OF POPULATION AGED 25 TO 64 WITH UNIVERSITY EDUCATION AND ENROLMENT RATES FOR PEOPLE AGED 18 TO 21 IN SELECTED OECD COUNTRIES, 1991

Country	Population 25 to 64 years of age with a university degree	Population 18 to 21 years of age enrolled at university
	(%)	(%)
Canada	17	22
United States	24	23
France	10	19
Germany	11	7
Italy	6	..
United Kingdom	10	12
OECD average	10	12

.. not available

Source: Organisation for Economic Co-operation and Development (OECD), *Education at a Glance* 1992, 201, 213.

Comparative data for different nations are also available over time. The education systems of different countries vary quite substantially and so while such international comparisons are of theoretical interest, there is always a risk of misinterpreting differences. However, these risks are reduced somewhat when we compare postsecondary enrolments since the demarcation between earlier years of schooling and higher education is the most similar across nations. To make the interpretation of enrolment numbers more comparable, the United Nations Educational, Scientific and Cultural Organization (UNESCO) presents postsecondary enrolments as a function of the population size of a country. This has the virtue of standardizing the numbers to a known base (enrolment per 100,000 inhabitants), but given that the age distributions vary by country, it would have been preferable if enrolments were standardized using a narrower age band. Such data, however, are not available.

TABLE 7.4

NUMBER OF STUDENTS ENROLLED (PER 100,000 INHABITANTS) IN POSTSECONDARY EDUCATION, BY SELECTED COUNTRY AND YEAR

Country	Number of students per 100,000 inhabitants			
	1975	1980	1985	1989
Canada	**3,600**	**4,040**	**5,100**	**5,030**
United States	5,180	5,310	5,120	5,600
France	1,970	2,000	2,320	2,840
Germany	1,690	1,990	2,540	2,840
Italy	1,760	1,980	2,070	2,380
United Kingdom	1,300	1,470	1,820	1,950[1]
Japan	2,020	2,070	1,940	2,180

1. Data for 1988 as opposed to 1989 (most recent available).

Source: United Nations Educational, Scientific and Cultural Organization, *UNESCO Statistical Yearbook*, 1991, Table 3.10.

According to the UNESCO data, from 1975 to 1989, both Canada and the United States clearly had higher enrolment rates at the postsecondary level than did other selected OECD countries (see Table 7.4). Indeed, even by 1989 no other country had enrolment rates that equaled the 1975 rates for Canada and the United States, despite the rapid growth in several countries, especially Germany and France. It is unlikely the differences are due strictly to different national education structures or age distributions. Notice, also, that when comparing Canada with the United States, the data again indicate that the education gap between the two countries is narrowing. In comparative perspective then, Canada has a well-educated population and the earlier worries about Canada lagging farther and farther behind the United States in terms of educational attainment are now history.

The above comparisons simply measure participation or attendance; they do not indicate the quality of learning. The latter, while a topic of intense interest in education circles, is beyond the scope of what we can undertake in this book (and at this time Statistics Canada is not directly involved in these international tests). Existing data on standardized achievement tests point to the differences between education systems, but simple comparisons of international test scores are highly problematic. Using the language of our earlier chapters, both Canada and the United States have postsecondary systems that are much more universal or mass-oriented in contrast to the more exclusive and, some would say, elitist systems of European and other industrial countries. Our point here is not to explain away differences between nations on international test scores, but to note that these structural and demographic differences are critical in interpreting Canadian educational performance in a broader international context.

7.3   CONCLUSION

Relative to the United States—a barometer Canadians frequently use to gauge our own success— we became a schooled society more recently. But now, as we move into the next century, Canadians are increasingly attaining levels of education comparable to American levels. Both nations remain, however, exceptional in terms of the length of time that young people spend in school. By spending greater periods of their lives in schools, Canadian and American children enter the paid labour force on a full-time basis later in life than their peers in other industrial countries.

ENDNOTES

1. For example, if we compare people aged 55 to 64, it could be argued that any of the differences found may have eroded for more recent cohorts. We could also compare people aged 20 to 24 but here the different ages at which Canadians and Americans typically complete their schooling could confound any attempt to interpret differences.

CHAPTER

8

DISCUSSION AND CONCLUSION

In this final chapter we conclude by highlighting some key issues elaborated earlier. We also take the opportunity to be more speculative, to push the envelope a bit, by going beyond our data to look at future challenges.

The Census of Canada provides a valuable barometer for measuring Canadian accomplishments in education. As demonstrated in Chapter 1, the census is a rich source of information on early educational experiences in Canada. Not only do early census documents record a variety of measures on literacy rates, school attendance, and school graduation, but they also provide interesting historical descriptions of the conditions of schooling in various regions of the country. This regional theme was discussed in Chapter 3 where we examined educational differences by region and the degree to which regional variations in education may be uniting or dividing the country. Our analyses of regional inequalities in levels of schooling cause us to worry that the futures of many young people in some remote parts of certain regions are not being sufficiently aided by the school system. Dropping out of school is, to a large extent, regionally concentrated.

Census data also permit an assessment of our collective success in delivering education to all Canadians. This is especially pressing in the context of our evolving economy, be it a "post-industrial" or "knowledge-intensive" economy. If certain groups of Canadians are isolated from the educational mainstream or fall behind in their attainment of schooling, their life prospects are likely to be impoverished. While Chapter 3 focused on regional differences, Chapter 4 highlighted the typical levels of schooling of members of different social categories, defined by gender, ethnicity, language group and so forth.

Most conspicuous here, because of their overall lower levels of school attainment, were members of various First Nations. From the vast amount of data we explored in the course of our research, this finding is one of the most striking and most worrying. Our educational systems have not served First Nations people well, and in our view this highlights a central challenge for all Canadians.

From the first European contact onward, a major concern was with "civilizing" the indigenous Aboriginal population. The Department of the Interior, which handled Indian affairs for the federal government, adopted this approach: "The Indian problem exists owing to the fact that the Indian is untrained to take his place in the world. Once we teach him to do this, the solution is had" (Department of the Interior 1895, xxi). Residential schools were invented as vehicles to promote assimilation (see Furniss 1995 or Knockwood 1992 for good discussions of residential schools). From the 1880s until the 1970s, many Aboriginal children were removed from their homes and sent great distances to boarding schools. While not all went to residential schools, a deliberate and concerted effort was made to remove thousands of Aboriginal children from their families and communities and immerse them in European traditions, thereby assimilating or "Canadianizing" large portions of the Aboriginal population. What this practice did, as the historical record shows, and especially as the testimonials of First Nations people reveal, was create a marginalized people who were in many ways stripped of their original culture. Pearl Achneepineskum, who attended Cecilia Jeffrey Residential School in Ontario from 1956 to 1978, captured one part of the failed policy: "You do not put a cat amongst a bunch of dogs and expect it to bark. Nor do you tell a fish to fly like an eagle" (1995, 2). Beyond failing as an immigration policy, a haunting legacy of residential schools and other education policies for First Nations people is that as a group Aboriginals receive far less schooling than do their fellow Canadians (Barman 1995). Few First Nations people, especially in rural regions, ever make it to college or university. This is, we think, a national tragedy that requires innovation and dedication by all Canadians, including First Nations peoples (see also Siggner 1983; Armstrong, Kennedy, and Oberle 1990).

The politics of identity, exemplified for us most vividly in the Commission of Inquiry on Equality in Employment (1984), assert that gender, race, and ethnicity are pivotal bases of inequality, including educational inequality. Although this perspective often proclaims a "class, gender, and race/ethnicity" trilogy to understand inequalities, we find that this perspective fails to account for recent changes in educational opportunities. Women, and most visible minority groups, have recently attained high levels of education, but social class remains a prominent and independent impediment to educational mobility. Canadians' chances of moving on to college or university are much more influenced by social class and geographical region than by gender or race/ethnicity. Indeed, class and region are the major fault lines dividing Canadian educational experiences, and these differences probably contribute significantly to the difficulties Aboriginal peoples and some ethnic groups face when trying to increase their educational levels.

Increasingly, the postsecondary level is where educational differences have the most impact on labour market outcomes. This trend occurs as more people (now well over one-half of all Canadians) continue their studies beyond high school. As we showed in Chapter 6, attainment of a secondary school graduation certificate is increasingly related to economic well-being. Fewer people can prosper economically without at least one degree or diploma from the education system. Consequently, the postsecondary system has increasingly come to perform the sorting function that secondary schools once did. More and more, the types of postsecondary institutions people attend and the programs they choose have an impact on their ability to find jobs and earn good salaries. The expansion and increasing differentiation of the postsecondary system is a theme we explored in Chapter 5.

These changes have a variety of consequences. First, they have the beneficial effect of providing people with greater opportunities and choices. However, the amount of actual choice that exists is debatable. Factors such as sex and social class affect not only where people study (Chapter 4), but also what they study (Chapter 5). Second, the expansion of the postsecondary system has come at a time when the rate of growth in secure, well-paying jobs has slowed and when government purse strings have tightened. Postsecondary institutions are increasingly told to do more with less, and hence class sizes have increased, contact between students and faculty has been strained, and colleges and universities have come to be seen as large and impersonal bureaucracies. Third, the more differentiated system and the scarcity of resources have heightened some types of competition between institutions and programs, often when co-operation would be the better strategy. Forms of competition such as advertising for students or offering more attractive scholarship packages may become more intense if the participation rate of the 18- to 24-year-old population should stabilize or decline. In recent years, colleges and universities have benefited from a greater propensity among smaller cohorts to continue studies at the postsecondary level. As unemployment and underemployment fears arise, future cohorts may have lower rates of participation in traditional postsecondary education if they search for alternative avenues into the labour market (although in our view the alleged paucity of prospects for postsecondary graduates is overblown in the popular media).

We also examined the changing dynamics of the teaching profession, showing how the system has evolved over time, paying particular attention to movement into and out of the profession (Chapter 2). Teaching is the largest profession in the country and increasingly the target of disgruntled parents and politicians. We explored both the demography of the profession and the relative earnings of teachers and others. Here, a key challenge will be to renew the teaching labour force while meeting the demands of multiple interest groups for a reinvigorated educational system. One possible solution is to hope new recruits will inject freshness into the profession. However, this is a potential folly if such hopes also raise expectations for better and better education, exerting ever more pressure on teachers, without a simultaneous reform of the system.

Finally, we briefly examined how Canadian educational attainments compare with the United States and other countries in the Organisation for Economic Co-operation and Development (Chapter 7). We have a long history in this country of looking south of the border to see how we are doing compared with our American cousins. This happens often in education. Comparatively, Canada has narrowed the historic gap in rates of education between the two countries. In a broader international comparison, Canada and the United States have the highest rates of postsecondary participation. Both countries are at the leading edge of the shift to mass education in the tertiary sector, though the United States is farther along in this process (see Griffith, Frase and Ralph 1989). Whether or not this expansion will continue is impossible to predict but as parents work harder and harder to ensure educational opportunities for their offspring, the pressure may mount. Parents want their children to fare at least as well as they did, and this adds an enormous amount of upward pressure to the education system. In the current context of smaller families, the educational fortunes of one or two children carry the full load of parental expectations—fewer brothers and sisters share the pressures.

DISCUSSION AND CONCLUSION

The themes of *change* and *comparison* have framed this monograph, and the changes and comparisons we identified are among the future challenges for Canadian education. The Census of Canada provides an effective data source for keeping abreast of the education system, for identifying pressure points requiring innovative solutions and, on a broad level, for assessing the success of our schools. We have used these data to trace the development of our schooled society, to map the fortunes of all citizens in the system, and to compare these patterns with other nations. As we move into the 21st century, an appreciation of current educational trends is important since these trends set the tempo for future change and form the loose boundaries within which change will occur. We have provided answers to a series of questions, as far as the data allow, while establishing baselines against which to assess these future challenges.

REFERENCES

Achneepineskum, Pearl. 1995. "Charlie Wants." In *Residential Schools: The Stolen Years*. Edited by Linda Jaine. Saskatoon: University of Saskatchewan, News & Publications Office, 1–2.

Akyeampong, Ernest B. 1990. "The graduates of '82: where are they now?" *Perspectives on Labour and Income* (Statistics Canada Catalogue no. 75-001E). 2, 1 (Spring): 52–63.

Alladin, Ibrahim. 1996. *Racism in Canadian Schools*. Toronto: Harcourt Brace & Co. of Canada Limited.

Allen, Robert. 1996. "The economic benefits of post-secondary education and training in B.C.: an outcomes assessment." Centre for Research on Economic and Social Policy (CRESP) Discussion Paper no. 34. Vancouver: University of British Columbia.

Andres Bellamy, L. 1993. "Life trajectories, action, and negotiating the transition from high school." In *Transitions: Schooling and Employment in Canada*. Edited by P. Anisef and P. Axelrod. Toronto: Thompson Educational Press Inc., 137–157.

Andres Bellamy, L. and Neil Guppy. 1991. "Opportunities and Obstacles for Women in Canadian Higher Education." In *Women and Education: a Canadian perspective*. 2nd ed. Edited by J. Gaskell and A. McLaren. Calgary: Detselig Enterprises Ltd., 163–192.

Anisef, Paul with Marie-Andrée Bertrand, Ulrike Hortian, and Carl E. James. 1985. *Accessibility to Postsecondary Education in Canada: A Review of the Literature*. Ottawa: Education Support Branch: Department of the Secretary of State.

Anisef, Paul, Norman Okihiro, and Carl James. 1982. *Losers and Winners: The Pursuit of Equality and Social Justice in Higher Education*. Toronto: Butterworths.

Anisef, Paul, Fred Ashbury, and Tony Turrittin. 1992. "Differential effects of university and community college education on occupational status attainment in Ontario." *Canadian Journal of Sociology / Cahiers canadiens de sociologie*. 17, 1: 69–84. [Abstract in French.]

Anisef, Paul, Fred Ashbury, Katherine Bishoping, and Zeng Lin. 1996. "Post-secondary education and underemployment in a longitudinal study of Ontario baby boomers." *Higher Education Policy*. 9, 2: 159–174.

Anisef, Paul and Paul Axelrod, eds. 1993. *Transitions: Schooling and Employment in Canada*. Toronto: Thompson Educational Publishing Inc.

Armstrong, Robin, Jeff Kennedy, and Peter Oberle. 1990. *University Education and Economic Well-being: Indian Achievement and Prospects*. Ottawa: Minister of Indian and Northern Affairs.

Ashton, David, Francis Green, and Graham Lowe. 1992. "The linkages between education and employment in Canada and the United Kingdom: A comparative analysis." *Discussion Paper No. 92*. Edmonton: Population Research Laboratory, University of Alberta.

Association of Universities and Colleges of Canada (AUCC). 1996. *Trends 1996: The Canadian University in Profile*. Ottawa: AUCC.

Baril, Alain and George A. Mori. 1991. "Educational attainment of linguistic groups in Canada." *Canadian Social Trends* (Statistics Canada Catalogue no. 11-008). 20 (Spring): 17–18.

Barlow, Maude and Heather-Jane Robertson. 1994. *Class Warfare: The Assault on Canada's Schools*. Toronto: Key Porter Books Limited.

Barman, Jean. 1995. "Schooled for inequality: The education of British Columbia Aboriginal children." In *Children, Teachers and Schools in the History of British Columbia*. Edited by J. Barman, N. Sutherland, and J. D. Wilson. Calgary: Detselig Enterprises Ltd., 57–80.

Beauchamp, Rachelle and Georgina Feldberg. 1991. *Girls and Women in Medicine, Math, Science, Engineering and Technology*. Toronto: Ontario Advisory Council on Women's Issues.

Beaujot, Roderic, and Kevin McQuillan. 1982. *Growth and Dualism: The Demographic Development of Canadian Society*. Toronto: Gage Publishing Ltd.

Beck, Nuala. 1995. *Excelerate: Growing in the New Economy*. Toronto: HarperCollins Canada Limited.

Beck, Ulrich. 1992. *Risk Society: Toward a New Modernity*. Theory, Culture and Society No. 17. London: Sage (originally published in 1986 in German; translated by Mark Ritter).

Bélanger, Rebecca and Teresa Omiecinski. 1987. "Part-time university enrolment." *Canadian Social Trends* (Statistics Canada Catalogue no. 11-008). Summer: 22–25.

Bell, Daniel. 1964. "The post-industrial society." In *Technology and Social Change*. Edited by Eli Ginzberg. New York: Columbia University Press, 44–59.

Bell, Daniel. 1973. *The Coming of Post-Industrial Society: A Venture in Social Forecasting*. New York: Basic Books.

Bertram, Gordon. 1966. "The contribution of education to economic growth." Staff Study, no. 12. Ottawa: Economic Council of Canada.

Betcherman, Gordon and René Morissette. 1994. "Recent youth labour market experiences in Canada." Analytical Studies Branch Research Paper Series no. 63 (Statistics Canada Catalogue no. 11F0019E).

Blau, Francine and Marianne Ferber. 1992. *The Economics of Women, Men, and Work*. 2nd ed. Englewood Cliffs, N.J.: Prentice-Hall.

Bohrnstedt, George W. and David Knoke. 1982. *Statistics for Social Data Analysis*. Itasca, Illinois: F.E. Peacock Publishers.

Bowlby, Geoff. 1996. "Relationship between postsecondary graduates' education and employment." *Education Quarterly Review* (Statistics Canada Catalogue no. 81-003-XPB). 3, 2 (Summer): 35–44.

Boyd, Monica. 1990. "Immigrant women: language, socioeconomic inequalities and policy issues." In *Ethnic Demography: Canadian Immigrant, Racial and Cultural Variations*. Edited by Shiva S. Halli, Frank Travato and Leo Driedger. Ottawa: Carleton University Press, 275–295.

Butlin, George, and Ian Calvert. 1996. "Interprovincial university student flow patterns." *Education Quarterly Review* (Statistics Canada Catalogue no. 81-003-XPB). 3, 3 (Fall): 30–42.

Cameron, David M. 1991. *More Than an Academic Question: Universities, Governance, and Public Policy in Canada*. Halifax: The Institute for Research on Public Policy.

Campbell, Duncan. 1984. *The New Majority: Adult Learners in the University*. Edmonton: University of Alberta Press.

Canadian Committee on Women in Engineering. 1992. *More Than Just Numbers*. Fredericton: University of New Brunswick.

The Canadian Global Almanac. 1995. General Editor, John Robert Colombo. Toronto: Global Press.

Canadian Institute of Child Health. 1994. *The Health of Canada's Children: A CICH Profile*. 2nd ed. Ottawa: Canadian Institute of Child Health.

Che-Alford, Janet. 1992. "Canadians on the move." *Canadian Social Trends* (Statistics Canada Catalogue no. 11-008E). 25 (Summer): 32–34.

Clark, Warren. 1991. *The Class of 1986 (A compendium of findings of the 1988 National Graduates Survey of 1986 graduates with comparisons to the 1984 National Graduates Survey)*. Ottawa: Employment and Immigration Canada, and Statistics Canada.

Cohen, Gary. 1990. *A Profile of Three Disabled Populations: The Health and Activity Limitation Survey*. (Statistics Canada Catalogue no. 82-559). Ottawa: Minister responsible for Statistics Canada.

Coish, David. 1994. "Trends in education employment." *Education Quarterly Review* (Statistics Canada Catalogue no. 81-003). 1, 3 (Fall): 17–29.

Collins, Randall. 1979. *The Credential Society: an historical sociology of education and stratification*. New York: Academic Press.

Commission of Inquiry on Equality in Employment. 1984. *Report of the Commission on Equality in Employment*; Rosalie Silberman Abella, commissioner. Ottawa: Supply and Services Canada.

Committee of Presidents of Universities of Ontario, Subcommittee on Research and Planning. 1971. *Towards 2000: The Future of Post-secondary Education in Ontario*. Toronto: McClelland and Stewart.

Corak, Miles. 1990. "Canadian Unemployment in Retrospect: 1977–87." *Working Paper no. 10*. Ottawa: Economic Council of Canada.

Creese, Gillian, Neil Guppy, and Martin Meissner. 1991. *Ups and Downs on the Ladder of Success: Social Mobility in Canada*. General Social Survey Analysis Series No. 5 (Statistics Canada Catalogue no. 11-612E no. 5). Ottawa: Minister responsible for Statistics Canada.

Crompton, Susan. 1995. "Employment prospects for high school graduates." *Perspectives on Labour and Income* (Statistics Canada Catalogue no. 75-001E). 7, 3 (Autumn): 8–13.

Curtis, Bruce. 1988. *Building the Educational State: Canada West, 1836–1871*. London, Ontario: Althouse Press.

Curtis, James, Edward Grabb, and Neil Guppy, eds. 1993. *Social Inequality in Canada: patterns, problems, policies*. 2nd ed. Scarborough: Prentice-Hall Canada.

Darling, A.L. 1980. "The impact of the participation rate—whatever it is—on university enrolment." *Canadian Journal of Higher Education / La revue canadienne d'enseignement supérieur*. 10, 1: 37–56. [Abstract in French.]

Davies, Scott. 1995. "Leaps of faith: shifting currents in critical sociology of education." *American Journal of Sociology*. 100, 6: 1448–1478.

Davies, Scott and Neil Guppy. 1997a. "Fields of study, college selectivity, and student inequalities in higher education." *Social Forces*. 75, 4: 1417–1438.

———. 1997b. "Globalization and Educational Reforms in Anglo-American Democracies." *Comparative Education Review*. 41, 4: 435–459.

Davies, Scott, Clayton Mosher, and Bill O'Grady. 1992. "Canadian sociology and anthropology graduates in the 1980s labour market. Part II: 1987 follow-up of 1982 graduates." *Society / Société*. 16, 2: 1–6.

———. 1994. "Trends in labour market outcomes of Canadian post-secondary graduates, 1978–1988." In *Sociology of Education in Canada: critical perspectives on theory, research and practice*. Edited by Lorna Erwin and David MacLennan. Toronto: Copp Clark Longman.

———. 1996. "Educating women: gender inequalities among Canadian university graduates." *Canadian Review of Sociology and Anthropology / Revue canadienne de sociologie et d'anthropologie*. 33, 2: 125–142. [Abstract in French.]

Day, Kathleen and Rose Anne Devlin. 1996. "Volunteerism and crowding out: Canadian econometric evidence." *Canadian Journal of Economics / Revue canadienne d'économique*. 29, 1: 37–53. [Abstract in French.]

Dei, George Sefa. 1996. "Black/African Canadian students' perspectives on school racism." In *Racism in Canadian Schools*. Edited by M. Ibrahim Alladin. Toronto: Harcourt Brace & Co. of Canada.

Dennison, John D., ed. 1995. *Challenge and Opportunity: Canada's Community Colleges at the Crossroads*. Vancouver: UBC Press.

Department of the Interior. 1895. *Annual Report*. Ottawa: King's Printer.

Dominion Bureau of Statistics. 1925. *Population*. Sixth Census of Canada, 1921, Vol. II (Statistics Canada Catalogue no. 98-1921 F). Ottawa: Minister of Trade and Commerce.

Dominion Bureau of Statistics. 1936. *Summary*. Seventh Census of Canada, 1931, Vol. I (Statistics Canada Catalogue no. 98-1931 F). Ottawa: Minister of Trade and Commerce.

Dore, Ronald. 1976. *The Diploma Disease: Education, Qualification and Development*. London: Allen and Unwin.

Drucker, Peter F. 1993. *Post-Capitalist Society*. New York: HarperBusiness.

Easton, Stephen T. 1988. *Education in Canada: An Analysis of Elementary, Secondary and Vocational Schooling*. Vancouver: Fraser Institute.

Economic Council of Canada. 1964. *First Annual Review: Economic Goals for Canada to 1970*. Ottawa: Queen's Printer and Controller of Stationery.

———. 1965. *Second Annual Review: Towards Sustained and Balanced Economic Growth*. Ottawa: Queen's Printer and Controller of Stationery.

———. 1992. *A Lot to Learn: Education and Training in Canada. A Statement*. Ottawa: Economic Council of Canada.

Foot, David K. 1996. *Boom, Bust and Echo: How to Profit from the Coming Demographic Shift*. Toronto: Macfarlane Walter & Ross.

Fortin, Michèle. 1987. "Accessibility to and participation in the post-secondary education system in Canada." In *The Forum Papers: National Forum on Post-Secondary Education*. Halifax: The Institute for Research on Public Policy.

Fournier, Élaine, George Butlin, and Philip Giles. 1995. "Intergenerational change in the education of Canadians." *Education Quarterly Review* (Statistics Canada Catalogue no. 81-003-XPB). 2, 2 (Summer): 22–33.

Fournier, Marcel and Michael Rosenberg. 1997. "School and the state in Quebec." In *Quebec Society: Critical Issues*. Edited by M. Fournier, M. Rosenberg, and D. White. Toronto: Prentice Hall, 123–141.

Furniss, Elizabeth. 1995. *Victims of Benevolence: the Dark Legacy of the Williams Lake Residential School*. Vancouver: Arsenal Pulp Publishing.

Gallagher, Paul. 1995. *Changing Course: An Agenda for REAL Reform of Canadian Education*. Toronto: OISE Press.

Gaskell, Jane. 1992a. "Issues for Women in Canadian Education." Working Paper No. 32, Economic Council of Canada. Ottawa: Economic Council of Canada.

———. 1992b. *Gender Matters from School to Work*. Milton Keynes, England: Open University Press.

Gaskell, Jane and Arlene McLaren, eds. 1991. *Women and Education*. 2nd ed. Calgary: Detselig Enterprises Ltd.

George, M. V., M. Norris, F. Nault, S. Loh, and S.Y. Dai. 1994. *Population Projections for Canada, Provinces, and Territories, 1993–2016* (Statistics Canada Catalogue no. 91-520). Ottawa: Minister responsible for Statistics Canada.

Giddens, Anthony. 1990. *The Consequences of Modernity*. Stanford: Stanford University Press.

Gidney, R. D., and W. P. J. Millar. 1985. "From voluntarism to state schooling: the creation of the public school system in Ontario." *Canadian Historical Review*. 66 (December) 443–473.

Gilbert, Sid. 1991. *Attrition in Canadian universities*. Research Report No. 1. Commission of Inquiry on Canadian University Education. Ottawa: Association of Universities and Colleges of Canada (AUCC).

Gilbert, Sid and Alan Pomfret. 1991. *Gender Tracking in University Programs*. Occasional paper No. 4. Ottawa: Industry Canada.

Gilbert, Sid and M. S. Devereaux. 1993. *Leaving school: results from a national survey comparing school leavers and high school graduates 18 to 20 years of age* (Statistics Canada Catalogue no. 81-575). Ottawa: Minister of Supply and Services Canada.

Gordon, David. 1988. "The global economy: new edifice or crumbling foundations?" *New Left Review*, (March–April): 24–64.

Gregor, Alexander D. and Gilles Jasmin, eds. 1992. *Higher Education in Canada*. Ottawa: Secretary of State.

Grenon, Gordon Lee. 1991. "Stigma at Work: The Consequence of Disability and Gender Inequality." Master's thesis, University of British Columbia.

Griffith, Jeanne, Mary Frase, and John Ralph. 1989. "American education: the challenge of change." *Population Bulletin*, 44, 4 (December). Washington: Population Reference Bureau.

Gunderson, Morley and Craig Riddell. 1991. "Economics of women's wages in Canada." *International Review of Comparative Public Policy*. 3: 151–176.

Guppy, Neil. 1989. "Pay equity in Canadian universities, 1972–73 and 1985–86." *Canadian Review of Sociology and Anthropology / Revue canadienne de sociologie et d'anthropologie*. 26, 5(November): 743–758. [Abstract in French.]

Guppy, Neil and Bruce Arai. 1993. "Who benefits from higher education? Differences by sex, social class, and ethnicity." In *Social Inequality in Canada: Patterns, Problems, Policies*. Edited by J. Curtis et al. Scarborough: Prentice-Hall.

Guppy, Neil and Scott Davies. 1996."Labour Market Dynamics in the Teaching Profession." *Education Quarterly Review* (Statistics Canada Catalogue no. 81-003-XPB). 3, 4 (Winter): 33–43.

———. 1997."Confidence in Canadian public education: Trends over time." Paper presented at the Sociology of Education Roundtable, 1997 American Sociological Association Meetings, Toronto.

Hagan, John, Ross MacMillan, and Blair Wheaton. 1996. "New kid in town: social capital and the life course effects of family migration on children." *American Sociological Review*. 61, 3(June): 368–385.

Haggar-Guénette, Cynthia. 1991. "Lifelong learning: Who goes back to school?" *Perspectives on Labour and Income* (Statistics Canada Catalogue no. 75-001E). 3, 4 (Winter): 24–30.

———. 1992. "Mature students." *Canadian Social Trends* (Statistics Canada Catalogue no. 11-008E). 26 (Autumn): 26–29.

Hargreaves, Andy. 1994. *Changing Teachers, Changing Times: Teachers' Work and Culture in the Postmodern Age*. London: Cassell.

Harrigan, Patrick. 1988. "A comparison of rural and urban schooling patterns of enrolment and attendance in Canada, 1900-1960." *CHEA Bulletin / Bulletin d'ACHE*. 5,3 (October): 27–48.

———. 1990. "The schooling of boys and girls in Canada." *Journal of Social History*. 23, 4 (Summer): 803–814.

Harrison, Brian R. 1996. *Youth in Official Language Minorities 1971–1991*. (Statistics Canada Catalogue no. 91-545E). Ottawa: Minister responsible for Statistics Canada.

Harvey, Edward B. and Lorne J. Tepperman. 1988. *Selected Socio-economic Consequences of Disability for Women in Canada, Aged 15 and Over: A proposal prepared for the research program of the Disability Database Program, Statistics Canada*. (Statistics Canada Catalogue no. STC0277).

Haveman, Robert and Barbara Wolfe. 1994. *Succeeding Generations: On the Effects of Investments in Children*. New York: Russell Sage Foundation.

Health Canada. 1994. *Suicide in Canada: Update of the Report of the Task Force on Suicide in Canada*. Ottawa: Minister of National Health and Welfare.

Hendrick, Dianne. 1995. "Canadian Crime Statistics, 1994." *Juristat* (Statistics Canada Catalogue no. 85-002). 15, 12: 1–37.

Herberg, Edward R. 1990. "The ethno-racial socioeconomic hierarchy in Canada: theory and analysis of the new vertical mosaic." *International Journal of Comparative Sociology*. 31, 3/4 (September): 206–221.

Hollands, Judith. 1988. "Women Teaching at Canadian Universities." *Canadian Social Trends* (Statistics Canada Catalogue no. 11-008E). 9(Summer): 5–7.

Human Resource Development Canada. 1993. *National Occupational Classification: Occupational Descriptions*. Ottawa: Minister of Supply and Services Canada.

Human Resource Development Committee. 1991. *Learning to Win: Education, Training and National Prosperity*. Ottawa: National Advisory Board on Science and Technology.

Hunter, Alfred. 1986. *Class Tells: Social Inequality in Canada*. Toronto: Butterworths.

———. 1988."Formal education and initial employment: unravelling the relationships between schooling and skills over time." *American Sociological Review*. 53, 5(October): 753–765.

Hunter, Alfred and Jean McKenzie Leiper. 1993. "On formal education, skills and earnings: the role of educational certificates in earnings determination." *Canadian Journal of Sociology / Cahiers canadiens de sociologie*. 18, 1: 21–42.

Indian and Northern Affairs Canada. 1993. *Basic Departmental Data—1993*. Ottawa: Minister of Indian Affairs and Northern Development.

Industry, Science and Technology Canada. 1991. *Women in Science and Engineering, Volume 1: Universities*. Ottawa: University and College Affairs Branch, Science Sector; Industry, Science and Technology Canada.

———. 1992. *Women in Science and Engineering, Volume 2: Colleges*. Ottawa: Minister of Supply and Services Canada.

Jasmin, Gilles, ed. 1992. *Continuing Professional Education in Canada. A Contribution to the OECD Study on Higher Education and Employment—Country Report: Canada*. Ottawa: Secretary of State.

Katz, Joseph. 1974. *Education in Canada*. Vancouver: Douglas, David & Charles.

Kerr, Clark. 1991. *The Great Transformation in Higher Education, 1960–1980*. Albany, N.Y.: State University of New York Press.

Kettle, John. 1976. "Direction Canada: People and Households." *Executive*. 18, 7/8: 32–40.

King, A.J.C. and M.J. Peart. 1992. *Teachers in Canada: Their Work and Quality of Life*. Ottawa: Canadian Teachers' Federation.

Knockwood, Isabelle. 1992. *Out of the Depths: The Experiences of Mi'kmaw Children at the Indian Residential School at Shubenacadie, Nova Scotia*. 2nd ed. Lockeporte, N.S.: Roseway Publishing.

Kominski, Robert and Rebecca Sutterlin. 1992. *What's it Worth? Educational Background and Economic Status: Spring 1990* (U.S. Bureau of the Census, Current Population Reports, Series P70-32). Washington, D.C.: U.S. Government Printing Office.

Krahn, Harvey, and Graham S. Lowe. 1990. *Young Workers in the Service Economy*. Ottawa: Economic Council of Canada.

———. 1991. "Transitions to work: findings from a longitudinal study of high school and university graduates in three Canadian cities." In *Making their Way: Education, Training and the Labour Market in Canada and Britain*. Edited by David. Ashton and Graham Lowe. Milton Keynes, England: Open University Press. 130–170.

———. 1993.*Work, Industry, and Canadian Society*. Toronto: Nelson Canada.

Lagacé, Michel D. 1968. "Educational attainment in Canada: Some regional and social aspects." Special Labour Force Studies, No. 7 (Statistics Canada Catalogue no. 71-512). Ottawa: Minister responsible for Statistics Canada.

Lawton, Stephen B. 1995. *Busting Bureaucracy to Reclaim our Schools*. Montreal: Institute for Research on Public Policy.

Leacy, F.H., ed. 1983. *Historical Statistics of Canada*, 2nd ed. (Statistics Canada Catalogue no. 11-516E). Ottawa: Minister responsible for Statistics Canada and the Social Science Federation of Canada.

Lewington, Jennifer, and Graham Orpwood. 1993. *Overdue Assignment: Taking Responsibility for Canada's Schools*. Toronto: John Wiley.

Li, Peter S. 1988. *Ethnic Inequality in a Class Society*. Toronto: Wall & Thompson.

Liaw, Kao-Lee. 1986. "Review of research on interregional migration in Canada." Report for *Review of Demography in Canada: Review of demography and its implications for economic and social policy*. Hamilton: McMaster University.

Liberal Party of Canada. 1993. *Creating Opportunity: The Liberal Plan for Canada*. Ottawa: The Liberal Party of Canada.

Lockhart, Alexander. 1979. "Educational opportunities and economic opportunities—the 'new' liberal equality syndrome." In *Economy, Class, and Social Reality. Issues in Contemporary Canadian Society*. Edited by John Allan Fry. Toronto: Butterworths, 224–237.

Lockhart, Alexander. 1991. *Schoolteaching in Canada*. Toronto: University of Toronto Press.

Looker, Dianne. 1992. "Interconnected transitions and their costs: gender and urban–rural differences in the transitions to work." In *Transitions: Schooling and Employment in Canada*. Edited by P. Anisef and P. Axelrod. Toronto: Thompson Educational Publishing Inc.

Lynd, D. J. 1994. "Increases in university enrolment: Increased access or increased retention?" *Education Quarterly Review* (Statistics Canada Catalogue no. 81-003). 1, 1 (Spring): 12–22.

Mandell, Nancy and Stewart Crysdale. 1993. "Gender tracks: male–female perceptions of home–school–work transition." In *Transitions: Schooling and Employment in Canada*. Edited by P. Anisef and P. Axelrod. Toronto: Thompson Educational Publishing Inc.

Marchak, Patricia. 1996. *Racism, Sexism, and the University: the political science affair at the University of British Columbia*. Montréal: McGill-Queen's University Press.

Mare, Robert D. 1981. "Change and stability in educational stratification." *American Sociological Review*. 46, 1: 72–87.

Matthews, Ralph and J. Campbell Davis. 1986. "The comparative influence of region, status, class, and ethnicity on Canadian attitudes and values." In *Regionalism in Canada*. Edited by Robert J. Brym. Toronto: Irwin Publishing, 89–122.

McDowell, Ramona. 1991. *The Flow of Graduates from Higher Education and their Entry into Working Life: a contribution to the OECD study on higher education and employment*. Ottawa: Department of the Secretary of State of Canada.

McNaughton, Craig, and John Thorp. 1991. *The Case of the Humanities and Social Sciences in Canada: a contribution to the OECD study on higher education and employment. Country Report: Canada*. Ottawa: Department of the Secretary of State of Canada.

Miech, Richard Allen and Glen H. Elder. 1996. "The service ethic and teaching." *Sociology of Education*. 69, 3: 237–253.

Mori, George A. and Brian Burke. 1989. "Educational attainment of Canadians." *1986 Census of Canada Special Report. Focus on Canada Series* (Statistics Canada Catalogue no. 98-134). Ottawa: Minister responsible for Statistics Canada.

Morissette, René, John Myles, and Garnett Picot. 1993. "What is happening to earnings inequality in Canada?" Analytical Studies Branch Research Paper Series, No. 60 (Statistics Canada Catalogue no. 11F0019E). Ottawa: Minister responsible for Statistics Canada.

———. 1994. "Earnings inequality and the distribution of working time in Canada." *Canadian Business Economics*. 2, 3: 3–16.

Myles, John. 1993. "Post-industrialism and the service economy." In *Work in Canada: readings in the sociology of work and industry.* Edited by Graham S. Lowe and Harvey J. Krahn. Toronto: Nelson Canada. 124–134.

Northrup, David and Anne Oram. 1994. *The 1993 Canadian Election Study: Incorporating the 1992 Referendum Survey on the Charlottetown Accord Technical Documentation.* Toronto: York University, Institute for Social Research.

Novek, Joel. 1985. "University graduates, jobs, and university–industry linkages." *Canadian Public Policy / Analyse de politiques.*11, 2: 180–195.

Ogmundson, Richard. 1990. "Perspectives on the class and ethnic origins of Canadian elites: A methodological critique of the Porter/Clement/Olsen tradition." *Canadian Journal of Sociology / Cahiers canadiens de sociologie.* 15, 2: 165–177.

Ontario Premier's Council. 1988. *Competing in the New Global Economy: Report of the Premier's Council.* Toronto: Government of Ontario.

Organisation for Economic Co-operation and Development (OECD). 1976. *Reviews of National Policies for Education: Canada.* Paris: OECD.

———. 1992. *Education at a Glance: OECD Indicators.* Paris: OECD.

Pagliarello, Claudio. 1995. "Employment income of elementary and secondary teachers and other selected occupations." *Education Quarterly Review* (Statistics Canada Catalogue no. 81-003). 2, 2 (Summer): 9–21.

Phillips, Charles E. 1957. *The Development of Education in Canada.* Toronto: W. J. Gage.

Picot, Garnett, and John Myles. 1995. "Social transfers, changing family structure, and low income among children." Analytical Studies Branch Research Paper Series No. 82 (Statistics Canada Catalogue no. 11F0019E). Ottawa: Minister responsible for Statistics Canada.

———. 1996. "Children in low-income families." *Canadian Social Trends* (Statistics Canada Catalogue no. 11-008E). 42 (Autumn): 15–19.

Pike, Robert. 1970. *Who Doesn't Get to University ... and Why: A study on accessibility to higher education in Canada.* Ottawa: Association of Universities and Colleges of Canada.

Pineo, Peter C. 1985. "Internal migration and occupational attainment." In *Ascription and Achievement: Studies in Mobility and Status Attainment in Canada.* Edited by Monica Boyd et al. Ottawa: Carleton University Press. 479–512.

Pineo, Peter and John Goyder. 1988. "The growth of the Canadian education system: An analysis of transition probabilities." *Canadian Journal of Higher Education / La revue canadienne d'enseignement supérieur.* 18, 2: 37–54. [Abstract in French.]

Porter, John. 1965. *The Vertical Mosaic: An Analysis of Social Class and Power in Canada.* Toronto: University of Toronto Press.

———. 1987. "Postindustrialism, postnationalism, and postsecondary education." In *The Measure of Canadian Society: education, equality and opportunity.* Carleton Library Series No. 144. Edited by J. Porter. Ottawa: Carleton University Press. 185–266.

Porter, Marion R., John Porter, and Bernard. R. Blishen. 1979. *Does Money Matter? Prospects for Higher Education in Ontario.* Toronto: MacMillan of Canada; Ottawa: Institute of Canadian Studies, Carleton University.

Potts, Margaret. 1989. "University enrolment in the 1980s." *Canadian Social Trends* (Statistics Canada Catalogue no. 11-008E). 15 (Winter): 28–30.

Prentice, Alison. 1977. *The School Promoters: education and social class in mid-nineteenth century Upper Canada..* Toronto: McClelland and Stewart.

Prosperity Secretariat. 1991. *Prosperity Through Competitiveness*. Ottawa: Government of Canada, Prosperity Secretariat.

Ram, Bali, Y. Edward Shin, and Michel Pouliot. 1994. *Canadians on the Move*. Focus on Canada series (Statistics Canada Catalogue no. 96-309E) Ottawa: Minister responsible for Statistics Canada and Prentice-Hall Canada.

Renner, Edward and Lorraine Mwenifumbo. 1995. "Renewal, costs and university faculty demographics." *Education Quarterly Review* (Statistics Canada Catalogue no. 81-003). 2, 3 (Fall): 21–34.

Richer, Stephen. 1988. "Equality to benefit from schooling: The issue of educational opportunity." In *Social Issues: Sociological Views of Canada*. 2nd ed. Edited by Dennis Forcese and Stephen Richer. Scarborough: Prentice-Hall Canada, 262–286.

Roberts, Sam. 1993. *Who We Are: A Portrait of America Based on the Latest U.S. Census*. 1st ed. New York: Time Books.

Ross, David P., Richard E. Shillington, and Clarence Lochhead. 1994. *The Canadian Fact Book on Poverty 1994*. Ottawa: Canadian Council on Social Development.

Ross, David P., Katherine Scott, and Mark A. Kelly. 1996. "Overview: Children in Canada in the 1990s." In *Growing Up in Canada: National Longitudinal Survey of Children and Youth* (Statistics Canada Catalogue no. 89-550-MPE). Ottawa: Minister responsible for Statistics Canada. 15–45.

Royal Commission on the Status of Women in Canada. 1970. *Report of the Royal Commission on the Status of Women in Canada*. Ottawa: Information Canada.

Sarlo, Christopher A. 1996. *Poverty in Canada*. 2nd ed. Vancouver: Fraser Institute.

Shamai, Shmuel. 1992. "Ethnicity and Educational Achievement in Canada—1941–1981." *Canadian Ethnic Studies / Études ethniques du Canada*. Calgary: Research Centre for Canadian Ethnic Studies at the University of Calgary for the Canadian Ethnic Studies Association. XXIV, 1: 43–57.

Shavit, Yossi and Hans-Peter Blossfeld. 1993. *Persistent Inequality: Changing Educational Attainment in Thirteen Countries*. Boulder: Westview Press.

Siedule, Tom. 1992. "The influence of socioeconomic background on education." Working paper No. 34. Ottawa: Economic Council of Canada.

Siggner, Andrew J., David Perley, Debra A. Young, Pierre Turcotte. 1983. *Regional Comparisons of Data on Canada's Registered Indians*. Ottawa: Research Branch, Corporate Policy, Indian and Northern Affairs Canada.

Siltanen, Janet. 1994. *Locating Gender: Occupational segregation, wages and domestic responsibilities*. London: University College of London Press; Bristol, P.A.: UCL Press.

Smith, Stuart L. 1991. *Report: Commission of Inquiry on Canadian University Education, 1991*; Stuart L. Smith, commissioner. Ottawa: Association of Universities and Colleges of Canada.

Stager, David A. 1996. "Returns to investment in Ontario university education, 1960–1990, and implications for tuition fee policy." *Canadian Journal of Higher Education / La revue canadienne d'enseignement supérieur*. 26, 2: 1–22 [Abstract in French.]

Statistics Canada. 1978. *Historical Compendium of Education Statistics from Confederation to 1975* (Statistics Canada Catalogue no. 81-568). Ottawa: Minister responsible for Statistics Canada.

Statistics Canada. 1980. "Part-time teachers—Growth and characteristics." *Service Bulletin: Education Statistics* (Statistics Canada Catalogue no. 81-002). 2, 3 (May 1980): 1-6.

Statistics Canada. 1982. *Population: Age, Sex and Marital Status*. National series (Statistics Canada Catalogue no. 92-901, 1981 Census of Canada). Ottawa: Minister responsible for Statistics Canada.

Statistics Canada. 1983. *Population: Mobility Status*. National series (Statistics Canada Catalogue no. 92-907, 1981 Census of Canada). Ottawa: Minister responsible for Statistics Canada.

Statistics Canada. 1984. "Population 15 years and over who worked in 1980 by sex and detailed occupation, showing 1980 employment income groups and persons who worked full-time, full-year (Number with and average 1980 employment income), for Canada and Provinces, 1981." Table 1 in *Population, Worked in 1980—Employment Income by Occupation.* The Nation series (Statistics Canada Catalogue no. 92-930, 1981 Census of Canada). Ottawa: Minister responsible for Statistics Canada, 1-1 to 1-180.

Statistics Canada. 1989. "Population 15 years and over with employment income by sex, work-activity and detailed occupation, showing number and average 1980 and 1985 employment income in constant (1985) dollars, for Canada, Provinces and Territories, 1981 and 1986 Censuses—20% sample data. Table 1 in *Employment Income by Occupation.* The Nation series (Statistics Canada Catalogue no. 93-116, 1986 Census of Canada). Ottawa: Minister responsible for Statistics Canada. 1-1 to 1-188.

Statistics Canada. 1992. *Age, Sex and Marital Status.* The Nation series (Statistics Canada Catalogue no. 93-310, 1991 Census of Canada). Ottawa: Minister responsible for Statistics Canada.

Statistics Canada. 1992. *Home Language and Mother Tongue.* The Nation series (Statistics Canada Catalogue no. 93-317, 1991 Census of Canada). Ottawa: Minister responsible for Statistics Canada.

Statistics Canada. 1993. *Educational Attainment and School Attendance.* The Nation series (Statistics Canada Catalogue no. 93-328, 1991 Census of Canada). Ottawa: Minister responsible for Statistics Canada.

Statistics Canada. 1993. *Employment Income by Occupation.* The Nation series (Statistics Canada Catalogue no. 93-332, 1991 Census of Canada). Ottawa: Minister responsible for Statistics Canada.

Statistics Canada. 1993. *Labour Force Activity of Women by Presence of Children.* The Nation series (Statistics Canada Catalogue no. 93-325, 1991 Census of Canada). Ottawa: Minister responsible for Statistics Canada.

Statistics Canada. 1993. *Mobility and Migration.* The Nation series (Statistics Canada Catalogue no. 93-322, 1991 Census of Canada). Ottawa: Minister responsible for Statistics Canada.

Statistics Canada. 1993. *Occupation.* The Nation Series. (Statistics Canada Catalogue no. 93-327, 1991 Census of Canada). Ottawa: Minister responsible for Statistics Canada.

Statistics Canada. 1994. *Revised Intercensal Population and Family Estimates, July 1, 1971–1991* (Statistics Canada Catalogue no. 91-537). Ottawa: Minister responsible for Statistics Canada.

Statistics Canada. 1994. Unpublished data. *General Social Survey, Cycle 9, Education, Work and Retirement (1994).*

Statistics Canada. 1995. "Annual Labour Force Estimates, 1946–1994." *Canadian Social Trends* (Statistics Canada Catalogue no. 11-008E). 36(Spring): 34.

Statistics Canada. 1995. *Births, 1992* (Statistics Canada Catalogue no. 84-210). Ottawa: Minister responsible for Statistics Canada.

Statistics Canada. 1995. *Divorces, 1992* (Statistics Canada Catalogue no. 84-213E). Ottawa: Minister responsible for Statistics Canada.

Statistics Canada. 1995. *Mortality—Summary List of Causes, 1992* (Statistics Canada Catalogue no. 84-209). Ottawa: Minister responsible for Statistics Canada.

Statistics Canada. 1995. *Women in Canada: A Statistical Report* (Statistics Canada Catalogue no. 89-503), 3rd ed. Ottawa: Minister responsible for Statistics Canada.

Statistics Canada. 1996. "Advance statistics." *Education Quarterly Review* (Statistics Canada Catalogue no. 81-003-XPB). 3, 3 (Fall): 62–70.

Statistics Canada. 1996. "Education at a glance." *Education Quarterly Review* (Statistics Canada Catalogue no. 81-003. 2, 4 (Winter): 77–86.

Statistics Canada. 1996. "University enrolment, 1995 (preliminary)." *The Daily* <http://www.statcan.ca/Daily/English/960108/d960108.htm>. Released January 8, 1996.

Statistics Canada. 1996. "University enrolment, 1996 (preliminary)." *The Daily* <http://www.statcan.ca/Daily/English/961204/d961204.htm>. Released December 4, 1996.

Statistics Canada. Various years. *Advance Statistics of Education* (Statistics Canada Catalogue no. 81-220). Ottawa: Minister responsible for Statistics Canada.

Statistics Canada. Various years. *Annual Demographic Statistics* (Statistics Canada Catalogue no. 91-213-XPB). Ottawa: Minister responsible for Statistics Canada.

Statistics Canada. Various years. *Earnings of Men and Women* (Statistics Canada Catalogue no. 13-217-XPB). Ottawa: Minister responsible for Statistics Canada.

Statistics Canada. Various years. *Education in Canada* (Statistics Canada Catalogue no. 81-229). Ottawa: Minister responsible for Statistics Canada.

Statistics Canada. Various years. *Education Quarterly Review* (Statistics Canada Catalogue no. 81-003-XPB). Ottawa: Minister responsible for Statistics Canada.

Statistics Canada. Various years. *Employment, Earnings and Hours* (Statistics Canada Catalogue no. 72-002-XPB). Ottawa: Minister responsible for Statistics Canada.

Statistics Canada. Various years. *Income Distributions by Size in Canada* (Statistics Canada Catalogue no. 13-207-XPB). Ottawa: Minister responsible for Statistics Canada.

Statistics Canada. Various years. *The Labour Force* (Statistics Canada Catalogue no. 71-001-XPB). Ottawa: Minister responsible for Statistics Canada.

Statistics Canada. Various years. *Universities: Enrolment and Degrees* (Statistics Canada Catalogue no. 81-204). Ottawa: Minister responsible for Statistics Canada.

Steering Group on Prosperity. 1992. *Inventing our Future: An Action Plan for Canada's Prosperity*. Ottawa: Steering Group on Prosperity.

Stehr, Nico. 1994. *Knowledge Societies*. London: Sage.

Stephenson, Bette. 1982. "Closing Address." In *Post-secondary Education Issues in the 1980s: Proceedings of the CMEC Conference on Post-Secondary Education, Toronto, October 19–22, 1982*. Toronto: Council of Ministers of Education, Canada, 249–258.

Sunter, Deborah. 1991. "Juggling school and work." *Perspectives on Labour and Income* (Statistics Canada Catalogue no. 75-001E). 4, 1 (Spring 1992): 15–21.

Tanner, Julian, Harvey Krahn, and Timothy F. Hartnagel. 1995. *Fractured Transitions from School to Work: Revisiting the Dropout Problem*. Don Mills: Oxford University Press Canada.

United Nations Educational, Scientific and Cultural Organization (UNESCO). 1991. *UNESCO Statistical Yearbook*. Paris: UNESCO.

Urquhart, M.C., editor, and K. Buckley, assistant editor. 1965. *Historical Statistics of Canada*. Toronto: MacMillan.

Vaillancourt, François. 1995. "The private and total returns to education in Canada, 1985." *Canadian Journal of Economics / La revue canadienne d'Économique*. 28, 3(August): 532–554.

Vanderkamp, John. 1984. "University enrolment in Canada 1951–83 and beyond." *Canadian Journal of Higher Education / La revue canadienne d'enseignement supérieur*. 14, 2: 49–62.

Wadhera, Surinder and John Silins. 1994. "Teenage pregnancy in Canada, 1975–1987." In *Perspectives on Canada's Population: An Introduction to Concepts and Issues*. Edited by Frank Trovato and Carl F. Grindstaff. Toronto: Oxford University Press, 205–213.

Waggoner, Dorothy. 1991. *Undereducation in America: The Demography of High School Dropouts*. New York: Auburn House.

Wannell, Ted. 1990. "Male–female earnings gap among recent university graduates." *Perspectives on Labour and Income*. (Statistics Canada Catalogue no. 75-001E). 2, 2(Summer): 19–31.

Wannell, Ted, and Nathalie Caron. 1995. "Male–female earnings gap among postsecondary graduates." *Education Quarterly Review*. (Statistics Canada Catalogue no. 81-003). 2, 1(Spring): 20–34.

Wanner, Richard A. 1986. "Educational inequality: Trends in twentieth-century Canada and the United States." *Comparative Social Research*. 9: 47–66.

———. 1996. "Trends in educational opportunity in Canada in the twentieth century." Paper presented at 1996 meetings of the Canadian Sociology and Anthropology Association. St. Catherine's, Ontario, June.

West, Edwin. 1988. *Higher Education in Canada: An Analysis*. The Economics of the Service Sector in Canada Series. Vancouver: Fraser Institute.

———. 1993. *Ending the Squeeze on Universities*. Montréal: Institute for Research on Public Policy.

Whittingham, Frank. 1965. "Educational Attainment of the Canadian Population and Labour Force: 1960–1965." Special Labour Force Studies, No. 1. Ottawa: Minister of Trade and Commerce.

Wilson, J. Donald. 1995. " 'I am ready to be of assistance when I can': Lottie Bowron and rural women teachers in British Columbia." Chapter 14 in *Children, Teachers and Schools in the History of British Columbia*. Edited by Jean Barman, Neil Sutherland and J. Donald Wilson. Calgary: Detselig Enterprises Ltd. 285–306.

Wilson, J.D., Robert M. Stamp and Louis Phillippe Audet. 1970. *Canadian Education: A History*. Scarborough: Prentice-Hall.

Winn, Conrad. 1985."The socioeconomic attainment of visible minorities: facts and policy implications." *Canadian Public Policy / Analyse de politiques*. 11, 4(December): 684–701. [Abstract in French.]

INDEX

Page numbers in italic indicate a figure or table. Figures or tables on the same page as a textual discussion of the topic are not differentiated. The letter "n" following a page number indicates a note; for example, "11n.2" indicates note 2 on page 11.

in Canadian ethnic hierarchy, 101, 102
levels of education, *103–4*, *112*, *114*
Germany, 175
Girls *See* Women
Globalization, xxxix, 21, 171
Grade schools *See* Elementary schools
Greek-Canadians, 102, *103–4*, 104–5, *112*, 113,
114, 115
Guidance counsellors
numbers, 30, *31*
visible minorities, *42*, *43*

Halifax, *76*
Hamilton, 76
Health profession programs
graduates over time, 139
income of graduates, *161–62*
labour force distribution of graduates, *152*
women graduates, 140, *141–43*, *162*
High schools *See* Secondary schools
History programs, *141*
Household science programs, 140, *141*
Humanities programs
graduates over time, 139
income of graduates, *161–62*
labour force distribution of graduates, *152*
women graduates, *141–43*, *162*
Hungarian-Canadians, *103–4*, *112*, *114*

Immigrants
as teachers, *51*, 52
children, *xxxiv*
levels of education, 77, 108–10, *112*, 113,
114, 126n.11–13
methodological cautions, 102
provincial levels, 25
school participation rates, 15, 16, 20, 25, 57
talent pool for labour force, xxxix, 20
Income
by field of study, 161–62
by sex, 163–65, 167
diminishing at all educational levels, 152, *153*
incremental with educational level, 154–55,
156, 159, *160*, 167, 169n.2–4
inequality of, xxxi
of families with children, xxxii–xxxiii, *xxxviii*
of teachers by age, 51, 59n.5
of teachers by occupation, *37–38*, 59n.3
of teachers by sex, *37–38*, 47, 49–52, 58,
59n.5
of teachers compared with other professions,
45, *46*, 47, *48–49*, 57–58
Interprovincial migration, 71–75
Inuit, 101

Irish-Canadians, *103–4*, 104–5, 113
Italian-Canadians, 102, *103–4*, 104–5, *112*, 113,
114, 115
Italy, *175*

Japanese-Canadians
as teachers, 41, *43*
levels of education, *106*
Jewish-Canadians, 102–3, *103–4*, 105, *112*, 113,
114

Kindergarten teachers
income trends, *37–38*, *50*
numbers, 30, *31*, *37–38*
sex, *37–38*, *40*, *50*
visible minorities, *42*, *43*
Korean-Canadians
as teachers, *43*
levels of education, 106

Labour force
children in, 4
education as job credential, xxix–xxx
149–50
education workers in, 2–4
educational distribution, 151, *152*
school drop-outs, 21–22, 154–55
Landscape architecture programs, *141*
Language
level of education, 93–101, 110–11, 122–23,
126n.9,14
of children, *xxxiv*
of teachers, *51*
Language programs, *141*
Latin American–Canadians
as teachers, *43*
levels of education, *106*, *112*, 115
Law programs, *141*
Level of education
Aboriginal Canadians, 111, *112*, *114*, 115,
123
age adjustments, 111, *112*, 114–16, *121*
by birth cohort, 12–13, *14*
by ethnicity, 101–5, 111–16, 123, 125–26n.8,9
by primary language, 93–101, 110–11,
122–23, 126n.9,14
by region, 62–68, 69–71, 77
by SES, 117–22, 123, 126n.16
by sex, 12–13, *14*, 83–93, 111, *112*, *114*, 115,
121, 122, 125n.2
Canada vs. other countries, 171–76
diminishing returns at all levels, 152, *153*
disabled persons, 116–17, 122
distribution of labour force, 151, *152*

Data in many forms

Statistics Canada disseminates data in a variety of forms. In addition to publications, both standard and special tabulations are offered. Data are available on the Internet, compact disc, diskette, computer printouts, microfiche and microfilm, and magnetic tape. Maps and other geographic reference materials are available for some types of data. Direct online access to aggregated information is possible through CANSIM, Statistics Canada's machine-readable database and retrieval system.

How to obtain more information

Inquiries about this publication and related statistics or services should be directed to the Office of the Director General, Census and Demographic Statistics Branch, Statistics Canada, Ottawa, Ontario, K1A 0T6 (telephone: 613 951-9589) or to the Statistics Canada Regional Reference Centre in:

Halifax	(902) 426-5331	Regina	(306) 780-5405
Montréal	(514) 283-5725	Edmonton	(403) 495-3027
Ottawa	(613) 951-8116	Calgary	(403) 292-6717
Toronto	(416) 973-6586	Vancouver	(604) 666-3691 .
Winnipeg	(204) 983-4020		

You can also visit our World Wide Web site: http://www.statcan.ca

Toll-free access is provided **for all users who reside outside the local dialling area** of any of the Regional Reference Centres.

National enquiries line	**1 800 263-1136**
National telecommunications device for the hearing impaired	1 800 363-7629
Order-only line (Canada and United States)	**1 800 267-6677**

How to order publications

Statistics Canada publications may be purchased from local authorized agents and other community bookstores, the Statistics Canada Regional Reference Centres, or from:

Statistics Canada,
Operations and Integration Division
Circulation Management
120 Parkdale Avenue
Ottawa, Ontario
K1A 0T6

Telephone: (613) 951-7277 or 1 800 700-1033
Fax: (613) 951-1584
Toronto (credit card only): (416) 973-8018
Internet: order@statcan.ca.

Standards of service to the public

Statistics Canada is committed to serving its clients in a prompt, reliable and courteous manner and in the official language of their choice. To this end, the agency has developed standards of service which its employees observe in serving its clients. To obtain a copy of these service standards, please contact your nearest Statistics Canada Regional Reference Centre.